REIMAGINE REWIRE RETIRE

CREATE YOUR BEST LIFE

TRUE STORIES FROM AROUND THE WORLD

AN ANTHOLOGY BY
VAL QUINN

KMD
BOOKS

Typeset in Adobe Garamond Pro 12.5/18pt

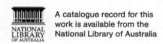 A catalogue record for this work is available from the National Library of Australia

National Library of Australia Catalogue-in-Publication data:

Create Your Best Life/Val Quinn

ISBN:
978-0-9942105-5-5
(Paperback)

Huge and sincere thanks to all the authors for so humbly and generously sharing their authentic stories in the pursuit of helping and inspiring others.

To my mum, dad and brother who inspire me daily.

FOREWORD

In this compelling compilation of true-life authentic stories from around the world, the authors share how they have navigated the pressures of day-to-day existence, work and the sometimes seemingly insurmountable challenges that life presents, to emerge with poignant journeys of self-discovery and the reignition of a spark.

Reimagining occurs when an individual, previously committed to a specific life path, makes the decision to diverge significantly by pursuing an entirely different and unrelated road.

Rewiring refers to individuals who have maintained a consistent career within similar fields for an extended period but choose to depart from that profession. They transition into a portfolio career, encompassing a diverse mix of full- or part-time work.

Retiring? How can we ready ourselves for this upcoming phase of life? Is retirement today comparable to the traditional concept observed by our grandparents and great-grandparents, or is it a distinct era, a 'third age'? Given our longer life expectancy, how can we satisfy our longing for leisure while also finding ways to contribute meaningfully to society during this extended lifespan?

Whether reimagining, rewiring or retiring, this book invites readers to explore the universal human experience of feeling, that perhaps, there is more to life, and we can embrace the opportunities and possibilities each day presents, regardless of age or circumstance.

Through the telling of their stories, the authors give us confidence that it's never too late to pursue our dreams.

CONTENTS

REIMAGINE

*'When it feels scary to jump,
that is exactly when you jump,
otherwise you end up staying in
the same place your whole life.'*
ABEL MORALES

LOST IN LIFE

People who took an indirect path to success

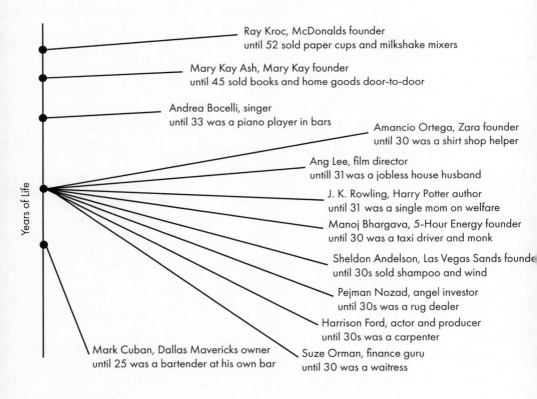

Years of Life

Ray Kroc, McDonalds founder
until 52 sold paper cups and milkshake mixers

Mary Kay Ash, Mary Kay founder
until 45 sold books and home goods door-to-door

Andrea Bocelli, singer
until 33 was a piano player in bars

Amancio Ortega, Zara founder
until 30 was a shirt shop helper

Ang Lee, film director
untill 31 was a jobless house husband

J. K. Rowling, Harry Potter author
until 31 was a single mom on welfare

Manoj Bhargava, 5-Hour Energy founder
until 30 was a taxi driver and monk

Sheldon Andelson, Las Vegas Sands founde
until 30s sold shampoo and wind

Pejman Nozad, angel investor
until 30s was a rug dealer

Harrison Ford, actor and producer
until 30s was a carpenter

Mark Cuban, Dallas Mavericks owner
until 25 was a bartender at his own bar

Suze Orman, finance guru
until 30 was a waitress

A CASE OF RESTLESS GENES

BY NORAH CASEY

I've always been obsessed about what motivates some of us humans to want to do more, to explore the unknown, to find out what's beyond the horizon. It intrigues me because I have an insatiable curiosity about stuff. If someone says I can't do something or go someplace, I see it as a personal challenge to do the opposite. I wonder about that. Thankfully I'm not alone and enjoy the company of fellow travellers on my novelty-seeking adventures. However, I also know others who implore me to 'take it easy'. To those who like a quieter life and a calmer pace, creatures like me are an anathema. Why would you constantly push yourself to try new things, climb over the ridge to see what's beyond or throw yourself into a mahoosive new venture you know absolutely nothing about? Then on one of my regular insomniac nights, I found the 'restless gene'. Well, I didn't quite find it, I found the scientists who found it – and it even has a name. The gene goes by the innocuous label of DRD4-7R. Only about 20% of the world's population have this little genome anomaly, some would say a curse. I like to think of it as an advantage.

No-one really knows why only a fifth of us have that restlessness, maybe something to do with our wider gene pool. I come from some good restlessness stock. My ancestors (two generations back) came from Kolkata in India and faced a perilous six-month journey by ship around the Cape of Good Hope, to land in Dublin, Ireland.

So maybe my restless genes are not so surprising. Whatever the genome pool, I have it in spades. If ever I feel a modicum of complacency might set into my life, I make a plan to do something that terrifies me. It could be white water rafting, learning to fly a plane (I have an abject fear of heights) or doing a stint of speed racing, but it could also just be switching things up a bit. If I notice a bit of a routine setting in, I catch myself on (as they say in Ireland) and change course. The idea of living my life by rote or sameness is a constant fear. And it is easy to slip into, especially as we age. So, keeping those neurotransmitters sparking, flooding my brain with dopamine, and staying curious, is what keeps me alive and ready for new adventures.

My life swerves, like no doubt most of you reading this, have been numerous. However, only some of those pivotal moments nudged me on to a different track, and along the way, I learned some important life lessons. The one I lean on the most, even now, is recognising the difference between the big boulders that come out of nowhere and land right in front of you making it impossible to continue on your chosen path and the little bumps we all get on our road through life. One will almost certainly derail you and force you into a different lane, while those smaller obstacles, though sometimes tricky to navigate, are worth riding through.

EARLY BEGINNINGS

My home was a lodge in the Phoenix Park, where my father worked as a gatekeeper and ranger, as his father had before him. You couldn't get a more magical upbringing than living there – the biggest city garden, right on our doorstep. There was so much wildlife and many unexplored jungles and ponds – it was the perfect upbringing for a child. I went to school at St Joseph's Convent, run by the Sisters of Charity, in Stanhope Street, near Stoneybatter. I wish I could say I studied hard, but I quickly learned, that with little effort, I could be average and if I wanted to impress (rarely), I could push myself to excel. Notes were regularly sent home from the nuns for being distracted or talking in class. One note arrived at the house regularly: *She does nothing but scribble all day long.* My mother laughs at that now (though she didn't then!). Those teenage years were about friendships mainly, but also that nagging notion that I needed to figure out who I wanted to be. It was a constant occupation: 'When I grow up, I want to be …' I think we all have some idea of what we want to be during our childhood years, but very often our lives don't follow that imagined path. For me, I was sure that when I grew up, I was going to be a vet.

MY ANIMAL LIFE

Dublin Zoo was my second home and right next door to our home in the Park. From a very early age, I spent all my spare time there and made myself useful. I cleaned out the guinea pigs' house, hosed down the rabbit hutches and de-liced the fantail pigeons. I learned how to milk goats and feed fledgling chicks with bread soaked in milk. My mother eventually got used to me arriving home with some tiny or sick animal that I couldn't leave overnight in the Zoo. My nights were often shared with poorly hedgehogs, baby rabbits and broken-winged birds and even, on one occasion, a baby seal. I was certain my future lay in working with animals. When I left school, I was still only sixteen and instead of heading to college, I worked in the quarantine section of Dublin Zoo, helping to hand-rear the first two Western Lowland Gorillas. It was a blissful time for me – any young animal lover's dream.

FOLLOWING FLORENCE

Choosing a career is rarely an exact science. What happened next was a bit of a curveball. I am still not entirely certain why, but I switched career track and enrolled as a student nurse at seventeen years of age. There weren't many jobs around at that time and I wasn't entirely sure I wanted to head straight back into intensive studying in college. Nowadays, going to university is an expectation, back then it was the exception – especially for kids from an inner-city school. That said, my parents were keen for all of us to do well, whether we went to college or, like many of our peers, landed a solid job in a bank or the civil service. My mother had trained as a mental health nurse in St Brendan's in Grange Gorman and her sister was an occupational nurse in Sligo, so maybe nursing was in my DNA. But to be honest, I think the decision to enter nursing had more to do with the fact I was going to train in a small hospital on the banks of Loch Lomond, in Scotland. Just far enough away to be exotic, but it still felt a bit like Ireland. I got caught up in it all – the heady journey on the airplane, stretching my wings, leaving the nest.

I figured anything that involved wearing a white uniform and broderie anglaise on your head couldn't be all bad.

THE FIRST PIVOT

I think I was a good nurse. I loved it, for the most part. Yes, it was tough dealing with illness and death at such a young age, but it was also a great foundation for life. It gives you a healthy perspective; nothing can ever beat the stress of those early years working in an environment that is quite often literally – life or death. I have never stressed over business decisions since. Over the course of the three-year education program, the elements I loved about nursing were slowly eroded by the petty rules that beset the profession at the time. When I trained, student nurses were part of the workforce and I was working in small hospitals in western Scotland, where nurses were often left alone at night in charge of a ward to cover mealtimes and shift changes. I remember vividly how frightened I was, being the only person minding these very ill patients at times. Those moments were slowly leading me to a quiet acceptance that, perhaps, this wasn't what I would spend my life doing.

Then I learned something important – overcoming fear is not an end in itself. All the way through my nursing education, if you had asked me if there was anything I was scared of, I would have told you categorically it was caring for a burns victim. So, I did something that was either foolish or courageous. I decided to confront my fear by doing a certificate in burns nursing in, what was then, Bangour Hospital, near Edinburgh. The course was combined with plastic surgery (not to be confused with cosmetic surgery), to encompass reconstructive work. It was a year of my life that changed me. I still remember seeing young children in Edinburgh's Royal Hospital for Sick Children, who were often orphaned by serious house fires – severely burned, but survivors.

As I went on to work in the outpatient department, I witnessed teenagers, nine or ten years on from these little children, who after multiple operations remained significantly disfigured – many suffered from serious depression, some had multiple attempts at suicide. At the end of that long year, I knew without a doubt I didn't have what it takes to devote my life to that. I overcame my fear but learned something far more important about myself. I was not destined to be a nurse.

THE SECOND CAREER

Sometimes you must start over. Nursing made me grow up and it also gave me the bedrock for my life and my various careers. It remained important to me for many more years and even now I feel at home when I am asked to talk to a group of nurses. Thus, even when our careers take a meandering path, that's not something to be frustrated by. Every job you undertake will teach you something – about life and about yourself. I was twenty-three and was ready to stretch in a new direction. Remember those notes about me scribbling all the time in class? Well, that little obsession became a lifelong career as a writer. If there is another trait that runs through the Casey gene pool, then it's writing and all things media (filming, photography, radio, digital – the whole package). After a few years as a professional advisor to the Royal College of Nursing in London, I took the plunge and enrolled in a postgrad in journalism at Harlow College.

ONWARDS & UPWARDS

By now you might detect a pattern. I think taking that difficult decision, from nursing to journalism, gave me the courage to embrace change throughout my life, even if it is stressful and difficult. Once I had completed my print journalism qualification, I studied television studio production and direction at the University of West London and learned radio journalism with the BBC. My career took a more linear path for the rest of my twenties, moving from news reporter to news editor, editor and then editorial director. But two things of note; I moved swiftly up the ranks enjoying every stage, but all the while was restless to move on. The constant companion of my life, at that time and since, was education and study. If I didn't know it, I went back to learn it. I remember thinking how fantastic it was to be a news reporter at the coal face, writing copy all day. In fact, I used to imagine how boring a life the poor news editor had, stuck to his desk and having to edit all of our copy. Then I became a news editor and pitied the reporters in the team who only saw that one piece of writing they produced and didn't understand the magic of creating headlines and structure and choosing the priority of where stories appeared. Finally, I was promoted to editor, which I believed at the time was the best job of all. To sit at the helm of a busy weekly, blending features and news and opinion pieces, creating the flow of the magazine, the images, the cover that might attract the eye at the newsstands – the whole picture. It was exhilarating. I had started a Masters in Journalism at the University of Wales. By then I was itching to expand my brain into the wider media. So, I spent weekends and evenings doing shifts and contributions at Sky, ITV, presenting radio shows and a late-night continuing education program for the BBC Two Learning Zone (as it was then).

BECOMING THE BOSS

One day, just before I reached my thirtieth birthday, I became CEO of the company. It wasn't quite 'just like that'. I was driven, hardworking and ambitious. I was also a fast learner and hungry for knowledge and new challenges. So, I stood out, put my hand up faster and higher than anyone else when it came to projects or going the extra mile. I delivered on time and with the precision of a homework assignment queen who knows the value of well-written concise proposals that hit the mark. Nothing prepared me for the role of CEO.

I was asked recently to name my worst and best boss. I nominated myself as the worst boss. I truly was. I couldn't make a decision. They wrote on the notice board one morning: *The Boss's Indecision is Final.* I would go round the boardroom table endlessly seeking everyone else's view, avoiding making difficult decisions and I kept interfering with the editorial director's job – because I knew it better than being the chief.

One day my senior team shuffled into the office and gave me a stern talking to about not dealing with a particularly difficult and often absent colleague. I didn't want to be the bad guy that started the disciplinary process. However, they graphically explained that my lack of leadership was adding to their work and stress.

So, I did what I did best. I went back to school. This time to study strategic management at Hult Ashridge, a global leader in business education, about forty minutes north of London. The stunning former thirteenth-century monastery set on National Trust woodlands, a family home of the British royal family, a former college for politicians and now my home-from-home for two years. We spent time crawling all over blue-chip businesses, engaging in all-nighters while running virtual startups and solving business challenges. I was locked in for three-week periods at various times (with only one Sunday off) for intensive learning. I was also able to use my own leadership strategy as the main focus for my qualification. It was gruelling, but what nursing did for the foundation of my life, Hult Ashridge did for my business life. I loved it. So much so, I went back to study advanced strategic management, and in recent years Hult Ashridge bestowed on me lifelong alumni membership. Being a CEO was really the best job of all. I never looked back.

TRANSITIONS

From nursing to journalist to CEO, my twenties were filled with life-enhancing energy and challenges. My brain was full of stuff, and I called on all of it at various times to navigate my course through that busy work-life. I switched companies, remained in London but reported to France and became CEO of a cluster of companies. I completed a global high-fliers program across various universities in Europe during that time. Among the most incredible nuggets of wisdom I gleaned from that intensive learning was the importance of diversity and equity, along with respect for different business behaviour in other cultures and countries. I was at that time working within a large team of CEOs (as the only woman), who came from a myriad of different backgrounds and spoke many different languages. It gave me the confidence thereafter to work globally and to prepare well in advance of meetings to ensure I was knowledgeable of my host's culture and language. I then became an even more avid proponent of diverse teams.

THE DRAGON ERA

In my thirties I transitioned from a country-based CEO in Britain to a global leader of multiple businesses. Now I was ready for the next step, from intrapreneur to entrepreneur. And very soon after that, on to my real passion in life – as an investor and mentor of fledgling and not-so-fledgling businesses and their founders.

In 2004 I bought my first business. I was CEO of a group of companies for the Jefferson Smurfit Group (now Smurfit Kappa), commuting weekly between London, Paris and Dublin and ready to be my own boss. Then came the opportunity to do a management buyout (MBO). As anyone who has gone down that road knows, it was a long and legally intricate process. Then at last came the day I signed all the legals and I was finally in charge of my own destiny (at least in business terms). So, Harmonia was born, and it became the largest magazine company in Ireland with a diverse multimedia portfolio.

I returned to Dublin with my husband Richard (Hannaford) and our young son Dara. I'd always wanted to work with animals so maybe it was unsurprising that I ended up working with dragons (except these ones answered back and sometimes quite loudly). I was the only female Dragon on the TV show, *Dragons' Den* at that time (in the US it is called *Shark Tank* and in Germany, *Lion's Den,* but they are all the same formats). Five stern-faced investors grilling those brave enough to enter the

Den to pitch for investment. It was a natural progression for me in terms of my entrepreneur journey. I was comfortable in front of the camera. I had been a presenter in the past and through all the intervening years, I was a regular contributor to national and international television and radio. It was a fantastic show and I loved working with the guys. My fellow Dragons (two of whom went on to stand for election as President of Ireland) were great to work with; Gavin Duffy (who started out as a radio entrepreneur), Seán Gallagher (co-founder of Smarthomes), Bobby Kerr (Insomnia Coffee Company) and Niall O'Farrell (Blacktie) and subsequently Sean O'Sullivan (who pioneered street mapping and cloud computing).

I wanted to invest in other businesses. While I had dabbled a bit in the past, *Dragons' Den* opened my eyes and my mind to the potential opportunities in a wide range of innovations and inventions – from the mad to the ingenious. I invested in some great people and businesses from my time in the Den. Harmonia was going from strength to strength and we were launching and relaunching new magazines and developing some of the areas of the business, particularly contract publishing and digital editions. Richard (who was a BBC correspondent for over twenty years) had joined me as editorial director and the long working hours began to ease a bit as the business became more stable.

WHAT DOESN'T KILL ME

The two most important catalysts for my career swerves came from dark periods in my life. The first I glossed over in my earlier preamble because I thought it might help to see the context of how my life turned out, to understand that while it devastated me, it did not destroy me. The reason for all that busyness in my twenties is because I had met and married a man who was violent and coercive. And while my home and personal life was controlled, stressful and frightening at times, I was given free rein in my work life and studies. When I remember all those evenings and weekends filled with learning and work, I feel exhausted. The busyness saved me during that period and helped to shape who I am.

I think sometimes there might have been another me, who didn't experience years of domestic abuse, who is still nursing and happily taking it easy in life. When I spoke on national television about my experience of domestic abuse, only in recent years, it was by far the hardest thing I've ever done in my life. I still find it difficult to recount the more violent episodes without being back there, reliving the trauma. So, I won't do so here.

I was asked to write a chapter for a book a couple of years ago on 'The day that changed my life'. I thought about that a great deal. I have had many phenomenal moments I could have chosen, but the only honest one is the day I left him.

That morning, when I drove away, I felt like I was diving headlong off a cliff. I promised myself over and over that no-one would own me financially ever again, that I would stand on my own two feet and keep my family and friends close. So, if you wonder how someone who went to a state-funded inner-city school for disadvantaged children, went from being a nurse to a Dragon, then that might well be the reason. It's not a very nice one but sometimes we grow stronger and shine brighter from the depths of adversity. Being a survivor of abuse changed me, but like many other survivors, I have gone on to lead a full and successful life. It also left me with a strong internal radar around people who bully, control and belittle others. I have got into hot water on more than one occasion in my personal and professional life for standing up to those who abuse their position of power. People say that's the Dragon in me, nothing could be further from the truth – it is the survivor in me.

LIFE SOMETIMES HAS OTHER PLANS

Now to my second catastrophe which catapulted me into a whole new world. Having spent over a decade running my own successful publishing business and investing in other enterprises, I believed that was my destiny. With my husband Richard (when God gives you a bad partner, he makes up for it by gifting you the most wonderful one) by my side, the next chapter was almost certainly going to be spent developing the business together and continuing to build a strong investment portfolio.

In 2011, however, I discovered that life sometimes has other plans. Tragically, at forty-eight years of age, Richard became suddenly ill with an aggressive cancer. He was dead within months and I, and my then-twelve-year-old son Dara, faced a dramatically different future. I returned to work within days of the funeral and Dara returned to school. We tried to put structure, routine and hard work into the vacuum left behind. I hoped the distraction and time-consuming challenges of everyday life would help us to bear the burden of grief. From those dark times, I began a journey of self-discovery.

This traumatic event acted as a catalyst to reappraising and reshaping the rest of my life. Richard didn't get the opportunity to do all he wanted to do in life. There are loads of 'Richards' out there as I am writing this, who through all manner of illness, ability issues and inequalities, will never get to fulfil their potential. That was a strong moral imperative for me to get out there and live every moment to the full. Out of the depths of grief that thought gave me the impetus and determination to change.

With renewed energy and focus, I underwent a transformation from businesswoman to broadcaster. Along the way I discovered it was still possible to live a rich and fulfilling life, filled with newness and challenges, regardless of age or circumstance.

BEING BUSY IS MY DEFAULT

So began a year of 4am starts on *Newstalk Breakfast,* Fridays in County Cork for the RTÉ One *Today* show, months of filming all over Ireland for RTÉ2 for *The Takeover* and juggling Harmonia, nine investments and a teenage son. Being busy at a whole new level was good for me at that time. I got to choose to shine a spotlight on issues where I hoped I could make a difference. I filmed with young women from the Traveller community for a four-part documentary series. I retraced my steps by going back to the hospice where Richard died. It was such a privilege to interview some very courageous people in the final stages of life about the importance of dying with dignity. I started my own Sunday morning show on national radio, wrote my bestseller book, *Spark!* (Penguin) and began working with and making documentaries with the incredible women who survived the Magdalene Laundries.

I made some big decisions, chief among them to sell the majority of the business assets of Harmonia to a US-based company. I am now working on some great projects in film and television. In an odd way, I am marrying all the different facets of my life. That nurse-dragon hybrid who set out in life to make a difference.

AND FINALLY ...

The swerve into a new path was not of my creation. It was because of that cataclysmic event in my life. We all experience death and bereavement on our journey through life. Sometimes the complexity of grief precipitated by loss causes us to careen into new life territories. There are, of course, other major life events that create an 'action and reaction' response. But this is my testimony about the nudges that pushed me into new life paths. Now I try to see the breadth of ordinary day-to-day events, to be inspired by natural beauty, to stay interested rather than interesting and allow emotions to flow as they come. Some days I don't have to climb mountains to feel I have used up all the space of the day in a good way.

I'm often asked what I might say to my younger self ... but I wonder more what my older self might say to me. Through the lens of age, maybe in the twilight of life, I imagine she would say 'take every chance'. Even if you worry about falling, take that leap. Quell the inner voices that whisper 'don't' and raise your hand high for every possibility that life throws your way.

To learn more about this author: linkedin.com/in/ norah-casey-1a16567

FURTHER READING
- 17 Remarkable career change statistics to know (2023)

- apollotechnical.com/career-change-statistics
- The science behind impact: Why we're compelled to do work that matters
- cmaconsult.com/the-science-behind-impact-why-were-compelled-to-do-work-that-matters
- This is what makes people happy at work, according to science
- fastcompany.com/90704833/this-is-what-makes-people-happy-at-work-according-to-science
- The science behind what motivates us to get up for work every day
- lifehacker.com/the-science-behind-what-motivates-us-to-get-up-for-work-5945221
- The surprising truth about what makes us happy at work forbes.com/sites/erikaandersen/2012/08/13the-surprising-truth-about-what-makes-us-happy-at-work/?sh=21da2595241a
- The 5 steps of effective employment pathways – forbes.com/sites/gradsoflife/2016/05/12/the-5-steps-of-effective-employment-pathways/?sh=4515e006df7f
- An 85-year Harvard happiness study found the biggest downside of retirement that no one talks about – cnbc.com/2023/03/10/85-year-harvard-happiness-study-found-the-biggest-downside-of-retirement-that-no-one-talks-about.html
- 5 Life-changing events that can shake us to our core – huffpost.com/entry/turning-50_b_4181486
- Are humans still evolving? – yourgenome.org/theme/are-humans-still-evolving
- Adventure is an important part of being human

bps.org.uk/psychologist/adventure-important-part-being-human

- 7 Ways to answer 'what should I do with my life?'– themuse.com/advice/7-ways-to-find-the-answer-to-what-should-i-do-with-my-life
- Theory of human motivation – us.humankinetics.com/blogs/excerpt/theory-of-human-motivation

THE EVER-EVOLVING CAREER PATH

BY CAROLE ANN (BYRNE) CLARKE

I'm standing in the corridor of my school, talking to my head mistress.

'What should I do?' I ask her.

'Go to college, of course!' she said.

I guess I should have known then that life was unexpected, opportunities would come my way and to take a leap of faith. Sports and music were what I lived for as a teenager. Whilst I had a best friend, I didn't feel like I neatly fitted into any particular friends' group in school, so sports and music were what I identified with. I worked hard at both and experienced some level of success, particularly in sport.

I never really considered myself academic and focused on the subjects I enjoyed, putting up with the ones I didn't. I filled out the CAO (college application form) just as a thing to do. The day I got into college, my dad had already paid a deposit for me to become a bilingual secretary. Two weeks later, I was standing on the concourse of University of Galway.

20

My dad gave me a hug and went on his way. I was alone.

My college years were so happy, meeting lifetime friends and experiencing real independence for the first time. I focused on languages which meant more lectures and tutorials than most of my friends. I definitely doubted myself early on and lacked confidence in my ability. Though, one day, I remember I told myself, *I was smart enough to get into to college, so I'm smart enough to get out the other side!* I carried that with me throughout my degree and subliminally it sank in because I've probably always considered myself smart since then (but definitely not academic).

College was much like school though, in that I could have studied harder, but again, sport was my focus, captaining the university, hosting intervarsities and playing interprovincial hockey at under twenty-one and senior levels. A short stint at rowing and acting in the drama society in my final year were fabulous distractions from academia too … and SO good for my mental health and wellbeing.

I loved my friends, my boyfriend and my life so much in Galway, I didn't want to leave. I went to a local college to do secretarial skills. I also decided to join a band at that time. We were good, solid musicians. I was the lead singer, and we wrote our own music. I still have a demo on my sports Walkman, would you believe! Clearly, I was convinced we had promise because I sat down and wrote a letter to my parents, thanking them for everything they'd done and the sacrifices they'd made, but I had decided to stay in Galway and make a go of it in music. A month later, I was standing in Paris with a big suitcase and nowhere to live, working for Disneyland Paris.

I was heartbroken but understood why my parents had

pushed back. I got on with it. Afterall, it was Disney, and who gets to dress up as an Arabian princess everyday as a job? I was also so lucky that, on my first day, I met one of my good friends from school who was as heartbroken as me. Both of us had left our boyfriends at home. After living in a hotel for a month, we moved into an apartment with no furniture and no money. Nothing like some camp beds, vegetable baskets and boxes as furniture. We were grand ... and we were. We had a ball. It was also a brilliant way to keep up my languages, learn communication skills, customer service at its best and discipline (some shifts started at 6am, some ended at 2am). And then there's the magic. Every day looking at life through the eyes of a child, an excited adult, delivering dreams to the world. That's where I learnt about the power of the collective to create and activate a mission or a vision.

Something happened to me when I was living in France. Maybe it was seeing the opportunity that if I harnessed my languages, I could work internationally. Or maybe I just wasn't ready to make a career decision. I applied for a Masters in applied languages for Business at the University of Ulster. With only twelve places in Ireland, I got in. I was delighted with myself. Gosh, it was tough. Long days of lectures, huge project load and lots of exams. Only two of us finished the full masters, whilst the other ten finished after their diploma. These two years were the foundation of my work ethic for the rest of my career. I worked harder than I had ever worked at my academia. Thankfully, I still had my college and representative hockey. And was introduced to rugby in my last few months there.

My first major fork in the road was when I was finishing at

University of Ulster. We were the supposed top 1% of the talent pool, and I could have been on my way to being an interpreter in Brussels. Yes, the money would have been fantastic and, yet, when I sat back and reflected on my life, it just didn't seem like me. Sitting in a booth, translating other people's thoughts and ideas. I had already done translation work and whilst I enjoyed it, it would not allow me to express my ideas and what I had to offer the world. I decided it wasn't for me. A risk, yes, because it was 1994 and there were not too many jobs for graduates in Ireland. I was turning down a BIG salary. I understood back then that, for me, money did not mean happiness nor success. It was more about finding my own path to fulfilment.

I applied for Ibec's EOP program and was accepted. In parallel, I saw an ad for Guinness Ireland Group. They were hiring twelve graduates. I applied along with over one thousand other applicants.

A PINT OF THE BLACK STUFF

January 1995, six female and six male graduates joined the Guinness sales team. Out of a salesforce of circa eighty people, there were eight women in total. A positive initiative by Guinness, and it meant changing times in the licence trade too. Some publicans who were used to men walking through their doors found it tough to engage initially. Loving sports helped create relationships, have fun with the locals and understand the power of connection.

My first couple of years as a trainee were varied and fun. Work ethic was drilled into you. I moved from Dublin and worked everywhere around Ireland. There were strong learnings for me in terms of respecting everyone, regardless of role, the power of community and supporting one another.

I secured my first cap for Ireland in rugby when I was at Guinness. I advocated for women's sports as much as I could, at the same time as delivering high-profile events and being visible in the organisation. Balancing an international female sporting career and a professional career in parallel was gruelling at times, so I had to build up my resilience.

I experienced the Guinness Ireland Group transition to Diageo. There was a restructure, which was an opportunity for me to move on. I had six wonderful years at Guinness and got to know my country (nearly every road of it), my culture and learn world-class skills from the sales and marketing disciplines of a famous brand. It's also where I met my husband.

IT'S AN AGENCY LIFE FOR ME

I moved from Diageo to a marketing agency. Agency life is like a roller-coaster. A lot of pressure, expect the unexpected, proudly winning pitches or awards to losing pitches and clients and having to bounce back. I had ten years of marketing agency life. Fast moving, demanding, creative, innovative, fun, long hours, agility, pivoting, lifelong friends. I really loved working with clients, creating long-term relationships and sustainable business and thus together delivering great work. I absolutely loved going from an idea to seeing our advertising work or our packaging designs. I was always so incredibly proud of the work we produced as a team.

Between Guinness and my agency life, I learned the importance of communication skills, bringing people on a journey with you, managing expectations and conflict, negotiating, emotional intelligence and leadership skills. I also realised I had a very strong work ethic and thus needed to ensure I take time for self-care too.

Our children didn't come easy for us. The workplace at the time didn't specifically support couples in this scenario. I was a female executive who wanted to be a mum. When I was offered a managing director role at a high-profile agency, I said no. If I took the job, the increased pressure, responsibilities and, most of all, my work ethic, could impact my ability to have children. This was the right decision for me and my family.

In 2010, there was an economic downturn, and agency cash-flows were tough. I made a move to Coca-Cola where I headed up large-scale global events and then digital transformation in Europe. Many flights a year, a heavy workload and a self-inflicted work ethic took its toll. I was, by then, questioning corporate life and its impact. In 2014, I felt exhausted and burnt-out.

THE IMPORTANCE OF SUPPORT SYSTEMS

A colleague reached out to me to check in. They were concerned. The impact was profound, as I realised I needed support. For someone who has rarely asked for help, I found it hard, but I did it. It's okay not to feel okay; it's okay to ask for help.

I went to my GP. I didn't want to take medication, but he insisted I needed to calm my body down. My anxiety was manifesting physically. I didn't want to go to counselling. I had done that back in my twenties, I wanted something that would help me move forward proactively. I was a sports person and was used to a certain approach to challenges and opportunities. I chose coaching. It was transformational.

TIME TO FOCUS ON MY VALUES AND WHAT I ENJOY

To think that, in my early forties, I had never really worked on *me* properly – my values and strengths, really thinking about what made me tick. Well, that's what I did, and it opened my mind to so many possibilities. The tools and exercises I worked with were like opening up a whole new world of myself. And one I liked.

I realised a lot of work I was doing was based on what I was good at but not necessarily what I enjoyed. My work ethic meant I ploughed on regardless, to the detriment of my own happiness and fulfilment. It also impacted my family life. They didn't see the best of me as I grappled with what was going on internally.

I thought about my favourite jobs and recognised they were when I worked at Next and Disney. Why? Because I loved helping people experience joy or feel better about themselves. It was that simple. I reflected on when I was in school, when I started Amnesty International or ran the Concern Fast for years. I clearly had a strong sense of justice and helping others.

Lastly, I focused on what made me proud throughout my career to date. In Guinness, it was where I discovered I was creative and brought ideas to life, delivering results. In the agency world, it was the MSR (mutual, social responsibility) projects we had worked on. At Coca-Cola, it was bringing joy to people through our experiences, as well as the MSR initiatives.

Coaching helped me to make the decision to leave my corporate job and do something completely different.

THE POWER OF A MIND MAP

I sat in front of a mind map I had created over a few weeks.

There were so many possibilities in front of me. A real confidence builder. It's like gathering all your skills, know-how, passion points and what you enjoy all together, and then combine it with what's important to you in this moment in time. It created a nice feeling when I was able to recognise what I had achieved over my career and reflect on my passion points. It gave me a sense that I could take on anything.

I did something I thought I would never do – go out on my own. I took on a few contracts over a few years and continued to study to transform myself. Executive and leadership coaching was the first course I did. I went on to study mental health and wellbeing coaching which made a real impact on how I could support individuals and teams. To add to my toolbox, I went on to become a senior resilience practitioner, a corporate wellbeing coach and, finally, I studied organisation development and culture transformation.

My transformation journey has been driven by my desire to 'help companies and leaders recognise that a workforce of wellbeing means a well business *and* healthy profits'.

STEELCAPPED SHOES AND HARD HATS

The world of organisational development and culture transformation has been my life since 2017, with particular focus on construction, steel, mining and utilities sectors, where there are concerning issues around mental health and suicide.

My time is now. I'm in the human design business (for profit or not for profit). Technology, the gig economy, globalisation, skills shortages, equality, diversity and inclusion, climate change, COVID-19 and war are all having an impact on how businesses need to be led and the new skill sets required to be successful. There is mounting data on how profit can be increased by focusing on a people culture and embracing new leadership skills throughout organisations.

Positive change is happening.

I've never had a clear pathway. For some reason, when I was a teenager, I knew I would arrive somewhere special in my midlife. How I knew, I do not know, but I did. I don't have any regrets – they'd eat me up. I do wish the education system had more focus on values, strengths, resilience and emotional intelligence, as I believe this could help future generations to thrive.

Everything I have studied, learned, experienced, fought for, made the best of, created, innovated, my networks – is for now. My adventure is far from finished.

To learn more about this author: linkedin.com/in/ caroleannclarke

THE WINDING ROAD
BY JAMES CLUSKEY

My career journey is one of many twists and turns along an ever-winding road. When we look back on life, we go through transitional moments. These moments can be both positive and negative. At times, it can feel like our world is ending, but it's how we move through these moments to reach a brighter side that counts.

My background is a little unconventional in that I chose professional sport as my discipline, specifically tennis. I come from a traditional Irish background. I grew up in the outskirts of Swords where my dad was a farmer and my mum a nurse. I was incredibly shy as a child, almost worryingly so. I was genuinely afraid of my shadow. I have two very early memories: one of which was hiding under the table when people came to visit; and the other was my great-aunt Angie, who was like a grandmother to me, throwing me a tennis ball one day and telling my mum I had great hand-eye coordination.

My parents signed me up for the Parks Tennis program in Swords. I would cry every time I left home for tennis but loved it when they got me on court. My passion for tennis grew and grew. I was hooked.

When I was fourteen, I was one of the top players in Ireland and playing tournaments every week of the summer. We all need a little luck along the way, and a couple of 'lucky' things happened for me. West Wood Clubs opened a venue in Clontarf, which had seven indoor world-class tennis courts. This meant I could train all year round, especially in the harsh Irish winter. The second thing was that a brilliant young Canadian coach moved to Dublin to head up the tennis facility. His name was Larry Jurovich, and he had a significant impact on my life and my tennis.

Larry thought differently and challenged a group of us players to think differently too. He had us reading books on Michael Jordan, Bruce Lee and one in particular I remember, called *Influence* by Professor Robert Caldani. It focused on how people make decisions. This was all to improve my tennis. Tennis is an individual sport, but Larry created a culture of performance. A culture where the group was competitive and players were pushing each other. We trained six days a week, including before and after school.

Life was good. I'm the youngest in the family and have one brother and one sister. Stephen is two years older than me, and Amy two years older than Stephen. As in most families, the youngest is the spoilt one, and the family revolved around my tennis.

However, that was soon to change. On the August bank holiday weekend, Stephen had been camping with friends when he suffered a freak accident and fell off a hay bale, breaking his neck.

He was paralysed from the neck down and it was an incredibly tough time for our family. He spent a year in a rehab hospital and my parents were there most days. It's times like these when you learn the importance of family.

I grew up quickly and threw myself, even more, into tennis. I believe I loved it, but it was also a coping mechanism. My tennis excelled and I received a scholarship to Louisiana State University to play college tennis for the LSU tigers.

I believe life is about making tough choices. Some we get right and some we don't, but still, we have to make them. I had to make one of those tough choices. I could choose to go to LSU who were ranked tenth in the country. The risk was, with twelve guys on the team, only six would make the starting team. My other option was to go to Indiana. They were ranked sixtieth in the country, but I would be their number-two player on the team of twelve. My philosophy was always to put myself around good people and the best players. So that is what I did. I chose LSU.

I had a good career at LSU where I was captain of the team and ended up individually being ranked number three in the US. I graduated from college in 2009 and played on the professional circuit from 2010 to the end of 2015. I reached a career high tennis ranking of 145 in the world, winning fifteen professional titles and playing Davis Cup for Ireland for ten years.

Tennis was my whole life, and it was all I knew. People struggle with transitions in their career no matter what the field, but especially professional athletes. It's your identity; *it's who you are.* I don't think I come from a traditional background, in that my dad is a farmer, but I'd say he's an entrepreneur at heart. At the dinner table he would always talk about his next deal and who he was renting his shed out to or what he was plotting next. I also think my mum is a very positive keep-moving-forward type of person. Maybe that rubbed off on me. A doubles partner I once had said I was the most positive person he ever met.

As I came to the end of my tennis career, I started to think about what I wanted to do next. I wanted to start my own business, but I didn't really know what in or what for. Initially, I coached tennis to get on my feet and earn a little bit of money. I was always thinking of ideas and tried a few things that didn't work.

If I go back to my philosophy upon signing for LSU, it was that I was committed to 'surround yourself with the people you want to become'. I knew tennis was my skill and I could add value to people. I reached out to a great executive coach who played tennis in my club. I asked him to go for a coffee and discussed if he coached me in business, I would coach him in tennis. He agreed. He had a hugely positive impact on me. He talked about having a number of coaching hours in the diary for cashflow, so I could use my other time to see what I liked and didn't like, work-wise.

I ended up doing a causal internship in LinkedIn HQ in Dublin where I could sit in on sales calls and learn from the team. I challenged myself to do things outside of my comfort zone. The easy option for me was to coach tennis. I had a good name and had access to more coaching hours if I wanted them, but I knew there might be something else out there for me. It was hard to replace my love of tennis, but I had to keep searching.

I was approached to work in a recruitment agency to help sportspeople transition out of their sport and support them in business development. I loved working with the sportspeople but there just wasn't the scale to fill my calendar. I loved the company culture and the people, but the job itself just wasn't for me.

My lucky break came when I heard, through a friend, about a tennis event on legendry entrepreneur Sir Richard Branson's island. I had a mutual connection to the co-founder of the event and contacted him about helping out at the event. My pitch was clear. I knew the calibre of players at the event were on holiday and didn't want to be standing on the court all day waiting to hit a ball with businesspeople. They wanted to be at the bar or in the pool. I suggested I could stand on the court all day and always be there for a guest to play tennis with. My philosophy was, *the worst he can do is say no.*

Tennis has opened a lot of doors for me, and this was a big one. I had the most incredible time on the island and met some amazing businesspeople and entrepreneurs, including Sir Richard. I also met Keny who runs Richard's island, and a few weeks after coming home from Necker, I got an email from Keny asking me to come back to coach Richard in tennis.

I've done several stints on the island with Richard and would typically play tennis with him twice a day. I've been to London with him too, and my tennis has given me the opportunity to spend time with one of the icons of entrepreneurship. One of the guests on the island said that spending time with him is like doing an MBA in business. I had that amazing opportunity.

While on the island, I had a eureka moment in that I decided I wanted to get more into the people performance arena. What were the lessons I learned from professional sports and how can I inspire people to live better? This has taken many forms, but I developed the business in many ways.

In a pre-COVID world, I hosted intimate events with CEOs and business leaders to discuss topics such as leadership and how to create a high-performance culture in an organisation. I completed my executive coaching qualifications, and CEOs started asking me into their companies to work with their teams.

I finally found a place, post-tennis, where I was happy. If I'm being brutally honest, I still wasn't *as happy* as when I was chasing a tennis ball around the world, but I was happy. I got engaged in December 2019 and life was good.

Then, in February 2020, everything went horribly wrong. I mentioned earlier my brother, Stephen, had his accident, and it was a pivotal moment in my life. Situations can go horribly wrong, and we have to respond. I think tennis teaches you that. I won fifteen professional titles, which is a lot more than 99% of players, but I played hundreds of events. We lose most weeks, and we have to bounce back the following week.

In February 2020, my fiancé broke off our engagement, and literally a week later, COVID-19 hit. My business effectively went to zero overnight. I had in person programs pulled. *Surround yourself with the people you want to become.* I'm lucky for my family and though we don't choose into what family we are born; I believe I won the lotto ticket on that. I was able to move home and regroup. I wrote a book on goal setting, called *Advantage,* and just tried to survive those initial months.

If I'm honest, I didn't really worry about work too much. I was worried about my parents or my brother getting COVID; that was my real focus. However, I slowly started to re-emerge. I moved into an apartment in Dublin and began to think more positively about the future. I'd had a small idea around where

I'd seen the educational and learning market go and decided to build out where I thought *I saw it would go*. What had I got to lose? I built out a performance platform for companies with live online classes on topics ranging from networking, listening and mental health. There are also breathing and meditation classes.

I've had good traction with companies coming onboard, and I'm absolutely loving what I'm doing. I feel like a tennis player again. Maybe sometimes we have to take a step back to take a few steps forward. I'm not saying I don't have challenges – because I do – but I'm very much enjoying what I'm doing.

I believe in having a vision and, yes, that vision can change but it's important to have a strong vision. When I played professional tennis, I was climbing a mountain. It was a big one and I just needed to find the next big mountain to climb. I feel I'm now at the bottom of the mountain again, but I've finally put on my mountain boots and I'm excited to start climbing again.

When taking any leap, it's important to protect the downside. The Hollywood story is you go all-in and give up everything. I'm a gut decision-maker and I do go 'all-in', but the way I protect the downside is to keep a number of tennis coaching hours in my diary to ensure I have cashflow. That way I can go off and do little internships or experiences, but still have the safety of some income.

I have several mentors and people who I ask for advice. I like people who encourage, support and tell me the truth. Personally, I think everyone should have a mentor. If you don't have a mentor, then go buy books or listen to podcasts. In my new COVID world I would go for a walk every day at lunch and listen to a podcast. We can all have a mentor in our ear and it's so important to listen to positive people. I'm also big on goal-setting. I will write down year, quarter and month goals, constantly monitoring and evolving them.

An interesting thing about change is how your habits can change. A lot of former professional athletes see significant body changes, like putting on weight, but I never struggled majorly with this. However, in the early years of my tennis retirement, I found playing tennis hard. I didn't have the same enjoyment. I played tennis to learn and to compete, and I wasn't having as much fun because I wasn't playing at the same level. It took time, but I ended up approaching tennis with more of a mental health focus. It was my happy place when I thought about my day and what I was doing.

Change is hard but we only have one life. When we know we are not living our purpose or our best life, then we must do something different. We need to put ourselves around good people, learn from others and live the life we want to live!

To learn more about this author: linkedin.com/in/ james-cluskey-5bb8376a

MAN, WHAT AN EFFING RIDE ...

BY ZOË DEAN-SMITH

Zoë is a Greek name meaning 'life' and it seems to fit! My life and career have been filled to the brim with surprises, twists and turns. My journey includes fourteen years in the field of architecture, working in the Kingdom of Eswatini (my home country, formerly known as Swaziland, in Southern Africa), South Africa and the UK; a fabulous year working as a waterski instructor at Club Med in Mauritius at the age of thirty; three years working as the human resource and administration manager of a microfinance institute in Eswatini; a year as country manager of an industrial catering company; thirteen years in the handcraft sector, with eight years as managing director of a handcraft social enterprise in Eswatini, a year launching a non-profit foundation and four years consulting work for women-led handcraft initiatives around the world. Then followed a year working as program manager of The Coca-Cola Africa Foundation in South Africa, before my current role at Vital Voices.

In the above career mix, one role was made redundant, I've

worked at three different organisations twice and I've resigned from three jobs (including two crappy bosses) without a clue what I was going to do next. I just knew I needed to make a change. In every instance, the universe brought me exactly what I needed next. I've also been shot at (the bullet just missed my leg), survived an attempted rape and am a breast cancer victress with fake boobs. Along that journey, I became a group fitness instructor in 1992 and still teach regular indoor cycling classes. I've also started writing two books.

Seven career chapters later, I've travelled the world, worked with inspiring women across our planet and eventually found my true north – working in the field of women's empowerment. Since March 2013, I've headed up the leadership and social impact department at Vital Voices Global Partnership, an international non-profit organisation based in Washington DC that invests in women leaders who are taking on the world's greatest challenges, from gender-based violence to the climate crisis, economic inequities and more. I oversee our social entrepreneurship capacity building, leadership development and mentoring programs, working with extraordinary women change-makers around the world.

I was born and raised in Eswatini and attended an all-girls high school in Pretoria, South Africa, with about one thousand girls. It was a prestigious and academic school. I drifted through, just barely doing enough work to pass my exams and without any desire to be a super-achiever. There were about two hundred of us in our 1980 school leaving year. Each of us had an *exit interview* with our formidable headmistress, 'Mully'. At that stage, I had no idea what I wanted to do when I left school. Having participated in quite a lot of sport, I figured I might pursue a career as a physical education teacher. When I shared this thought with Mully, she said, 'That is just as well, because you won't amount to much more in your life.' Talk about a slap in the face. In retrospect, I consider her remark to be a gift because my immediate thought was, *Oh yeah, I'll show you.*

CAREER CHAPTER ONE: ARCHITECTURE

During my school leaving year, I did an aptitude test. It was suggested that I pursue a career in either architecture, quantity surveying, law or occupational therapy. As I used to doodle in my schoolbooks, my dad suggested I follow the architecture path. This was literally why I pursued this first career chapter. I completed a three-year diploma, graduating as an architectural technician and spent the next fourteen years working in several architectural practices in Eswatini, South Africa and London. I worked at two of these practices twice.

During this time, I continued with my sporting activities. I became an aerobics instructor, played squash regularly, had two fabulous off-road motorbikes, spent weekends exploring our beautiful Swazi mountains with friends, competed in a handful of four-wheel drive off-road car rallies and participated in numerous amateur theatre productions at our local Swaziland Theatre Club – dancing, acting, set building and painting – eventually producing and directing many shows. My two proudest achievements in amateur theatre were producing *The Rocky Horror Picture Show*, which led to a surprising career opportunity and playing the role of Shirley Valentine in the one-character play by Willy Russell.

CAREER CHAPTER TWO: WATERSKIING AT CLUB MED

In my late-twenties, I had a gorgeous adrenaline-junkie boyfriend, Justin, who taught me to waterski well. At the age of thirty, after we separated, I decided I wanted to be a waterskiing instructor at Club Med. I knew they would be looking for multi-talented people, so I put together a ten-page booklet of everything I had ever done or thought could be of interest, including all my sporting and other achievements. I got the job without an interview. I left my architectural job and headed off to Mauritius – an island nation in the Indian Ocean, on the eastern side of Madagascar. I spent the next year working as a waterskiing 'GO' (gentil organisateur), teaching literally thousands of people how to waterski, participating in the stage shows every night and making many fabulous friends from around the world.

I stayed in Mauritius for two six-month seasons. Towards the end of a season, each GO can request which village they would like next. At the end of my second season in Mauritius, I requested either Moorea or the Club Med II ship that cruised the waters of Micronesia and the east coast of Australia. Neither option was available and as I didn't like or respect my second season chef de village (Club Med boss), I decided to go back home to Eswatini to wait for my next Club Med village assignment and was able to secure my previous architectural job. I found a lovely house to share with a friend, bought a car and got my first dog, a beautiful Alaskan Malamute, Heathcliff. About three months after I got Heathcliff, I received a call from Club Med with great news! They had both options for me. You can imagine my anguish; I could sell the car, but I couldn't possibly give up my new puppy, so I turned them down. I sometimes wonder how different life might have been, but I have no regrets.

CAREER CHAPTER THREE: HUMAN RESOURCES AND ADMINISTRATION IN MICROFINANCE

When I rejoined the architectural practice, the construction industry in Eswatini was not as bustling as it had been and my workload was split between architectural work and taking on some administrative roles within the business. I was subsequently included in a group of staff members who were being let go as the business downsized. My boss helped me secure my next job, working as the admin and human resources manager for a USAID funded microfinance organisation, Swazi Business Growth Trust (SBGT). I managed the HR and admin for a staff of sixty people, two offices, several vehicles and staff housing.

It was during this time that I produced *The Rocky Horror Picture Show.* Our Rocky Horror family was made up of about thirty-five cast members and a large stage crew. It was the biggest production I had ever embraced and was hugely successful, by our small-town standards. We sold out every night. It was a riot with audience participation.

In January 1998, SBGT went into liquidation and my role ended, along with all sixty staff members who lost their jobs. My biggest learning during this time was focused on industrial relations and establishing relationships with the local unions. I also learned that you never know where an experience might take you i.e. producing *The Rocky Horror Picture Show* – a life moment that would eventually take my career path into the field of women's empowerment.

CAREER CHAPTER FOUR: INDUSTRIAL CATERING

Soon after I lost my job with SBGT, through a childhood friend connection, I was headhunted to be the operations manager for Eswatini for an industrial catering company. As country operations manager, I was responsible for overseeing catering contracts at several factories, country clubs and hospitals around the country. I had been recruited for this job because of my organisational skills. However, having no previous experience in catering and food management, within a few months I realised I was out of my depth, so I resigned with no job to go to. I just knew I had to get out before I screwed up.

CAREER CHAPTER FIVE: THE HANDCRAFT SECTOR

Within a short period of time, two options presented themselves. The first was to become the office manager of a local computer business. The second, through the late Jenny Thorne, whom I had cast to play the role of Magenta in our *Rocky Horror Picture Show,* invited me to use my organisational skills that she had seen in the Rocky Horror production to help her to scale up Gone Rural – an economic empowerment social enterprise. She had started the enterprise in 1992 and was working with six hundred rural women artisans, making tableware and homeware products, for export, from the local *lutindzi* mountain grass. I remember thinking, *Hmm, computers or handcrafts, which feels better?* The idea of working with women artisans sounded like a more attractive option. So, in January 1999, I joined Jenny as general manager at Gone Rural. Taking over the administrative reins allowed Jenny to spend more time on the design and rural outreach that she so enjoyed. Jenny gave me every freedom to bring more order and efficiency to the wholesale operations and to scale up our business.

In our first year of working together, we formalised the business into a (Pty) Ltd company. Jenny gave me 10% shares in the business and each year I purchased a few more shares. Within my first four years, we tripled our annual revenue and quadrupled our customer base to over eight hundred outlets in fifty-six countries worldwide. One of Gone Rural's greatest recipes for continued success in a competitive global market was the strong focus on product design and development. Jenny recruited design interns from St Martin's Art College in London. They would come and spend six months with us, learning about Eswatini, the history, culture and handcrafting techniques. Philippa arrived at Gone Rural as a design intern in late 2001 and later became our full-time creative director.

In March 2003, Jenny passed away unexpectedly from a leukaemia diagnosis she had received just six weeks earlier. At this time, I owned 29% shares in the business. After this devastating loss, I stepped into the role of managing director and invited Philippa to become my partner in the business. Phillipa and I set up a 'sister' non-profit organisation to implement the social upliftment projects that Jenny had planned in her last couple of years of life, to provide community development support to our artisans, their communities and families. We would source donor funding to implement projects including HIV/AIDS support, access to clean drinking water, food security and orphan scholarships.

In 2004, through a World Bank Development Marketplace competition, the Grassroots Business Initiative (GBI) arm of the

International Finance Corporation (IFC) found us. This new relationship impacted both Gone Rural and my career path. The immeasurable assistance we received from the IFC included a sizeable grant, a working capital 'soft loan', a tremendous amount of capacity building support and training, the pre-financing of many large-volume orders for overseas customers, multiple opportunities for me to travel internationally to showcase our social enterprise business model and the introduction to similar social enterprises around the world and potential support partners. Gone Rural started receiving global recognition as a social enterprise.

In September 2005, I was invited to attend a conference in Accra, Ghana, and it was at this gathering I initially met Alyse Nelson, president and CEO of Vital Voices, the Washington DC based organisation with whom I currently work. I also came across a holistic life map exercise. I was going through a phase of feeling that I had reached a career plateau. It was during a kinesiology session when I was introduced to a visioning exercise that required me to assess myself in seven areas of life and to then write down goals in each of those areas. It was the first time in my forty-two years that I had ever stopped to think about what it was I intentionally wanted to do with my life. Up until that point I had bumbled through life, almost on autopilot. That session and my subsequent goal-setting turned out to be life-changing. As I completed the exercise, I realised this was a formula I wanted to share with others. Since then, I have taken that framework, evolved it, introduced additional life categories and presented it to multiple audiences around the world. I've also manifested some great goals of my own.

As Gone Rural continued to grow, we hired a third person into our management team: Julie. In April 2006, we legally registered our 'sister' non-profit organisation, Gone Rural boMake (GRB), now known as BoMake Rural Projects. Towards the end of 2006, I felt I had made all the constructive changes I would make and was starting to feel a little stagnant within my work. We had also reached a stage where we couldn't afford to have three people in management. As I reflected on this, I realised that Philippa and Julie had much to offer within the business, with new ideas and new energy. I made the decision to step out as managing director and make space for Philippa to move into that role.

I retained my shares in Gone Rural for a number of years. When I decided to sell them, a handful of Gone Rural's long-term staff members had established an association and were interested in buying shares. I followed Jenny's example and gave 10% of my shares to them. I loved the idea of staff having part ownership and soon started seeing the impact of that investment. Those staff members were thinking more strategically about efficiencies and started coming forward with new and innovative ideas.

In that same year, three consulting opportunities presented themselves, providing me with global development work in the handcraft sector that would take me through the next four years. Between 2008 and 2011, I spearheaded Vital Voices' Global Women Entrepreneurs in Handcrafts Leadership & Business Development Program, developing a week-long business bootcamp for export-ready handcraft entrepreneurs which eventually evolved into a train the trainer program, as well as working with Technoserve and the IFC.

I am so thankful to Jenny for bringing me into the world of women's empowerment. She gave me the opportunity to work in a space where my daily input would directly impact the lives of others and to think more broadly about what more we could all be doing to bring positive measurable change. I also realised that the more I tuned into my true north, the more opportunities would present themselves to me.

CAREER CHAPTER SIX: THE COCA-COLA COMPANY

In mid-2011, I realised that the funding for all three of my consultancy projects was coming to an end and began to think about my next step. I heard about my next career opportunity through a friend. It was a position with The Coca-Cola Africa Foundation (TCCAF) in Johannesburg. They were seeking someone to manage their projects across the entire continent of Africa. I thought, *Why not? I've got nothing to lose in applying. This would be so cool.* I had initiated the Gone Rural BoMake NGO in Eswatini. This was a similar focus, just on a larger scale.

I was beside myself with excitement when I was offered the job. I really felt that Jenny and the universe had conspired to help me to grow and to amplify the impact I could have on the world. I was going to work with one of the largest, most well-known brands in the world. How awesome was that? At the time, TCCAF was working in forty-two African countries, funding programs which included access to clean drinking water, malaria and HIV/AIDS prevention and treatment and education. It was with an equal mix of excitement for the unknown and sadness at leaving behind my friends and my beautiful home country, that I packed up my house and my two dogs and set off on our next adventure.

Working at TCCAF taught me many things. I loved the corporate culture as well as being a part of what felt like a cohesive, large extended family, working within a well-oiled machine. Seeing for myself the incredible difference the Foundation investments were making in communities across the continent, I will forever be a loyal Coca-Cola fan.

About six months into the job, I realised my work scenario was not turning out to be what I had expected, but I couldn't figure out an alternative that would suit my skill set. Hence, in October 2012, I handed in my resignation without having a plan B – no next job to go to. I believe that one needs to firmly close a door before the next opportunity will present itself. Just as when I resigned from Gone Rural, I needed to make the decision to change my situation before the next opportunity would come along. There is no room for procrastination.

CAREER CHAPTER SEVEN: VITAL VOICES, ONCE AGAIN

The day after I resigned, totally out of the blue, I received an email from Alyse at Vital Voices (VV). She wanted me to apply for a position to run the organisation's global leadership development and mentoring programs. My primary role would be to take over the reins of The Global Ambassadors Program, a partnership between VV and Bank of America, bringing together the amazing women leaders in the VV network with some of the most powerful and impressive global women executives, for an intensive mentoring experience. My response was, 'Let me think about that ... YES!'

After a phone interview, a couple of months applying for an O1A visa and a month of nail-biting waiting, I got the visa and relocated to Washington DC. I love my job. As I write this chapter, I am still doing that same work – heading up Vital Voices Leadership and Social Impact department. It was easy to settle into life in Washington DC. I found a great house, got to travel a lot, started teaching indoor cycling classes at a handful of gyms and began building my network of friends and colleagues. I was well settled in my life and my job for several years.

Then COVID happened. The late Queen Elizabeth II used the phrase *annus horribilis* in her 1992 Christmas message, where she said: '1992 is not a year I shall look back on with undiluted pleasure.' 2020 was my *annus horribilis,* the year in which I manifested DCIS – ductal carcinoma in situ, a non-invasive breast cancer that starts in the milk ducts. I believe that my journey with DCIS started back then, in March of 2020.

During COVID lockdown, as many of us adapted to working from home, I discovered I really do not thrive living in isolation. I missed having daily in-person contact and conversations with my great work colleagues, with the community I had built and my fab spin class family.

Living in Washington DC, a lot of focus is placed on politics. Soon after the COVID outbreak, George Floyd was murdered, and the Black Lives Matter movement had me reflecting on how I show up as a white African woman coming from a very different lived experience, compared with what I was seeing in the US. In late July of 2020, my brother Mark, who lives in South Africa, got a bad case of COVID and suffered a massive heart attack. Fortunately, his doctor had sent him to the emergency room that morning and I'm so very happy to say he is still with us, but it was tough being so far away.

It made me ask questions, 'Am I living in the right place? Am I doing work that I love?' I realised I needed to make a change. I love my work, but I needed to change my physical environment. I was looking for somewhere with a great outdoor lifestyle.

My fab friend Nadine from Eswatini lives just outside of Denver, Colorado. I visited her in October 2020 with the intention of figuring out whether Colorado might become my next home state. She did an excellent sales job, taking me to visit spectacular places like Rocky Mountain National Park and the amazing Red Rocks Amphitheatre. I was sold. I immediately made the decision I would move to Denver. I was enormously relieved when our Vital Voices CEO, Alyse, gave her blessing. This way, I could continue doing the work I love as well as live in a beautiful part of the United States that feels like a very big Eswatini, with its chilled people, magnificent mountains, unlimited outdoor activities and big open spaces.

I planned to move in late January 2021 and would share a house with Nadine and her housemate Mary. Towards the end of 2020, I started getting some odd muscular sensations in my chest, so I had a mammogram in early December and received a diagnosis of stage zero DCIS breast cancer, with grade three cancer cells in my right breast. While we had caught this at an early stage, the cancer cells were very aggressive, so this was not a time to dilly-dally. I left DC on 6 January – the day that the US Capitol was stormed … a good day to get out.

In Denver, they couldn't pick up the full extent of the breast cancer from either mammograms or an MRI thus we didn't know if the cancer was present on just the right side or in both breasts. My options included (i) another lumpectomy, (ii) a single mastectomy or (iii) a bilateral (double) mastectomy.

For me, it was a quick and easy decision. Over a phone call, I made a decision which went from 'hell no!' to 'hell yes, and while you're at it, make it a double!' I knew if I didn't opt for the bilateral procedure, I'd spend the rest of my life worrying whether there might still be some breast cancer cells lurking. My breast surgeon, Dr Widner, works alongside a fabulous plastic surgeon, Dr Hunsicker. Between them, they've been doing what is called 'one and done' reconstructive mastectomies, where Dr Widner performs the mastectomy removing the breast tissue and Dr Hunsicker does the reconstruction during the same procedure. I elected to have this 'one and done' procedure which was a great success, followed by a couple of months of recovery. I didn't need radiation or chemotherapy.

I did, however, experience 'survivors' guilt'. When I think about strong women like Mary (also a cancer survivor) who have undergone radiation and chemotherapy to overcome this disease, I believe I got off very lightly.

I feel very strongly that if you're living a life with constant stress, then change your circumstances. Don't wait. Don't procrastinate. Make the change. Go for all your regular medical checkups (ob-gyn, mammograms, dentist etc.), perhaps on your birthday month, as a gift to yourself.

It's been interesting reflecting on my very chequered career path and recognising that each position brought me a skill I would need in my future career chapters. I encourage you too, to take opportunities as they arise, which I have no doubt will build the foundation for future experiences and ensure a life of fun and friendships. Enjoy the ride.

To learn more about this author: linkedin.com/in/ zoe-dean-smith

REIMAGINE & REIGNITE YOUR LIFE!

BY CATHY DERKSEN

'How does one become a butterfly? You have to want to fly so much that you are willing to give up being a caterpillar.' – *Trina Paulus*

I gave up being a caterpillar over a decade ago. No more *just doing life*. It was time to take on the transformation required to fly, living a life with passion and intention.

This quote has been hanging on my wall for years, and it's been featured in many of my books, as it has been a key factor in my ability to reimagine and reignite my life. It drove home to me the fact that we need to be willing to leave behind our past in order to truly step into the life we want to create. We need to reimagine what our life could look like, make the decision and take the actions necessary to move forward.

In my late forties, I came to the realisation I was feeling stuck and numb, living a depressing life which had evolved over decades of living in an abusive marriage and working in a toxic environment. In 2008, my family was involved in a fatal car accident. Luckily for us, everyone in my vehicle was physically unharmed, but the shock of witnessing the sudden death of another driver was the wake-up call that sparked the massive changes I've created in my life since then. Life is too short and too precious to stay stuck and numb.

This new clarity set me on a path to reimagine what my life could be. Over that next year, I found the strength and resources to leave my abusive marriage and take on a complete career transformation. I reassessed my experience and skills. I looked deep within to expose layers of my interests and passions. Up until that point, I had spent twenty-five years working in medical genetics. Although the fields of biology and genetics will always be passions of mine, the isolated, toxic work environment was not a good fit for me. My self-reflection process had allowed me to see that my innate gifts were centred around being of service to others and building connection. I felt a calling to focus on supporting women to create a better life for themselves. Through courage and tenacity, I took on the challenge of reimagining and reinventing my life.

I have been blessed with the intuition and confidence to know that I can take on any challenge. I trust that I will figure things out. I threw my life in the air and reinvented it on the way down. I started my life as a single mom with two teenagers, left my toxic workplace and completely changed my career from medical genetics to financial planning. My mission, as I went all-in with this change, was to create a positive impact on the lives of women by supporting them in creating financial success for themselves.

The process of reimagining life involves ongoing reassessment and review. After a decade of working in the big banks and investment companies, I did not feel I was having the massive impact I felt called to create, despite having assisted many people in improving their life situation. I had supported my clients in understanding their accounts and building wealth but there were so many aspects of creating true financial success I wasn't able to address in those roles. The time limits and compliance details of this professional environment did not allow me to support people in truly understanding the critical factors in their relationship with money, as well as the deep stories that keep so many of us stuck in our current situation, both in finance and in life. I knew it was time to reimagine my life again.

Now in my late fifties, I have dug deeper into the process of listening to my intuition and asking myself the critical questions around my own gifts and passions. What am I capable of? What is the impact I want to have? What is the legacy I want to create? Who am I here to serve? What do they need from me?

My dedication to helping women create a life they love has stayed strong, and I began to imagine doing this on a global scale. As my ability to connect easily with people all over the world has unfolded, I find myself building a global community of women who are keen to shift the world in a positive direction. I allowed myself to think big and step into the vision of new possibilities ahead of me. Knowing I could not fulfil my vision while working in my role as a financial planner, I summed up the courage and took the leap into entrepreneurship. This adventure has been filled with many ups and downs, challenges and thrills, and it has given me the freedom to solidify how to bring my vision into reality.

I am now the founder of my company, Inspired Tenacity Global Solutions. I focus my work on supporting midlife women create success on their own terms and to step into the bigger vision of the life they want to create. While continuing to follow my intuition and listen to the global community I have created, I now focus my business on creating platforms for women to share their stories, support each other and amplify their message to the world. Creating collaborative book projects has become my main service. I create new books on themes that women want to write and read about such as embracing courage, taking on midlife transitions, transforming leadership, overcoming barriers to success and many more inspiring subjects. I have discovered this to be the sweet spot in bringing together my skills, passions and new possibilities.

I've had many people ask me how I have been able to take on such massive changes in my career and in my life. Here are a few of my top suggestions for reimagining your life and stepping into new possibilities.

The first step involves giving yourself permission to think bigger and to allow yourself to see these ideas as possible for you. As women, many of us have spent decades looking after everyone else and putting our own life on the backburner. It's time for us to step into our own vision for the future.

Don't get stuck by limiting beliefs and stories you tell yourself. Know that you are never too old to start something new and that your wisdom and experience are valuable gifts to share with the world.

A critical factor in my success has been the global community of positive, supportive people I have built around me.

Surround yourself with people who encourage you to step into your dreams. Very often, our closest family and friends are not supportive when we start to take on changes in our life. In most cases they are not trying to harm you, they are just trying to keep you safe. This is why it's so important to reach outside of these circles to connect with people who see your vision. Your family and friends will catch on later.

Don't limit your dreams to things you've done before. Allow yourself to think beyond your current situation. Start taking steps in that direction. Reimagining your life and taking on new possibilities can be scary and overwhelming at times, but you can create outcomes beyond your wildest dreams.

To learn more about this author: linkedin.com/in/ cathyderkseninspiredtenacity

REROUTING

BY LORETTA DIGNAM

When we use Google Maps, sometimes we take a wrong turn or take a different route. Google then gets busy rerouting us to get us to our intended destination. When I reflect on my life and career, I see a common theme, a lot of rerouting – whether by accident or by choice.

No-one in my immediate family had ever gone to university. It wasn't a natural progression from my all-girls Catholic convent school, St Pauls, in Greenhills. It was not the norm for me or my classmates to discuss their preferred university course. The expectations for a 'bright girl' where I lived, were to get a job in the civil service or in the bank – permanent and pensionable. But I had other ideas. I saw education as my ticket to life out of my working-class world. My ambition was to go to university and get a degree. By the time I finished school, I applied for law through the university application process, driven by watching *Crown Court* on BBC 1 TV. My first taste of disappointment and failure in my life plan came when I added up my leaving cert results points – I was one point short for my law degree course.

Tears fell immediately. By contrast, my parents were chuffed and so proud of me. But I was devastated. What next? I needed to reroute.

My parents couldn't afford to send me to university, but we were lucky enough to qualify for a grant. Living at home, plus my part-time job, made it just about affordable. I started my second-choice university course, a Bachelor of Commerce degree in UCD and my plan was to switch into law at the end of first year, however, I decided I liked consumer behaviour and marketing. I partied hard, worked hard and rowed with the UCD women's boat club. I loved university life, socially, academically, sports-wise, romance-wise; they were the best days of my life. So much so, I decided I would do a masters and then a PhD. The thought of being 'Doctor Dignam' appealed to my ego, but I needed a second-class honour or above in my degree to get into my chosen masters course. As I had failed at my last major academic hurdle, I was surprised when I got a first-class honours and came tenth in a class of three hundred. A proud moment. My next goal was secure!

Next up was my Masters in Business Studies. I loved that too, confirming my desire to be an academic and to do a PhD. I also enjoyed the entrepreneurial studies we did; I could see myself being an entrepreneur. A friend advised me of the 'Milk Round' of graduate program jobs. She drew my attention to one specifically, with Mars Inc. The Mars graduate recruitment roadshow gripped me. The opportunities were endless, and the pay was incredibly attractive. I fell in love with what they had to offer. I could just do my PhD later, right? I received the results of my masters – first-class honours and joint first in the class. I was on target. Of the thousands who applied to Mars Inc, only two of us were offered a job on their graduate program. Boy was I proud! So, I took the job with Mars, rerouting, with a plan to defer my PHD.

Joining Mars Inc, starting at Pedigree Petfoods, involved me leaving my boyfriend of three years and moving to London to initially take up a sales role, as part of the graduate program. I was driving 1,000 miles a week, selling dog food and cat food out of the boot of my car, having just passed my driving test six weeks prior. Not quite the sexy job I had envisaged at my masters graduation! I didn't particularly enjoy the sales role, finding it quite lonely. After two major car crashes, where I wrote off both cars, I was moved from sales to marketing and into the head office. Accidental or subconsciously intentional, who knows? An extreme tactic, nonetheless, to get out of sales.

I went on to work for thirteen years with Mars Inc in the UK, Ireland and Sweden. What a company! 'Best in class' is how I would describe everything about Mars. The best years were when I was working in Dublin. I worked with a team of people who were smart, determined, hardworking and such fun. We had an enviable culture and always celebrated success. I especially loved working in the food business at Mars/Masterfoods. I launched Dolmio in Ireland and, with my colleagues, built the Uncle Ben's brand. We even made it into the *Guinness Book of Records,* building the world's largest lasagne in 1990, a challenge but incredible fun! We gave the very edible lasagne away to Meals on Wheels and other charities. The food business in Ireland was one of the most successful in the Mars Masterfoods group at the time. It was a thrill to lead out on that.

What happened to my PhD? Well, once again I reimagined and rerouted. I was enjoying working with Mars Masterfoods so much. I was earning good money and travelling. The idea of going back to academia after the excitement of this commercial world was no longer appealing. So, I kicked the proverbial can down the road.

I met my German husband and got married in 1992. In 1993, I had my son Fabian and that changed a lot for me. I took up a promotion with Masterfoods Sweden and we moved there when he was only six months old. It was a challenging time, as motherhood and career were a conflict for me. I felt guilty throughout my career for being a working mother. I had my gorgeous daughter, Enya in 2001. Very soon after that, our marriage ended. When my ex-husband and I separated, then divorced, I was a single parent with two children, working full-time outside the home. I had to work as I had no financial support. Guilt continued to plague me. I looked at the other mums with envy, as they collected their kids from the school gate. I often wonder if men experience the guilt that many women do?

After four years in Sweden, I was ready to come home. I had reached marketing director level in both Ireland and Sweden, and it was time for something else. I identified the businesses I wanted to work for in Ireland and set about making it happen. ESAT (a new mobile phone company) rejected me, but Guinness Ireland (now Diageo) offered me a senior marketing role, looking after the 'declining brands' in the portfolio. The optimist in me thought that with these brands, the only way was up. Smithwick's was part of the portfolio and under my tenure, we saw the brand turn around to very profitable growth. I took on some other roles after that, including the head of consumer communications, a generalist in charge of a team of specialists and a huge marketing budget. Those were the days!

After Diageo came Kerry Group, where I headed up marketing for their Food-to-Go business, which was comprised primarily of pre-packed sandwiches. Growth was meteoric for the four years I worked there. From August 2008, however, we could see sales fall off a cliff. It was the beginning of the big crash. Our hi-vis customers (construction workers) stopped buying our sandwiches and the rest is economic history. Cuts ensued, and I was a casualty. Once again, I had to reroute.

Within jig time, I had another two roles: marketing director and board member at Jacob Fruitfield and part-time lecturer at the Michael Smurfit Business School on their Msc program. A lot of late nights and juggling followed, as I never intended to take on both roles simultaneously. At Jacob Fruitfield, I worked with an old university classmate. Whilst there I brought 'Chocolate Mikado' to market. For its full 360 marketing program and turning the Jacob's biscuit brand around, I won Marketer of the Year in 2011. That peer-awarded accolade was something I will always treasure. I participated in the sale of Jacob Fruitfield to Valeo Foods, and my departure was then inevitable.

At this point, I yearned for something broader than food businesses, so began consulting across a variety of sectors. I was again attracted back to lecture in the Michael Smurfit Business School on their MBA program. I also applied for a ministerial position on the board of the Abbey Theatre, our National Theatre, and was successfully appointed in 2015. I had inadvertently adopted a 'portfolio' career. I had variety, stimulation and it was financially lucrative. What more could a woman want? I was able to be around for my kids, as my hours were flexible, which assuaged some of my guilt.

The Abbey Theatre board position was hugely exciting and stimulating for me. I was working with a group of eclectic board members, from playwrights to actors to judges and high-profile CEOs. Within six weeks of joining the board, the Abbey Theatre's 2016 centenary program, 'Waking the Nation' was announced, to commemorate Ireland's 1916 rising. But it contained only one play written by a woman. The reaction was explosive, led by a newly formed group called Waking the Feminists or #WTF (genius!). Given my experience in communications, I ended up on the newly formed committee for gender equality and was appointed chair at our very first meeting. Together, the members of our committee, with whom I have made friends for life, successfully introduced the first Abbey Theatre Gender Equality Policy, which subsequently became part of the DNA and culture of the Abbey and spilled over into the rest of the theatre community. I was part of history in the making. Being part of driving change gave me a new sense of excitement and achievement. My appetite was whetted.

In 2017, I got a call from the CEO of Ardagh Group, asking if I was interested in joining him there. He was a highly successfully ex BComm classmate, and after some consideration, I rerouted. I resigned my clients and went back into the corporate sector in a B2B role. This was not something I'd planned for nor envisaged happening but seemed like a great opportunity. Unfortunately, or fortunately, it was to be short-lived. We were both ex-Ardagh Group five months after I started. This unexpected and new-found freedom (or unemployment, as was the reality), meant that I had to think long and hard about what I wanted to do next. This would require some serious rerouting.

What should I do at fifty-three years of age? I started looking for jobs. Either I was too senior, too old or too junior. I spent a few months coming second in interviews. One piece of feedback I got was that I was capable of so much more and that by taking that job, I would limit my possibilities. Intriguing feedback. Or maybe I could go part-time or retire early? I was at a crossroads. My rerouting app was working overtime trying to figure out a way forward.

In parallel, over the previous four years, I had been on a sort of health journey that had taken me by surprise – MENOPAUSE! A month before I turned fifty, I had what was to be my last menstrual cycle and very soon the hot flushes started. That was all I knew about menopause – hot flushes and no periods. But surely, I was too young? Didn't that happen to much older women than me? I had never heard the word *perimenopause* and so missed the myriad of symptoms that affected me throughout my forties. How was I, an intelligent, educated and experienced woman of the world, so ignorant and blindsided? I was all in favour of treating my menopause symptoms the 'natural' way, including buying magnets that I put in my underwear to help with my hot flushes. The magnet cost €35 in Boots. Bargain! But all that happened was that the supermarket trolley chain stuck to my tummy – *voom!* I put up with three years of hot flushes (twenty to thirty throughout the day and night) in my quest to find a natural solution. I eventually 'gave in' and went to my GP looking for HRT. I was terrified of HRT because of the mythical narrative in my head; *HRT causes breast cancer and makes women put on middle age spread.*

Was this based on fact? Every time I consulted Dr Google the answers were conflicting. I didn't know what to believe and I chose to believe the information that supported my own fictional narrative. My visit to my GP was short and sweet and I left with a prescription not suited to me. Three weeks later, I tore off the unsuitable patch and consulted a hormone specialist. I had a transformational consultation that took an hour, and cost a lot more than a GP visit, but I left knowing so much more than I'd started with. I left with separate hormones (oestrogen and progesterone).

This appointment changed the course of my life. Within weeks my symptoms abated. At my three-month review, testosterone was added to my regime; a hormone I was unaware women needed. That was the last missing piece of the jigsaw for me. I was back! I was transformed from a woman who described herself as being like a 'slow puncture', to a vital woman who had her mojo back. This prompted my own market research among other menopausal women, and about their experiences, which were similar.

The seminal moment came when I met an influential and successful businesswoman for coffee in Bewley's of Grafton Street, Dublin, to discuss 'opportunities'. Remember, at this time I was unemployed and trying to find my North Star. At the meeting, she picked up her menu to fan herself, as she was telling me her plans for her sixtieth birthday. I thought she was feeling faint, so offered to take her outside for air. She told me there was no need to fuss, she was 'just having a hot flush'. I was gobsmacked and asked her where she'd gone for help. She had seen no-one and had been experiencing symptoms for ten years! I decided there and then that I needed to help women manage their menopause. That day I decided to open a clinic, dedicated to 'all things menopause'. The idea was born. My rerouting was beginning.

I went home to let the idea percolate and take shape. I had seen firsthand at the Abbey Theatre the power of policy to change workplace and societal outcomes. Surely, I could try to do something to help make the lives of menopausal women better? I had witnessed my daughter go through puberty and thought about what lay ahead for her as a woman and the impact of hormones and periods every month, pregnancy (maybe) … and eventually menopause. Her experience needed to be very different than mine and my mother's and grandmothers', and I needed to start 'today'. This became my imperative. I put all my energy into starting my own menopause clinic. I had some savings I could invest. I felt in my gut that this is what I *had to do,* and I had a sense of peace with this decision.

I spent some months researching menopause, educating myself, checking out what services were available in Ireland and internationally. I talked to doctors, nurses, colleagues, family and friends, bouncing the concept off them all. I watched videos, read books about menopause and went on a course in the UK, where I was the only non-clinician. I just knew this was the right thing for me to do. I had decided to rewire and not retire or take the easy route forward.

I had years of business experience, so I knew how to do a lot of things. I got support to help me with branding, web design, plus medical help to get the clinic set up, painting work, building furniture and so on. It was all hands on deck. It took nine months from inception to opening the doors of the clinic. It felt exciting and energising to be working on something new, something with purpose.

I decided to call the clinic 'The Menopause Hub'. It was a name that offered the opportunity to expand the services and products that women might want. I wasn't financially independent, nor do I have a life partner who supports me financially, so I still needed an income, however, I was ready to take a risk. I wasn't expecting to earn any income from this venture for the foreseeable future. Sometimes not everything can be aligned perfectly, sometimes you just have to take a leap and hope your judgement works out and that some money will follow. I jumped.

It was exciting and scary in the lead up to the opening … but mostly exciting. I was kept going by the adrenaline surge. My kidults (my adult children) and friends were so incredibly supportive. I was energised by the prospect of a new direction. Hard to believe, as I was in my fifties, but it felt easy somehow to put in the effort needed for something I believed in. It also helped that the hardest days of my parenting were behind me. My children were no longer as dependent on me, and I had the motivation and freedom to pursue my purpose. It was such a buzz. I admire those entrepreneurs who embark on their journeys with young children in tow.

In December 2018, we opened the doors of The Menopause Hub. It was a bittersweet moment. Sadly, the night before, my mother, Frances Dignam, passed away (aged ninety-one). I considered postponing the opening, but my mum was passionate about women's rights and supporting women, so I went ahead in a numb daze. As you can imagine, the anniversary of the opening will always be bittersweet and tinged with sadness. My mum would have loved to see what I am doing now. And she would be so proud.

Had I known then what I know now, I'm not sure I would have taken the same path in becoming an entrepreneur. It seems so sexy a concept … running your own business, but the learning curve was steep. Very steep! I was a non-medic in a medical world. Did I have doubts? Of course, I did! My biggest doubt was whether we would have enough patients to sustain a business, despite the numbers on paper in my business plan. But that has never been an issue, surprisingly. The biggest hurdle I had was recruiting doctors. This was much harder than I thought it would be, particularly as there is a shortage of GPs in Ireland, and a dearth of doctors who want to specialise in menopause. As the business grew, there were more hurdles to overcome, some big and some not so big, and other problems to be solved. At times it felt like whack-a-mole.

I admit that after the first year I was emotional and exhausted, but I never considered giving up. Family and friends continued to encourage me to keep going and reassured me that what I was doing was a 'good thing'. I just kept my eyes and laser-sharp focus on my vision and goals.

The fact that I am a menopausal woman and a patient gave me some core insights, resulting in us having a patient-centred approach. We brought onboard additional doctors, a psychologist, a dietitian and nutritionist, a women's health physio and an acupuncturist, to offer an holistic, evidenced-based approach to menopause care and management. The clinic is now going from strength to strength. We opened a second clinic on the north side of Dublin in Autumn 2022, though two years later than planned, thanks to COVID-19. And we opened our third clinic in Ballincollig, Cork, in October 2023.

There comes a point in life for some of us where we have reached a career cul-de-sac. I felt like that. I had accumulated so many skills and experiences outside of the marketing discipline and believed I had much more to offer. I felt I had reached the end of the road in what I was doing. Rerouting on this scale felt challenging, daunting but exciting. So, if you have a yearning for a different direction, my advice is to wholeheartedly 'go for it'. There is no point having regrets.

I, personally, didn't want to go to my grave with my epitaph being: *Here lies Loretta who sold Mars bars, dog food and beer all her life!* I wanted to leave a legacy of change. But I had no idea what that might be. In my role as chair of the gender equality committee at the Abbey Theatre, with my contribution to improving gender equality in the wider theatre community, I felt I had left some small legacy. This gave me the courage to try something else and on a bigger scale, in menopause. At least my epitaph would read a little differently.

I know I'm not alone in wanting to give back and leave a legacy. Whatever you do, surround yourself with radiators, not drains. There's a saying, radiators generate energy and drains suck you dry. Having positive, supportive people around you is critical. Even the most optimistic of us have days of self-doubt! There were times when I was exasperated, times when I was frustrated, times when I was exhausted and times when I doubted myself, but I never thought of throwing in the towel.

I've regularly asked myself in life, at different stages, whether the benefits outweigh the costs? I have asked that about my relationships, my friendships, my hobbies, my volunteering work. When the costs outweigh the benefits, it is time for a decision of some sort. So far, for me, with The Menopause Hub, the benefits outweigh the costs.

They say that hard work, luck, and timing are everything. When I started, menopause was taboo. Now, thanks to the advocacy of people in the UK like Davina McCall, Meg Matthews and some key medics, and in Ireland too, thanks to advocates like me and a handful of others, menopause is spoken about more. We still have a very long way to go to normalise and to destigmatise menopause. Often people say to me, 'Your timing was excellent' … they do not realise that The Menopause Hub and the work I've been doing has been a catalyst driving that change.

When I let myself reflect, I am proud of what I'm doing and what I've accomplished so far. To me, the image of being an entrepreneur used to sound sexy and fun. The reality couldn't be further from the truth. Using the *Headspace* meditation app has been hugely helpful for me to allow some quiet brain time. I now earn an income which is still less than when I was working in the corporate sector, but I don't mind. Each year my income increases as the business grows and continues to be successful. At this point in my life, my worth isn't valued by 'material goods'. I feel I have enough of everything.

Five years on, I have absolutely no regrets. I am glad I took the plunge. I have a team of great staff, which makes life easier. I see infinite possibilities to grow the business and infinite ideas of how to expand. Given how much I enjoy what I am doing, how we are changing women's lives and the buzz of being an entrepreneur, I have decided to go to the next level, and I am on the international expansion trail now. This will keep me energised, challenged, focused and rewarded for the next five years. In addition to work, all I want now are experiences; to travel, to eat out, to go to live entertainment, to experience culture, to hang out with family and friends. I can afford to do that, and I make the time. I am happy.

To learn more about this author: linkedin.com/in/ lorettadignam

CAREER WITH PURPOSE – CAN WE BE HAPPY WITH THE 'ONE'?

BY CHARLOTTE DOYLE

This life will pass by no matter what you do, so how are you going to choose to spend it?

Choosing a career is one of the most important decisions you will make in life. A career gives us a sense of direction and purpose. It's about so much more than deciding what you will do to make a living.

While some people are lucky enough to know what they want to do, and end up in satisfying careers, many of us are not. Is it nature or nurture that determines our choice? Many people don't put any effort into selecting their occupation or even choose them for the wrong reasons. They may choose careers that seem secure or pay well, but this often leads to unhappiness.

Can we be happy with the 'one' career choice we make? With this question in mind, I'd like to share my journey.

One of the most common questions we hear as children is *what do you want to be when you grow up?* The environment we are exposed to growing up greatly influences our career choices. Mothers are a big influence on our career choices, and it has been scientifically proven that childhood fantasies of what we want to be are well developed by the age of fourteen. Back then, I knew what I wanted – to play golf and to marry John.

'Be an accountant,' my mother solemnly said to me, 'then you can do anything you want.'

I read an interesting article explaining how we determine our careers based on the survival strategies we develop as children. For example, if we learned that being seen and not heard was a safe way to navigate our childhood household chores, odds are we'd opt to work in accounting. The child who spent most of their childhood trying to cheer up their depressed mother might become a stand-up comic, a psychologist or a caregiver. To survive as children, we learn to look externally for feedback about what we should or should not do – especially for how we *should* make a living. We learn these lessons well and they are stuffed deeply into our unconscious. Years later, as we try to figure out what career path to take, these learnings push us toward certain occupations and away from others.

In 1988, the last year of school, I was a high achiever with good grades. I was elected head girl and travelled to Lourdes representing Killaloe parish. I was winner of Ulster Bank's Student of the Year and finalist in the All-Ireland School Public Speaking competition. It was happening to me, and I thought I was the 'one'.

In a decade with no exposure to mobile phones, Google or social media platforms, TV, radio, books and magazines were our channels of knowledge. My years of reading *Jackie* magazine fuelled my thoughts, and it was in those pages that I'd decided to set up my own company running events; it was in my genes after all, so why shouldn't I? My mother owned a grocery shop, my grandmother was a publican and my grandfather owned and operated Melia Coach Tours.

My career guidance counsellor was a nun who had joined the Sacred Heart from the age of eighteen. Although educated and well-read, she had no grasp of what was out there for the taking, especially for convent girls from Tipperary. Her words to me were, 'Lovely, dear, but when you marry, who will mind the house and children?' I turned on my Dubarry loafers with my mind set on proving I could do it.

However, as a people pleaser, I gave in to my mother's ambitions for me and went off to Limerick to become an 'accountant'. Within the year, I was elected class president organising our refreshers week. It was in Limerick that I would start to hang out with the 'creative' types, as they were known back then; students who were more mature, a bit different in the way they dressed and spoke, and certainly more at ease with their sexuality. They oozed confidence and being surrounded by passionate and creative people made me realise there was more to life, and being your authentic self was important.

However, I was wearing my 'party pants' far too much and failed my first-year exams. My mother was disappointed, to say the least. I was 'a college dropout' and hauled up to Dublin to stay under the watchful eye of my godmother to finish my accounting exams. It was the nineties, and Dublin, I was coming for you.

I enrolled in Dublin Business School part-time, and quickly realised I needed a job to fund my social calendar and keep me in style. I landed my first job with Henry J Lyons & Partners, a high-profile architects practice, working as a trainee account assistant. I told them, in an interview, I was studying at night to become an accountant, and they believed me. At the time, I believed it myself. So how do we choose our first job? The simplest answer, in my experience, is they hire you and you are grateful.

In our first job, we are keen to make an impact and progress fast. We may have to sacrifice our social lives or engaging hobbies over studying for professional exams. The 'party pants' were put away and I embarked on evenings spent preparing for my ACCA tax exams. There was no choice – I had to get these exams, if not for my mother, then to give me the ability to do what I wanted.

I enjoyed working with Henry J Lyons and came to understand if you surround yourself with creative and passionate people who inspire you, then you are more positive in your outlook and the work you do. Yes, I was still a reluctant accountant, but I felt lucky to have a good job and live in the epicentre of the capital. All I needed was one thing: more money.

At the age of twenty-four, I had two choices; travel or commit to my relationship and my career. Some of my friends were heading to America, as back in the nineties, it was THE place to go. The lure of sunny California and Florida and the excitement of New York and Boston was enticing; they left, and I stayed. I focused on building a career and saving for a house, wanting to settle down.

When I had finished my accountancy exams, I secured a

well-paid account executive role in my second job with ABB Reinsurance – it almost killed me! It meant eighteen-hour days and weekends, working with a small team in Dublin, with the head office in Zurich. The money was the draw, for sure, and the people were, again, passionate about what they did for the company. It was the early nineties, and in the words of Fat Boy Slim, I would 'eat, sleep, work, repeat'. The culture was that you stayed 'till you got it done'.

At this stage, I hated everything about accountancy; Excel spreadsheets, reconciling figures, reporting and analysing figures. But I wanted to 'prove' I could do it and not let anyone down.

I was binge drinking after work and smoking to alleviate stress. My relationships suffered outside of work and were on the slippery slope. I had piled on weight and developed panic attacks and constant headaches. I was doing something I didn't like, and it was taking a toll on my body. A dislike of your job is likely to manifest itself in your body – I didn't leave the job, it left me.

Throughout this four-year period, a constant support in my life was John McLoughlin. Yes, my fouteen-year-old fantasy and ambition had become a reality … plus he played golf. John my rock. They say great soulmates make great motivators, and this is true. Psychologists have discovered that people with supportive partners/spouses are more likely to take on potentially rewarding challenges – including challenges at work – and that those who take on such challenges experience more personal growth, happiness and better psychological well-being. I might have not wanted to be an accountant, but I had someone in my life who believed and supported me.

Then my world crashed.

My amazing father, Charlie, died suddenly, two weeks before my wedding. It was a complete shock, and I was numb. I idolised him.

The loss of a parent must be the closest thing to a universal emotional experience that humanity has. The trauma of the event, though, can affect the rest of our lives. The loss of my father changed my perspective on my career and life, I didn't care any longer to impress anyone with my job title or money.

Grief is like breathing, you must do it.

I know life is not perfect and we can't be happy all the time, but we can find joy in what we do. I knew I wanted to find that joy. We proceeded with the wedding as planned and nine months later, still in the 'fog' of grief, our only and wonderful son Cathal was born. He was our joy and the one.

I was fortunate enough to get a package from ABB as we had relocated to the Channel Islands during my pregnancy. We bought a house and decided I would take time to support my mother, as during that two-year period, we had lost my grandmother and grandfather, as well as my husband's father. It was a tough time, but my Cathal was the choice I made, and one I did not regret. In the words of Billy Ocean 'when the going gets tough, the tough get going', and that I did. I was twenty-eight.

At this point, there was another type of grief I was also experiencing – losing my career. It's important to grieve when you transition through various stages in your career and life – it helps you understand more about yourself and deal with the feelings of loss. How do you move on?

When we meet new people, one of the first questions asked is, 'What do you do for a living?' Our job defines us; we say, 'I'm an accountant,' 'I'm a nurse,' or, 'I'm a solicitor.' People we meet make assumptions about our character based on our occupation. It's little wonder we tie up our self-identity with our job.

Going to work gives us a sense of purpose and ritual – we get up, get dressed and go into work. It defines what we do with our day. As humans we need to connect. How do you talk about yourself and your life when you're not working?

I immersed myself in charity work and volunteering and felt fulfilled. A year after Cathal's birth, I was approached to join RTÉ (Ireland's public service broadcaster), as accountant/event manager in the RTÉ Sports and social club located on the Montrose site. It was the offer I was waiting for, combining my passion for working with creative people, my passion for events and using my skills as an accountant. I spent sixteen years in RTÉ Montrose and loved every day. They were supportive to me when I suffered three late miscarriages. I got involved with the creche and credit union onsite as a board member and made friendship bonds that, to this day, are in my close circle. My mother was right, *be an accountant and you can do anything*. This was the one for me.

However, times changed in Montrose and, in 2014, they were selling land and making cuts to staff, offering redundancies. I was no longer happy at work, not because of the people I worked with, but the *purpose* had gone from my career. As things were winding down, I became bored, and the lure of a substantial package was enticing. But RTÉ carried a prestigious name, and I was nervous. I would no longer get invited to the film premieres, the launches and the balls, but I also knew it was the one chance for me to have another career. I was forty-four.

A career change can be daunting at any point in your journey. However, in your forties, you are likely to have two decades of experience in your work history, which can feel hard to leave behind. In your forties, you're also likely to have more responsibilities, including financial, family and relationships.

The good news is that experience and those responsibilities also indicate a highly developed skill set, and your desire for change points to a growth mindset and willingness to work. This perspective may come in handy when you're tempted to ascribe any age-related negative narratives to your career. Likely, it's not your age that's the problem; the story you believe is.

Whatever the obstacles stopping you from making the one change, only you can make it happen. For me, I knew I had to speak to someone – other than my mother, my husband and friends. They knew me too well. It could be the right time to invest in yourself. I firmly believe that life coaching or mentoring is crucial to anyone with self-doubt. Finding the right person to seek advice is important. In recent years through the *Image* business women's network, I came across Niamh Ennis , a change and transformation coach. Her book *Get Unstuck* has been a huge influence on how we must be willing to do hard things and stretch ourselves, if we want better outcomes. Because it is in the doing, the action, that we discover we are truly capable of achieving what we want. I met Niamh this year and was struggling with a job offer and her poignant question was, 'What if you say "no"? How will you feel?'

Knowledge is power. As a mature student, I headed back to college and enrolled on an Honours Degree in Business Studies. I loved it and it loved me. I wasn't working during this time and could devote time to my son and husband, as well as giving me the time to develop in something that wasn't accountancy. I graduated in 2015 with first-class honours and went straight to Osborne recruitment agency with clear demands. I laid down where, what and who I wanted to work for. I didn't want to make a mistake. I knew the one thing that was most important and would find me joy: a career with a purpose.

I remember 8 August 2015 well. It was the day I started in Tuath Housing in Merrion Square, Dublin 2. I met the chief executive, a social entrepreneur with a funny, warm disposition who radiated empathy for the people who worked under his leadership. I knew that day I was in the right place with the right people.

However, I had to know where I was going to fit in this work, and felt I had to be visible and shine, and that I did my best to do. I did this by volunteering to help organise events, joined work groups and took on extra responsibilities. I spoke up at meetings and was always well-presented and on time. Maya Angelou said, 'Try to be a rainbow in someone's cloud. I've learned that people will forget what you said, people will forget what you did, but people will never forget how you made them feel.' The culture at Tuath Housing was supportive and caring, and I felt valued. I had found purpose, and it was the one for me.

How do we find purpose in our career? Remember chasing butterflies? The more you ran, the more they flew to escape you. But sometimes, when you just sat on the grass and watched, they'd come to rest on your leg – if only for a moment. Finding purpose in your work can have a lot to do with your attitude and the need to understand what's truly important to you. Step back a little. It's possible to see that, no matter what you're doing, you can incorporate meaning into it.

I have been with Tuath Housing through almost nine incredible fast-paced years of growth. From a part-time reception cover to human resources manager with a team supporting almost two hundred employees over four offices, delivering nearly eleven thousand homes to 26,500 tenants. There is no shortcut to promotion, you must put in the work. During this time, I completed CIPD fellowship in HR, along with a management diploma and was shortlisted for four various HR-related accreditations. In 2022, I was honoured to win Human Resources Rising Star. I get to work with caring, passionate people and feel supported in what I do in a career with a purpose.

When do you know it is time for a change? It's how you feel on a Sunday night. If you have doubts going into work on a Monday morning, then the truth is you already have made up your mind you need to make plans and do something about it.

At fifty-two, my story is far from over. I have begun studying a postgraduate diploma in innovation, creativity and social development at Trinity College, Dublin. I am surrounded by a diverse group of creative people with a passion and drive for purpose. Tangent in Trinity encourages idea makers and disruptors; I have found my tribe.

In May 2023, we moved to Menton, south of France, on a one-year career break focusing on self-development and travel. I made the sacrifices in my twenties not to travel, to progress in my career and, I gained in return, early motherhood and a wonderful son.

I do not have any financial commitments, and this has given me freedom to do what I want.

In life you need three things:

1. Someone to love.
2. Something to hope for.
3. Something to do.

Can you be happy with the 'one'? I leave it with you to answer.

I am fortunate not to be tied to any financial commitments and with wise, early pension advice, can now enjoy this career break. This break has given me valuable family time and strengthened my relationships. I have volunteered, travelled and acquired new skills and overall improved my self-doubt.

To learn more about this author: linkedin.com/in/ charlotte-doyle-ba11a1148

DON'T STAND IN YOUR OWN WAY

BY GILLIAN DUGGAN

About ten years ago I found myself at a crossroads. I was about to be made redundant for the third time in as many years, each time, without a big sexy payment. My family had flown the nest, my marriage was empty, and I was at a low ebb – feeling lost and, undeniably, lonely.

While I needed a new job, I also had to leave my marriage, my home and, at the age of fifty-five, live on my own for the first time. Having put out some feelers, no-one in my network came knocking. Recruitment agencies offered me more of the same and wanted a one-page CV. How do you reduce thirty-five years employment to one page? This made me feel old and useless, and even more miserable.

With hindsight, I was going round and round in circles in my head, wearing myself out.

Nowadays, I am working in a different area as a national tour guide, a hiking guide and driving buses of all sizes. I was able to retrain, through my local ETBI (Educational Training

Board of Ireland) and obtained a Fáilte Ireland recognised qualification as a national tour guide, a lowland leader award from Mountaineering Ireland and the D category on my driving licence permitting me to drive the big buses. And most of this happened during the COVID lockdown.

One of the elements included in the training was help creating a CV, which got me over the one-page hump, when I realised enthusiasm and willingness to learn is never going to come across in a CV.

However, I didn't get here by doing a formal interview but rather because I reached out and built up a relationship, did some (enjoyable) work without payment (thanks to the government supports in place i.e. social welfare) and showed I was a good communicator and tour guide.

So how did I get to where I am now?

I have always loved history and geography and combined with my hobby, hillwalking, I loved examining the outdoor environment as I moved through it. I had completed mountain skills courses over the years, plus I had been guiding in the mountains on a volunteer basis. Once, I met a guide with two tourists on the Brockaghs near Glendalough, and I thought, *Wow* – that was *the* job ... being paid to hike!

Mark Twain said: '*Find a job you enjoy doing, and you will never have to work a day in your life.*'

Through my local ETB (education and training board), I found a national tour guide training course. I applied and was accepted, and noticed I was the only one in my class who had this outdoors skill set. I did not see myself as a professional hiking guide until one of my tutors told me that a tourist's idea of a hike and my idea were two different things. They wanted the low Brockaghs not Carrauntoohil, the highest mountain in Ireland.

I saw another opening. If I got my bus driving licence, I had a better chance of getting year-round work as a driver/guide. Through the ETB again, I learnt how to be a professional driver, got my CPC (certificate of professional competence), learnt about the tachograph amongst many other relevant elements, all whilst getting lessons driving a fifty-seater bus around Dublin.

As an aside, I was not the first in my class to do the driving test, but I was the first to pass it. I'm very proud of that. However, I decided that morning, I never wanted to drive one of these monsters ever again. So, these days, I stick to the minibuses and smaller coaches.

While I was on my driving course, I spotted an outdoor adventure minibus parked at the woods behind my house and I emailed them my new CV. We arranged a meeting, and as we talked about the work and my experience, I realised I recognised my interviewer. Terry offered me a job starting as soon as I finished my bus course. I told him I had met him once before – on top of the Brockaghs with two tourists!

Unfortunately, COVID hit and disrupted everything, which sent me into another slump.

I walked around the garden every morning and even though it was early in the year, I kept finding mushrooms. I knew all the plants and trees in the garden, but not the mushrooms, so I found something with which to distract myself.

Over the course of that summer, during a lift in the lockdown, Terry offered me my first professional hiking guide job;

bringing a group up and over the Brockaghs where I had first met him. It was a wonderful experience, for lots of reasons.

That lockdown autumn, I continued learning about mushrooms and started to experiment with spore prints. Firstly, to help me identify species but, having forgot about a set, I found it had made a fantastic design in the interim. I experimented and framed some to give as Christmas presents to family and friends. They encouraged me to take it to the next level and I created a website, www.mushroomart.ie. I had a very sharp learning curve in website design, marketing and sales.

It was around this time that my mother died, alone, in her nursing home. I found this very difficult to come to terms with and still do. I also damaged my knee so was on crutches for her funeral, which meant I could not go on my distracting mushroom hunts. I remember the sorrow and pain being tortuous.

While I was on crutches, I saw another ETB course called Tracks and Trails; a lowland leader Mountaineering Ireland qualification. I felt it would square my circle of new qualifications – tour guide, driver and now hike/walk leader. The online interview was over Teams, and I enthusiastically answered all the questions with a smile, while my crutches were under the table!

Thankfully, the commencement of the course was delayed due to another lockdown, and I had recovered from the operation by the time it started. We had a wonderful group of mostly tour guides and despite lockdown, spent the next five months walking the Wicklow Hills learning all about tracks and trails. It was educational, so we all had a permit to travel! It was the most fun and we still keep in touch sharing information and work referrals.

I'd done some work for Terry before and during COVID, but

I'd never sent in an invoice. The poor man's time was spent doing refunds for all the forced tour cancellations and I just couldn't ask for payment. Terry was very faithful to me and kept offering me work whenever the lockdowns were lifted. Finally, in May 2022 when the Irish lockdown was lifted, it went crazy. Normally, there is a build-up, but the tourists were like greyhounds out of a trap and I was working flat out between driver/guiding day tours and guiding walkers.

I have been honing my craft and have received great reviews for my tour guiding and driving. I have travelled all over this beautiful island, explaining our cultural highlights both on and off the beaten track. I have met interesting people, been to interesting places and am still learning, still walking the hills and feeling energised and happy, confident and self-assured.

The ETB and the Department of Social Protection provided me with these opportunities for which I will always be grateful, plus may I point out that for me and many others, lockdown was productive.

My daughter got married last summer to the most wonderful young man. I am very much on speaking terms with my husband and considerate of his pending retirement, since he was married to his job for all these years. I still have my mushroom art and look forward to mushroom hunts every autumn.

I have found a new romantic relationship too, with a loving, rewarding and respectful bond. They saw something in me and have been a constant positive and encouraging influence. It works both ways and we are a mutual appreciation couple. It is warm and caring.

Some people have thought me brave to retrain for a new

career at my age, and I admit there were days when I thought it wasn't meant to be. But I will say it – don't stand in your own way.

Some ask me if I should be putting my feet up now, but I feel too young to retire.

Some say I am inspirational, for which I am flattered, and if my story inspires one person to change their life trajectory, then I will be happy.

I can't call this new career a job, I enjoy it far too much.

To learn more about this author: linkedin.com/in/ gillianduggan

UNCONVENTIONAL SELF-EVOLUTION

BY MARK FARRELL

Imagine this: tomorrow morning you wake up and perhaps dress differently, commute to a new location or simply just open your laptop and start working in a field you have longed for. If that sentence got you more excited than your favourite decadent over-priced coffee drink, then you are ripe for change. Simply writing that sentence gives me excitement, thinking back to when I had an epiphany to delve into another industry. One not entirely removed from my profession, though the platform and audience I wanted to serve and how I would serve them was vastly different from what I was accustomed to.

It's widely known that the field of broadcasting, in particu-lar radio, is unstable and fiercely competitive. The number-one broadcast market in the world takes this to an even higher level. When this very cool middle-aged motivational speaker was a twenty-year-old college kid, I landed an internship at a New York ʳ radio station through a connection from my big brother. I ᵛer the moon with the opportunity that ultimately became a twenty-year career with one radio station. My tenure involved two ownership changes, four format changes (adult contemporary, smooth jazz, chill and alternative rock) – and it was one hell of a ride. As an intern, I began doing the most basic of tasks in production. After a few years, the program director wanted me to produce promos. That was something I had longed for and so began a period of substantial growth where I started to flourish creatively.

I was a happy young man, cutting my teeth in NYC radio where everyone in the world wanted to work. From conducting live broadcasts at legendary NYC venues in a state-of-the-art mobile recording truck, to meeting artists including Sade, George Benson, Diana Krall and countless more, it was an exhilarating time. However, over years of producing much of the same type of material, I started to consider the work more and more mundane, as the day-to-day recording and producing was losing its pizzaz. I was offered an opportunity to host a public affairs show which I wholeheartedly embraced. I elevated the show to an entirely new level by having celebrities on and developing solid interviewing chops!

Life was great. Then the bottom fell out. My brother Mike died by suicide when I was twenty-five and it was devastating for my family and me. Mike was a huge fan of the radio station. As sad as I was, I felt there was a little bit of Mike that lived on through the music. Even though I received support after Mike died, it wasn't that long after that I myself experienced anxiety and depression. Thankfully, through hard work on myself, including therapy, I persevered and kept working. I am very much an extrovert, and it began to dawn on me that being tucked away in a sound-proof studio for ten hours a day wasn't good for my mental health. That, coupled with the feeling I was meant for more, always had me pondering my next move. I wish I had been able to break free of radio sooner. It was a confluence of events that set my new trajectory in motion. Likely something similar will push you closer to reimagining, like your inner voice saying, *It's time!*

My wife has changed my life exponentially for the tremendous person she is, and unbeknownst to her and me at the time, she introduced me to the person who was pivotal in me becoming a motivational speaker. 'Mark, you should have this guy on your radio show,' were the words that led me to interview a spectacular talent and someone I liked and respected. Mykee Fowlin educates audiences on diversity via brilliant character acting. He had appeared on my show a few times. Through his sharing of personal struggles, combined with the notion of helping people, it was that which sparked the idea in me to become a speaker. I asked Mykee if he would read my life outline, highlighting my adversity. I wanted to determine if my personal experience of continually propelling myself forward in life despite daunting circumstances could be an experience to benefit people. After he read how my brother Mike died by suicide, how I struggled with anxiety, my love affair with alcohol (and more), my reckless lifestyle, how my father died of Alzheimer's, my rare visual disability and more (though you'll need an uplifting talk yourself if I continue), his response was something like, 'Oh yeah, there's a lot of material here.' That was the first major component that had me consider reimagining in the form of becoming a motivational speaker.

I was sensing that traditional radio was going to decline due to the digital medium which would reduce and reshape the radio industry as a whole. That was the second component that sealed the deal for me. The radio station was sold once again, and this time I, Mark Farrell, did not make the cut (nor did anyone). Reinvention (gulp), here I come!

Having Mykee as an industry source was advantageous as I could bounce ideas off him. Regardless of what connection you may have – you must roll up your sleeves and put in the long hours to create what you want. Fortunately, I was attracted to a field that was not a far leap from radio. I had some experience hosting events and concerts, so it wasn't like I had to be concerned about the potential of stage fright.

Outside of radio, I would combine my advocacy for persons with disabilities and positive mental health, as well as develop a stage presence by emceeing events for Special Olympics, American Foundation for Suicide Prevention, Foundation Fighting Blindness, Achilles International and other organisations. If there's a way for you to dabble in the field where you want to land, perhaps as a volunteer or in a part-time capacity, that is ideal to test the waters before making a big career change.

When the radio station was sold, I had already been developing speaking topics and designing a website, so the transition was a combination of planned and bumpy. None of this would have been possible if not for my incredibly hardworking wife who earned a good salary and made it possible for me to build a speaking business.

If you are an industrious person, it is a major asset in reinvention, especially if you have to seek any job to bring in money prior to the job or business you desire. I think grit and hard work are in the Farrell DNA as I have been a garbageman, landscaper, woodworker, janitor, cashier, dishwasher, bookstore manager, bouncer, bartender (including a stint with Club Med – a story for another time).

If you want to become an entrepreneur, ask yourself if you possess the discipline to manage yourself (not always easy), multiple tasks, schedules, deadlines and the ability to sell and/or market yourself (again, not easy). When I started in radio I made mixed tapes, really good ones, selling them by going door to door in NYC after work. Roles like that may not initially seem like they offer benefits aside from money, however, there were many gains for me including being out of my comfort zone, learning to pitch a product in front of a perspective client, how to cajole a client into a different mindset and negotiation tactics including bartering. Through your various roles in life, chances are you have valuable skill sets you may take for granted.

As a lifelong cyclist, triathlete and marathoner, I had a long desire to become a spin instructor and set about to finally attain a spin instructor certification. The fitness component had been the main draw. Then I had a realisation that teaching spin requires the ability to communicate in a clear and concise manner (while not sounding too winded), while simultaneously motivating and entertaining riders – so this could serve as a close second to performing on stages, just sweatier!

In the summer of 2011, Mark Farrell Motivation came to fruition. My goal was to book school talks for the autumn, through utilising contacts of my mother, Peggy Farrell, who had a long tenure as a beloved high school nurse and advocate for all. I was able to connect with school psychologists and decision-makers to pitch them on my talks that included overcoming adversity, celebrating differences, mental health and a bevy of other vital topics. All my topics and talks were, and are, based on a plethora of personal experience through my varied life.

I believed that would set me apart from most speakers who don't have anywhere near my experience, charisma and stage presence. After all, how many speakers are visually impaired and compete in triathlons without being able to see the swim course, place second to an Olympic silver medalist (in cycling in the NYC Cycling Championship), succeed as a NYC creative director and on-air radio personality, can make top-notch wood-working projects with the aid of dual magnification (handheld magnifier with magnifier glasses)? I would also be original with my telescopic devices (like what a surgeon wears) that I legally must use to drive (part James Bond, part nerd) that would both confuse and shock audiences. Well, I was over the moon as I landed my first few school talks rather easily (with good compensation). I thought, *Wow, I am on my way.*

Reinvention to lights, camera, action! I was off and running and psyched with my performance. But I found out quickly that getting school contacts to answer the phone or return multiple emails was not easy. I have natural sales skills, however, I quickly learned that decision-makers in schools typically like to use the same speakers/presenters repeatedly because they are 'safe'. That bothered me and fuelled me simultaneously.

My mantra – My difference makes me stronger – encapsulates how everyone is different. All audiences I present to (from eight to ninety) embrace that line. Unlike how society often views a 'difference' as a weakness or character trait that someone who is successful doesn't possess – I stress the opposite … that someone's difference actually makes them stronger. That's what this speaker, booker, speech writer, salesperson, logistics expert, social media guru, researcher, graphic designer, networker, athlete (entertainment and motivational field places great emphasis that a performer be in great condition), media specialist, audio/video editor and so much more – must excel in for Mark Farrell Motivation to maintain success.

I must confess, I greatly underestimated how layered and how difficult it would be to land clients. My mindset was like this: *Hey, I have great stories to share, laced with vital nuggets of information that will benefit students (k-twelfth grades). Who wouldn't want to hear them delivered by an effervescent radio personality? It'll be easy to book speaking gigs with those two aspects alone.* Wrong! It takes outreach, follow-up and more outreach, with more follow-up and still typically little-to-no response. Though I completely understand that this is how the world of business operates, one can take it personally from time to time. How much rejection can one person handle?

So, let's discuss more of the mindset that'll fuel you for success in your next endeavour. Looking back, I would say I was 1,000% confident that Mark Farrell Motivation would be successful (let's go with the monetary definition of success for now). That provided a great deal of drive for me when I was making connections and booking gigs – and when the speaking landscape was arid. When you share with family, friends and perhaps current colleagues that you're going to reinvent yourself by launching a business or quitting your well-paying position to become a _____ [fill in the blank] – you will likely hear people say, 'Oh, that's great but how are you going to make money?' Or maybe one of these lines: 'Why would you give up your job to start over?' 'How long are you going to give it?' Those people are envious. They probably do care about your wellbeing though they are also scared of anything unconventional.

Adapt or perish is cliché, and though perish is an embellishment, not escalating your skill set and, most importantly, not being true to yourself is a form of slow decline. I have been at my business for over a decade. Mostly everyone else I know (and don't know) is ecstatic over how I positively impact lives and let me know via social media, to having complete strangers recognise me, sharing how they (or maybe their child) saw my talk and that it really reverberated with them.

We are human and resilient by nature, though even this motivational speaker gets down about business occasionally and thinks about packing it in to work for someone else full-time. Then I quickly regain clarity by thinking of the random kids I bump into who recite my mantra, 'my difference makes me stronger', years after they saw my talk. That resets my focus a gazillion times over. And then there's this. I gave a talk to students with special needs, and when I was done, two teachers approached me, and they were crying. They shared that one of the students who commented from the audience how much he liked my talk during the Q&A portion – had not spoken to anyone in seven months. I got choked up too and quickly thought about the ramifications my words had on him, how they penetrated him so profoundly that he stood and opened up after being silent for an extended period! Am I happy that I reimagined myself? Hell yes! You will experience both lows and highs when you reimagine, and it's then you must remind yourself why you made the decision and rock on.

I knew I was capable of more; I knew I wanted to connect and contribute to the success of people's lives in a greater way. I knew my voice had to be shared with the world. I didn't reinvent myself to become a speaker overnight. An important reimagining note – when pondering your next move, it's okay to keep one foot firmly planted temporarily or permanently in your existing area of work as it can provide solvency. When I started my speaking company, I wasn't in radio, though I missed it and decided to re-enter. I love being on the air. I love speaking to fifty or five thousand people live in-person – there's nothing like it in the world for me.

It's ironic how either my speaking opportunities lessen and more radio opportunities are presented, or vice versa. Ebbs and flows typically work in my favour since I always have many irons in the fire. I imagine that stems from learning how to create opportunity for myself through getting my first job at ten. Even when the world was turned upside-down in March 2020 and all my talks were cancelled, and even my radio shows were greatly diminished – I conceived a way to bring hope to isolating seniors through the power of music and connection, which I aptly named 'Mobile Music & Positivity'. Though unplanned, this was yet another way I reimagined myself. I was determined to make people and communities feel the power of music – regardless of restrictions, I just needed to be creative, and I was up for the task. Afterall – I am in the 'improving lives' business. I strapped professional speakers to the roof of my SUV and secured a generator to power all the audio equipment in the rear of the truck – I was then ready to rid fear and uncertainty from people's lives if only for several minutes.

My mother was living in a senior community. This was a way for me to bring Maggi music, and boy, did she love it. Maggi danced and sang outside her apartment as I circled her building and played Frank Sinatra, Dean Martin, Tony Bennet and more. I would visit different locations in the community and then hop out of my truck and run around with a wireless microphone and say things like 'life is grand and I'm here to remind you just how precious it is, how resilient you are, and there's no better reminder than the power of music'. I had countless lines I shared that made people beam. People made thank-you signs, waved and cheered. Those moments of the pandemic are forever etched into a part of my brain that makes me elated.

Have I had moments where I second-guessed my decision to leave radio full-time to start a speaking business – yes. Though the pros far, far outweigh the cons. Just ask my family how I am after I return from a speaking engagement – they say I float through the door, just like I did when the student spoke for the first time during my talk after months of silence, and just like today, when a member of my spin class said, 'Mark, you live to make people's day.' Super proud moment.

Ten years into my business, and I still occasionally do free gigs. I cannot decline a gig because a school or small non-profit doesn't have the money. It stings a bit, but what's really important is that students have the opportunity to experience my message which could make a tremendous difference, if even just for one student. That's priceless. I hope to be able to earn enough from corporate talks that I can offer free school talks to struggling districts. You too may have to work for free, donate your service or product when you start, and that's okay.

We regularly change our minds, clothes, cars, homes, partners and so much more. Though changing careers can make someone quake in their boots. I totally get it – leaving a field that provides stability can be daunting. Though never knowing your full potential or permitting yourself a chance of professional exploration is perhaps a life not fully lived.

My story can be considered one of reimagining. I consider it also as growth events, where my passion of connecting with people is the nucleus and the concentric circles surrounding my core is the audience I serve, in turn making me an improved version of myself while positively impacting lives.

I believe in you because your eyes are on this page demonstrating your zeal and passion for change. I believe in you because you're allowing yourself the opportunity to consider an unconventional path. Do it on your terms. Terms that don't have to be drastic, it can be subtle. Aside from ethics, I believe there are no rules or standards when it comes to your goals, health and financial wellbeing.

On your path of major or minor reimagining, I give you five words that will hopefully serve you well: 'My difference makes me stronger!' This will remind you of your unwavering resilience, fortitude and stellar leadership.

To learn more about this author: markfarrellmotivation. com

GROWING IN SPIRALS

BY JANE FEIGHERY

In May 2015, I finally acted on a niggle that had been present for some time and handed in my notice to LinkedIn. After spending eight years in the UK, France and Spain, I had moved back to Ireland in 2012 to join LinkedIn's talent solutions sales team. The 3.5 years I spent with LinkedIn were formative and transformative. I have been leaning on the learnings I acquired during that time ever since, and I am forever grateful for the friends I made and the skills I learned.

The decision to leave was informed by some form of quarter-life crisis. To counterbalance the pressure of being in a full-cycle sales role, I had begun a daily ashtanga yoga practice in 2012 and had gone on to train as a yoga teacher in early 2015. Meanwhile, I had been attending many yoga retreats and thought-provoking events about the future of Ireland, while devouring books about social entrepreneurship, conscious business and purpose. I realised I felt quite disconnected from Irish cultural, political and economic life, and that this was something I wished to remedy.

After attending a particularly inspiring talk by Dylan Haskins at a 'Trailblazery' event in Dublin, I decided it was time to begin investing in work that was creating the type of Ireland I wanted to live in. Dylan had raised a powerful point around how much of a positive impact could be had on Ireland if the many talented people working for US multinationals were to instead work for Ireland. This comment strongly resonated with me and provided me with great clarity. I decided it was time for me to take a leap from LinkedIn and begin teaching yoga as a means of supporting people to transform themselves physically, mentally, emotionally and spiritually.

In retrospect, I have looked back somewhat cynically on that idealistic version of myself, and on the lofty idea that I could change the world through teaching yoga. Nonetheless, I still stand by the principle at the core of my objective. To transform the world, we must first transform ourselves. All change begins from within the individual. While yoga is not a silver bullet or a one-size-fits-all solution, an ashtanga yoga practice is an incredibly powerful tool to optimise one's mental, emotional and physical state. I had witnessed the mental clarity and peaceful, highly powerful energetic state of those who had dedicated them-selves to an ashtanga yoga practice and I could see how much more effective this allowed them to be in their lives and work.

The niggle that it was time to move on was present for at least six months before I plucked up the courage to act on it. I remember an emotional conversation with a friend on her last day with the company. I was voicing how frustrated I was with myself, that I knew I needed to hand in my notice and, yet, just couldn't seem to act on it. She assured me it would feel entirely right when the time came, and her advice was spot on. A few months later, I knew 100% that the moment had arrived. I sat with it for a weekend, and then handed my notice in on the Monday.

Eight years later, I feel nostalgic for that naive, idealistic, younger version of myself who believed that one's purpose related to the company you were working for and to the mission and stated impact of that company. At the time, I had decided my vision was to be part of creating the type of Ireland I wanted to live in, and that my purpose was to support people to transform their lives through yoga.

However, our purpose is not static. It is ever evolving as we grow and as the circumstances of our lives evolve. One's purpose may relate to parenting for a given phase of life and to building a business during another. It simply articulates the impact we wish to have on the world and through what means or action we will affect this.

Before I had a chance to embark on launching my yoga teaching, I stepped into a new role as director of development with Social Entrepreneurs Ireland (SEI), and again threw myself head over heels into work. I had long admired the work of Social Entrepreneurs Ireland, and this new role seemed like the perfect fit. I spent another four years moving in the world of social entrepreneurship, not-for-profit and social change, between that first role with SEI and a stint with The One Foundation.

Interestingly, I realised I had felt more alive, more impactful and more at home in a US multinational than I did in the not-for-profit space.

On leaving LinkedIn, I had asked myself if I would have a

greater impact on the world by continuing to work my way up the ladder in a tech company while growing my skills, experience and wealth in the process, or if bringing my skills to a not-for-profit organisation would enable a greater impact.

At the time, I decided I would invest in the latter option, but after only a few years in the not-for-profit sector my view changed entirely. Whether or not we are willing to admit it, wealth, connection, status and valuable experience equate to power, and that power can create significant positive impact when used wisely.

Irrespective of the sector or organisation, it was the integrity, abilities and intentions of leadership that truly enabled positive change in the right direction.

I began investing again in building my own freelance business, and in 2019 launched as a self-employed consultant, coach and yoga teacher. At this stage, I had completed an Advanced Diploma in Coaching with Neuroscience along with many additional yoga teacher trainings and had been teaching yoga on a weekly basis for more than three years.

As I entered 2023, psychotherapy training was taking a large chunk of my time and energy, while yoga teaching had taken a back seat. My yoga practice, however, remained the most important support for my wellbeing and therefore overall clarity and sense of purpose. Values discovery, alignment and execution became a focus of my consultancy and coaching work, shifting my perspective on who I was and where I want to go.

I discovered that values exploration is immensely powerful work and that the simplicity of this work belies its profundity. Getting clear on your values, i.e. on your highest priorities in life and then showing up for these values day in, day out in your words, actions and decisions, leaves no room for escapism or bypassing. While it may be simple work, it is certainly not easy to engage in, and when we commit to it, we are forced to face ourselves, our BS and our hypocrisy.

There have been many learnings over the past eight years. I have begun holding my opinions and views more lightly over time, as I've learned that the more you know, *the more you know you don't know*. I am therefore cautious to provide any specific advice. I will share some of the reflections that feel true for me now, with the knowledge that in five years' time, my opinion on these may well have changed, and also under the proviso that this is just the experience of one person at a given point in time.

The following are a few reflections on what to consider when planning a leap from a secure job:

• First, do the inner work.

   Often when we feel a niggle of dissatisfaction, we assume this relates to our external reality. We make the mistake of blaming factors in our current set-up rather than doing the inner work to ascertain what is truly going on. In doing this inner work, we may discover we are on a career path that is not true to our heart and soul, that we have outgrown a romantic relationship or a way of life. Alternatively, we may discover we simply need to make a few edits to our existing circumstances. We could, for example, simply need to set stronger boundaries in work and create time for our hobbies, relationships and passions outside of working hours.

   Investing in therapy and doing this inner work is costly in terms of time, energy and money, and there is nothing like self-employment and selling your own brand to bring any and all unaddressed issues to the surface! It's a good idea therefore, to begin working with a therapist or a coach while in stable employment and arriving at some clarity through this process as to what you truly need and want.

- Appreciate the truth in the 'grass is not always greener' adage.

There is no one-size-fits-all when it comes to how a person defines 'success' in life. And there is nothing inherently superior about setting up your own business versus working for a large company. Being an entrepreneur is so frequently glamorised and romanticised in our culture that those who have not taken a leap out of employment can, by default, feel like they must be failing in some way. This is not the case. It all depends on your own values and priorities in life. Your current job may well allow you to live in accordance with your purpose, much more so than self-employment or being an entrepreneur would. Your purpose may not relate to your paid employment. It may instead relate to your children, your family or your hobbies outside of work. Familiarise yourself thoroughly with the potential consequences of stepping away from a comfortable (or stressful!) job and remind yourself of the parts of that reality you enjoy. The aspect of being an employee that I miss most is being part of a team and working towards company goals. Until you have a team around you, working for yourself can be a lonely pursuit which requires an ability to face the mundanity of day-to-day tasks by yourself and for nobody but yourself!

- Know and align with your values.

There is more to be said on this topic than I can possibly cover in a short paragraph, but in brief – it is of vital importance to know what matters most to you in life and then to ensure you are honouring these values in your current reality as the first step. I did a values exercise in 2015, and while my values have remained unchanged since then, I have gone through various phases during which I have forgotten about one or several of my values and consequently strayed off course. A simple first step you can take without making any radical changes is to define your values and commit to showing up for them.

- We grow in spirals.

    Our physical growth in the womb occurs in spirals, and so too does much of our spiritual and emotional growth. What does it mean to grow in spirals? It means that the growth trajectory is not linear, rather it can involve finding ourselves time and time again in familiar situations, relationships or patterns we thought we had outgrown. As noted previously, life continues to send the same lessons our way until we finally learn them, and hence, the growth pattern of the spirals. Acknowledging, appreciating and surrendering to this phenomenon has brought me great peace in recent years. Rather than beat myself up and feel like I'm regressing, I now know I am simply following a typical pattern of growth which is perfectly valid and normal. Each turn of the spiral brings a little more self-awareness and clarity and allows for the right amount of growth in the right direction.

- Make sure you have a net before you leap.

    Mark Manson recommends we choose the 'pain' or the 'struggles' we are willing to contend with, irrespective of the path we choose in life.

Unless there is a pre-existing pot of money, stepping out of a secure job can genuinely be a highly risky endeavour. Often those who make this choice have already saved enough to live comfortably until the end of their days or have financial support behind them to ensure they maintain a roof over their head, food on the table and keep the lights and heat on.

Many life coaches selling the dream of 'taking the leap' are quite literally making a living by selling you this dream. There is often privilege behind the scenes when people can step freely out of steady employment, and there are also varying levels of risk tolerance and responsibilities to take care of for different people.

I set myself up to leave stable employment by getting a mortgage I would be able to repay through the rental of a room in my house. This decision has served me greatly, and alongside it, there has also been a lot of compromise and belt-tightening that has consistently happened during periods of uncertainty. I've become very familiar with the importance of stability to support my creativity and expansion. Creating, selling yourself and investing in the long game can become quite challenging when you're living month-to-month and it's cold and dark outside!

This reflection is not designed to dissuade you from following a dream, rather to encourage you to first do your homework and preparation on the lived realities of that life path and to ensure you will be happy to embrace the lows as much as the highs.

To conclude, an excerpt from Antonio Machado's *El Caminante:*

Traveler, your footprints are the only road, nothing else. Traveler, there is no road; you make your own path as you walk.

For anyone considering making a big career/life change both for inspiration, and to develop some frameworks for decision-making, I recommend the following books:

- *The Dip* by Seth Godin
- *The Subtle Art of Not Giving a F*ck* by Mark Manson
- *The Practice* by Seth Godin
- *The Power of Regret* by Daniel H Pink
- *The Way of Integrity* by Martha Beck
- *Everything is Figureoutable* by Marie Forleo
- *The War of Art* by Steven Pressfield
- *Essentialism* by Greg McKeown
- *Range* by David Epstein

To learn more about this author: linkedin.com/in/ janefeighery

LIFE AFTER PROFESSIONAL SPORT

BY JAMIE HEASLIP

When growing up, professional sports may not exactly be a path that one would choose. For me specifically, as the sport wasn't professional in Ireland until late August of 1995, I didn't know it was a path to consider for my future. It was just something I played on the weekends, as it was a lot of fun. Ironically, at that time, my older brother was one of the first to go professional in Ireland. I was around thirteen years old, and in secondary school I didn't really give a whole lot of thought to it. It wasn't really until I was in college that I could see a path forming as an option for me.

At the start of my third year of college, I was offered two contracts, basically to go professional then. I turned them down as I wanted to finish my degree. I was offered a contract again in my final year. So, in my fourth year in college, I signed a contract at Easter time. I went pro in the June of 2005. I hadn't really appreciated that it was a career path until 2002 or 2003. I was studying medical engineering in DCU; that was my direction of travel. I don't know if I would have worked in medical engineering or that

I would have stayed long in it. It was something that I progressed, having been to the school guidance counsellor. The results of the aptitude tests seemed to gear me that way.

If I hadn't progressed my rugby career at the end of college, I believe I would have tried to do something sports science related off the back of my degree. Or I could have pivoted into something like physio. But none of that was to be at the time, as I was lucky enough to be able to play professional rugby. For me, it was a childhood dream come true. As a youngster, I dreamt of playing rugby for Ireland, and then to achieve that and get paid to do it! I got a really good run at it too. I am proud I was a fully senior professional for thirteen years, which is a long run, as I think the average professional career is about six years.

During my time I gleaned a great knowledge of rugby rules and really enjoyed it. Obviously, one can stay in the sport and become a coach afterwards but I never really wanted to become a coach. I like the business of sport, however, there are quite limited options in Ireland in that regard. I believe I probably would have had to go to abroad and I didn't really want to do that.

It is definitely a challenge of being a professional sports person. If, for example, you don't want to be a coach, you will finish your professional career after around ten years. Everyone else is going to have those ten years of experience in their certain chosen field e.g. business. You will have gained a lot of experience in other skills or softer skills, however, you won't have the hard skills in the businesspersons' comparable fields.

Sport demands everything from you at a professional level. It's all-consuming and touches all facets of your life. It's hard to pull yourself out of it to make time to plan for possible future avenues. There are a lot of studies available about the importance and benefits of being a well-rounded athlete and student. We discussed these in the team and management try to facilitate it. However, it is hard to do when you're playing a sport that has a commitment of playing thirty to thirty-five games a year and going on tours and camps. It doesn't easily lend itself to allowing time to commit to learning and development for other things outside the sport. It may be a bit different now.

When I was there, the Rugby Players' Association had people who would try to help you. They try to find a suitable course or work with your college to persuade them to allow more flexibility in terms of projects and deadlines. They also try to create options on college work to submit to get certain credits to obtain a qualification.

The time required is the REAL challenge. The association have mentor programs too. Ideally, you should know what you want to get from a mentor. You must bring something to them. I think initially players thought these business mentors would have the answer for them and tell them, 'This is what you're going to do,' but that's not how it works. You have to have an idea of what you want to do.

Unless you want to get into something very specific, like for example, to be an accountant or a doctor, I think it's hard for professional sports people to really know and to wrap their head around something that prepares them for the future. It is only when they finish that they can try to find a North Star and to transition.

In 2017, I was a year married and signed a three-year contract that was going take me up to September 2020. About three weeks later, I got an injury in a warm-up game against England. A year later, in 2018, I was told to hang up my boots.

So, my last game was played in 2017. The original plan was

to play under contract until September 2020. I would then have liked to go to Japan, the southern hemisphere, or maybe both, to play rugby there. I thought perhaps I could come back to a club in France and play in France for a year or two and finish with international duty. I thought then, the year I finished, I could do a full-time MBA and try to figure out a direction and next steps then.

That would have taken me up to 2021/22. That was the original plan. You've got to factor in that I would have made a lot of financial decisions off the back of that plan as well; where I would be laying the foundations for my life, with houses and all sorts of different things like that.

By 2018, I was two years married, and we were expecting our first kid. So, finishing professional rugby that year moved up the time frame of my original plan and forced my hand. Even though I thought I was prepared, in a lot of ways, I learned I was unprepared. Quite a year. It was a rough patch. They say some of the most stressful things in life are 'change career, have a baby and move house' – well we did all three within nine months of me retiring from rugby. So, yes, it was a bit of a stressful time. A year and a half after finishing rugby, COVID hit. It was an isolating time; a rough two to three years. It took time for some things to pan out, like insurance. I tried to use my coping mechanisms, such as help from my network, but COVID certainly interfered with everyone's network. So, I developed new coping mechanisms.

My coping mechanisms included trying to bounce ideas off different people, finding different mentors, trying to develop a North Star to aim towards, and then working back off that in terms of milestones towards it.

Once you finish rugby, or any professional sport, that's it. You can't be as selfish as you had been when you were playing. That can be a bit of a shock. It's no longer about you and playing on that Saturday. It's a whole other dynamic that's going on. That's just one of many things professional sportspeople find quite challenging and have to wrap their head around.

The things that stick in my mind are things that my dad said to me. From his 40+ years in the army, establishing the Ranger Wing to postings abroad and being a Brigadier General. He said that talent is nothing without discipline. I developed a few others while playing, 'Discipline equals freedom. Consistency equals compound interest.' Those are core beliefs of mine. I've come across many guys over the years who were way more talented than me coming through, but they lacked discipline. Talent is nothing without discipline. The best thing you can do when you're creating your own story for your life is to be the lead character. So, lead by example. You are what you repeatedly do. Work on it. I am very disciplined, very focused. I put a plan together over time. It's not what always materialises, but one needs something to aim for.

You need to know what you're going towards, but you equally need to make choices of things that you won't go towards. I made loads of the same mistakes as many who have finished a career suddenly, whether from redundancy or for other reasons. I heard guys say, 'Don't say yes to everything, when you finish, you know, think about it, take some time away. Think about the direction that you want to go.' People can be tempted to say yes to everything and do all sorts of different things. Then you're in danger of just being a busy fool for a while. I probably didn't give myself enough time to let the whole body and mind relax and see which way I wanted to go. So, my advice is to take your time.

It probably took me up until the end of 2022 to really get a base and foundation in place to be in a more solid spot right now.

My wife Sheena was a big help supporting me through this time being my North Star!

I continue to work with a coach, Mick Todd, on leveraging my strength and being authentic. I met him following my professional rugby career. I recommend finding a coach or an expert in each of the areas or fields that are important to you. My financial advisor is someone I met afterwards. He's someone I wish I had met five to ten years ago while playing. That's definitely a recommendation I would have for others. Coping mechanisms are like having a plan, yet not being too rigid with the plan. Having some sort of plan is good, but you have to be adaptable with it too. And that's what helped me cope.

When I played rugby, I focused on goal-setting and how to get the most out of myself while playing. As I look at my life now, I use the same format. I distinctly remember Michael Phelps' book *No Limits: The Will to Succeed*. He was very methodical in his approach to the Beijing Olympics. For me, I use the imagery of the Olympic rings and have combined them with the Japanese thinking of *ikigai*. I find the *ikigai* philosophy a good way of framing my thoughts. I have five rings, and they're all different, important parts of my life. I need them all to be strong and balanced for me to be my best.

I did that during my time in sports; I had rings for 'rugby', 'recovery', a ring I called 'Jamie Inc.' (elements outside of rugby), 'family' and 'friends'. I've used that approach now for my life post-rugby. I have the current one now hung on my wall. The current rings are 'family', 'health and wellbeing', 'growth', 'career' and 'Sabra' (which is the name of my company). These are the five areas I now look to be working on constantly. I set my goals based on those five rings. I have created long-term ambitious goals – my 2030 goals. I name them and then I work back to what that means for this year and then for today. I work with a coach on this. I am starting to put together 2024 goals now. It all works back to that for me; I have a plan.

That's how I operate now. I am lucky I have a variety of interests. I now work in Stripe as the Irish strategic growth lead. This is currently my main job. I manage the go-to-market strategy and help with growing the revenue number. I help manage the go-to-market strategy, while managing our various key stakeholders in the ecosystem. That's what I do Monday through Friday. In addition, I continue to do a little bit of punditry which keeps me interested in rugby. I also have my different business interests and companies in which I have invested. I do a lot of sports training because I need to keep fit and healthy myself. That's another important element in terms of one's own mental wellbeing.

I get to spend a lot of time with my family, which is great. I'm working from home today and have painted fingernails! My eldest daughter is five and she's very much a girly girl. She's very similar to her mother. She likes all things sparkly and glittery. It gave me quality time with her and half an hour of peace. I'll take that!

Would I recommend professional sports as a career to my kids? To be honest, I'd like to let them figure out their own path. I have two girls and both have very different likes. We get them to try everything – whatever sticks, sticks.

I just want an easy life now. The last couple of years of rugby was all-consuming and selfish. I very much do not want to fall back into a career path that is as consuming. I want it to be something that is energising an challenging. It's the only way that I will keep growing. I'm very much trying to create a world where if I can take semiretirement earlier than others might have the opportunity to. If I can, I will. I'm working towards creating that sort of environment where I have interests that keep me engaged but also allow me to have free time.

I want to be able to create an environment that enables others to thrive – enables my kids to thrive. To leave the jersey in a better place. Do I know what role I will play in that? I don't have a clue. But that's the North Star I'm working towards. I set my goals around that. Sometimes opportunities may arise. That's where flexibility and adaptability come in. Know where you want to go. Reflecting on this in relation to rugby, I've always said, 'I want to leave the jersey in a better place.' Now that's the foundation I'm building on for my family, for the girls to have a better launchpad for themselves.

I've always believed in having good coaches. These need to change depending on what is required. So, when you're a small business starting out, you know the team you need – a startup team, that's the founders. Let's say now you're a high-growth company, you're scaling your revenues or scaling your user acquisition, whatever the metric, that team is not going to be the same in eighteen months. So, you need different coaches at different stages over time. Thus, I needed very different coaches when I finished my rugby career than when I was playing. That's my personal take; I think one needs different coaches at different stages. I need a different strength conditioning coach now than I did when I was playing. I need different mentors, depending on the business opportunities and if it's a startup or even a VC-backed businesses.

I invested in pubs. We have just opened our fourth in August.

I know, for now anyway, that I don't want to take on or set up a business myself. I'm more than happy to be involved in and invest in various other businesses. Setting up my own business is not part of my plan. Many people may want to do that, in which case, they would need a very different mentor than me.

I've done a lot of groundwork early that will pay up as I had a pension from twenty-one, believing in that compound interest. We over estimate what we can achieve in the short-term, but under estimate what we can achieve over the longer-term. I maxed it out for as long as I could while playing. Now I don't have to worry about it. Many people are bad at making these longer-term bets and long-term thinking outcomes. Many are not good at understanding the compounding effect of different investments that you can place now. We underestimate the power of that. I'm thirty-nine now, so let's say in ten years' time, I'll be forty-nine and our daughters will be fifteen and eleven. I would love to be semiretired and have time to be able to hang around with them, because once they hit college, they're gone. That is one of the goals I'm working towards. That I can spend time with them and create some amazing memories. It comes back to the goals. I am creating a plan of amazing family experiences they'll always remember. They will be able to do different things at different stages over the ten-year period, like a Disneyland trip in the shorter term and then later a safari, Japan, Australia and New Zealand. I'd also love to do the northern lights. Great things to do as a family. I encourage you too to set your goals and make your plans.

To learn more about this author: linkedin.com/in/ jamie-heaslip-33319157

THE BRAIDER, THE BAKER, THE BREAST CONFIDENCE MAKER – FROM VILLAGER TO VITAL VOICE

BY NICOLE JOSEPH-CHIN

You can dream anything – just remember to dream brilliantly, with splashes of colour sprinkled on everything you touch.

It started in a village in the outskirts of the capital city of Port of Spain, in the twin island republic of Trinidad and Tobago. I aspired to become a teacher. As a little girl, aged nine or ten, I would talk to the furniture in my home and give assignments to my dolls. Homework was corrected and math sums were worked out on the wall, until my father made me a blackboard because, of course, I was leaving chalk everywhere.

I also dreamt of teaching my dolls and teddy bears how to spell and to speak another language. Grammar was the first rule each time we had doll school. I would ask the dolls if they were ready to change the world. Little had I envisioned the self-talk that was embedded in the imaginary classroom. I didn't really know what they were going to change, but I knew they had work to do.

Fast-forward to my teenage years and my imaginary classroom changed. My aspirations changed, and there was now an opportunity to participate in learning another language, as well as participation in public speaking. My curiosity shifted from the village girl to the dreamer, dreaming and envisioning the ways I could add my experiences to the many other girls who were examples of living a dream.

I admired a woman called Dawn who had been part of the village I was raised in. She had become a household name with her beautifully handmade wearable art clothing. I definitely wasn't a designer or artist, but her vision told me that girls in my village of Barataria were equally capable of the pursuit of unconventional paths to success.

THE BRAIDER

Loving to experiment with hairstyling, I'd put extensions in my dolls' hair and would cut their hair into styles, even playing barber one day when I cut the hair of my neighbour and she cut mine. We had matching bangs at eight years old and, of course, got into trouble when our parents discovered our hair a day or so later. Except by then, there was nothing to do but wait for it to grow back!

My escapades into hairstyling gave me opportunities to earn income, create interesting styles for friends and gain clients – parents who would bring their daughters to get their hair done for school.

Was hair for me? My desire to become a teacher was still a real thing at that time.

THE BAKER

One of my greatest passions as an adolescent was baking cakes. I would bake cakes every weekend as a tradition of being in the kitchen with our mother on the weekend. No doubt, I'd create a few lovely cakes, share with friends and neighbours and, *voila,* cakes were the thing to look forward to every weekend.

Then, two experiences became the determining factor of a future of dessert making. As a lover of dessert, I was on my way to *dessert hobby adventures* when the aunt of a friend tasted my cake and hired me on the spot as the dessert supplier for their resort.

Months later, another aunt of my friend asked me to do a Valentine's Day bake sale for her office and gave me a request for one hundred cakes. The overwhelming feeling to deliver and excel was tortuous and exhausting. So, she came by to help me, and together we baked a little over the one hundred cakes ordered. Thereafter, baking became overwhelming, draining and a chore; the effects of too much of one action, not leaving room for grace and joy. Large batches of cake batter took the joy out of creating something special. I didn't bake another cake until decades later, during the pandemic in 2020.

I definitely had no aspirations of becoming a Caribbean version of Julia Child.

THE BANKER

Fast-forward to 1990 and all the eventualities and activities of that year. My graduation from secondary school after A-levels, a coup d'état in the latter days of July, parents overseas worried sick whilst they were abroad during the coup and good ol' me getting a call about a vacancy in the bank for a temporary position. A temporary position that would become a beautiful career spanning fifteen years as a full-time adventure in financial planning, financial services sales, VIP banking – high-end clientele portfolio management and business development. Somewhere in-between, I'd decided I would never let boredom set in.

THE BREAST CONFIDENCE MAKER

Fast-forward again to the decision to work for myself and embark on a new pathway, hanging up my formal career and ditching the rigid work environment. Now my days are set in a lovely boudoir-styled room with women talking about their comfort with their brassieres. I have never been so happy. I am the founder of Ms. Brafit, a globally recognised social enterprise focused on women's health and education. My vision is to help change the world, teaching valuable lessons and weaving a culture of care.

Today my work makes sense. It brings confidence to women and elevates hope. It is part of an important undertaking to empower women and girls at varied stages of life.

To learn more about this author: linkedin.com/in/ nicolejoseph-chin

TRANSITIONING FROM A HIGH-FLYING CAREER

BY EMER KENNEDY

'The richest and fullest lives attempt to achieve an inner balance between three realms: work, love and play.' – Erik Erikson

For most of my career, I thought I was exactly where I wanted to be; I had a great job at a great company doing something that I loved. As a senior HR director at Google with a global remit, being busy gave me a purpose and an identity. However, working at top speed along with late-night calls and crazy deadlines was also part of it. It was exciting, dynamic and adrenaline filled but it was also nonstop and all-encompassing.

When the pandemic hit and life came grinding to a halt, I literally felt like I'd fallen out of an airplane. I can distinctly remember saying to my husband over breakfast that for the first time in years, I didn't have jet lag anymore. Theoretically, this shouldn't have been a huge surprise: In the twelve months prior to lockdown, I had circumnavigated the globe at least five times and was on a three-week travel schedule. Only then and there, at the breakfast table with my husband, did I realise how big a part of my life travel had been. With this part being abruptly removed from my life, I was suddenly able to centre myself. Over the following weeks and months, I started along a path of self-questioning that ultimately changed my life.

I loved my job, I loved what came with it: recognition, status, security. However, what didn't come with it was time – time to think, time to reflect. What was it that I liked about my job? About working with a team of global executives, with bright and brilliant colleagues? What was it that I liked about travelling? The answer came down to one single word: coaching. I realised I wasn't in it for the recognition, the status, the dizzying lifestyle after all, I was in it for the interactions, for the meaningful personal exchanges, because I enjoyed coaching others and because I could learn from them at the same time. And so, in the middle of lockdowns and virtual globetrotting, Mind Canopy, an executive coaching company, was born.

'Awareness is the greatest agent of change.' – Eckhart Tolle

The feeling of knowing that I wanted more from life was probably there before the lockdown, but I was just too scared to admit it. Whenever I had time for myself – sitting alone in airport terminals or during a yoga class – I invariably pondered whether or not I was truly happy. Gradually, I realised how precious time was and how thoughtlessly I sometimes had been using it. I also started to think a lot more about my wellbeing.

Contemplating change is not linear. For a time, I simply went over and over things aimlessly in my head, and hence without conclusion. During this period, I read a lot of books, meditated and occasionally raised the topic hesitantly with some close friends. It was not until I completed the LifeForward program at the Hudson Institute in Santa Barbara, California, that – by learning and using great frameworks – I was able to make sense of things. As uncomfortable and unsettling as this period in my life was, it eventually allowed me to move towards change across four main areas: job, finances, identity and the fear of the unknown.

'Seek your calling, even if you don't know what it means, seek it.' – Phil Knight

At first, I was unclear about what I wanted to do next. I had a general idea that I wanted to advise and help people in their careers, but my North Star was rather vague. Also, every time I thought about leaving my permanent job, the question of money came up. At home, I'm the main breadwinner, so getting my head around the numbers and allowing for some in reserve was a priority. Thirdly, my sense of identity and who I was had been very much tied to my job. I didn't want to be one of *those people* who seem to be stuck talking about their past lives. I wanted to live now, own my new identity and feel comfortable with it, while embracing the future. Finally, there was the fear factor – the fear of failure, the fear of regret, the fear of making a mistake. Depending on my mood, this fear could become an all-encompassing feeling of anxiety. It's important to remember that these four things aren't solitary and independent from each other, but rather interconnected and sometimes hard to discern.

This is why – when I set out to change my life – I decided to change them one by one, while always being aware of how the fear and anxiety of one area, could spill over into another.

CHANGING JOBS

For most of my career, I'd worked with various coaches and had been one myself, so the territory of career and personal transformation was familiar to me. Thus, my search for a role I felt passionate about led me to pursue an executive coaching program at the Hudson Institute. I loved the training, the readings and the lectures. I was also encouraged by the positive feedback from my early clients which gave me confidence I was going in the right direction.

If I was going to give up my great job, I really wanted to invest in myself. Going back to being a student was therefore something I was keen to explore. I researched various courses, talked to different universities and eventually landed at the Masters in Change at INSEAD in Fontainebleau, Paris. It felt complimentary to my work as a coach, especially with regard to personal change and transformation.

CHANGING FINANCES

Knowing what you can afford and what you need to plan for is both clarifying and reassuring. So, when it came to a source of income, I worked with a financial advisor to get my head around the numbers.

A lot of people asked me if I would be able to give up the lifestyle I was used to. The reality is a lot of my spending was in service to my high-flying career. I spent a lot of money on convenience. I was always desperately short on time, so spending money on services or shortcuts was a necessary expense. The more stressful a day, the stronger the need for instant gratification. A long day at work would often lead to a spontaneous online purchase. Now, I control my time and my days which allows choices around how I want to spend money much easier.

CHANGING IDENTITIES

I did worry about how I would be perceived after my career at Google. The old nagging voice of *is this good enough?* was a regular visitor in my head. One of the best books I read around identity is called *Working Identities* by Hermione Ibarra. In this book, Ibarra describes everyone as each having several imagined 'selves'. There is the self that wants to be a yoga teacher, the self who thinks about owning a business, the corporate self, the landscape photographer self and so on. Ibarra recommends to first identify all of these selves and then use *safe to fail* experiments to test them out. This not only allows you to see if you like something, but also gives you an opportunity to flirt with a new identity. I started coaching on the side during my last year at Google. At the same time, I began a course to become a yoga teacher. As a result, I found I had a strong affinity with being a coach but less with being a yoga teacher.

CHANGING FEAR

I won't lie, I did have more than a few sleepless nights and it took many months before I felt confident with voicing my decision to leave my job out loud. So, the final shift was addressing my own behavioural response to fear. The two techniques I used were meditation and taking excruciatingly small steps. With meditation, I allowed myself to sit with fear, to acknowledge it, feel it and simply be with the discomfort. It wasn't pleasant but it did allow me to recognise it, observe it and not be completely flooded by it. Many people say the way to work through fear is to act on it, although that in itself can be daunting. I took things one conversation at a time and worked at a slow enough pace, so that the feeling of change was very gradual. Even when I eventually had exhausted all conversations and completed all my actions, I still sat for another month or so with the decision.

I vividly recall the day I handed in my notice at Google. I met with the amazing leaders I had worked most closely with and had what I can only describe as beautiful conversations. I know it sounds cheesy, but these conversations, ones I had dreaded for weeks, flowed easily and that to me was a sign I was doing the right thing.

'Fear is not the enemy – waiting to stop feeling afraid is.' –
Maria Forleo

After giving my notice, I worked a further six months, ensuring a smooth transition for my successor and finishing all outstanding projects. My last day at Google was a Friday. On Monday morning, I started my new business. It's probably best to take a break or a holiday, but I was so energised I didn't want to stop – and I haven't stopped since.

Life is about balance. Therefore, I revisited my love affair with yoga. While I discarded my earlier plans to become a qualified yoga teacher, I eventually started Ayurveda with YogaVeda

Living in Dublin. This proved to be a real game changer for me personally. Not only did it help to get my own wellbeing back on track, but it was also helpful in my understanding of wellbeing and how it underpins everything we do in our lives.

Since creating *Mind Canopy*, my life has transformed on so many levels. I still love doing what I'm doing, but now I do it in my own time. I still look forward to getting out of bed every day, but now I distinctly know why. I still get to work with many interesting and incredible people, but now I feel a huge sense of purpose being able to help them manifest change and growth in their lives, because I can directly see the result of my work.

Running my own business, I have learnt so much more about being a small business owner than when I was leading the small business sales unit at Google. I am in charge of my own time, and I work at my own pace. While my days are still busy, I rarely do late-night calls and I'm in control of my own schedule. The impact this had on my energy levels was unequivocally positive. I now have more time for exercise, for my husband, for myself. I now have more time for living my own life.

'What is meant for us flows freely in harmony with us, not against us.' – Cleo Wade

If I was to summarise what I now know about changing careers and stepping out of the corporate world, I would say you need time. Once you give yourself time and space, you can chip away on both the practical side of things as well as the range of emotions that will naturally emerge. This life transition is an entirely individualist path, which means you have to trust yourself and let your own inner voice help you. A coach can be a great guide to walk beside you, but ultimately, it's your journey and you are the one who needs to go up the mountain, no matter how hard it might seem. My biggest fear in life is always that I will reach old age and have regrets. Following your dreams and chartering your own course in life is about holding a vision for yourself and then putting one foot in front of the other, no matter how long it takes, to achieve it. If you do this, the rewards will be beyond your wildest dreams.

To learn more about this author: mindcanopy.com

A JOURNEY TO FREEDOM AND FULFILMENT

BY MAIREAD MACKLE

Reflecting on the incredible journey that has brought me to this point, it's a journey that has spanned my initial aspirations as a podiatrist, to the exhilarating life of entrepreneurship and, ultimately, the discovery of how freedom and flexibility in life can be achieved.

The story began with the dreams and ambitions of a young, newly trained podiatrist. I had invested three years of study and dedication (with a lot of parties thrown in, of course!), culminating in my graduation day and attaining a qualification in podiatric medicine. The future appeared bright, brimming with possibilities, and I embarked on this new phase of my life with boundless enthusiasm. I had it all mapped out, get a job as a podiatrist, and happily work away, as my main financial ambition at that stage was to be able to afford central heating, having lived for 3 years in Belfast as a poor student!

But life has a way of throwing unexpected challenges in our path. In my case, these challenges took the form of rejection letters. Podiatry was a young profession and the jobs were few. Despite my academic achievements, interview after interview ended in polite but disheartening refusals. These were trying times, testing my resilience and making me question the career path I had chosen.

They say every cloud has a silver lining, so instead of wallowing in the rejections, I decided the only thing I could do was to forge my own path and create my own business. In researching what I could do, I came across a new community service that would allow people who suffered from injury or illness the choice to stay at home instead of going into residential care. I loved the idea and got started straightaway researching the concept and planning. I borrowed £10,000 from the local bank and when I look back now, I wonder if it was my naivety or my mindset but I didn't even consider the risk of failure! As they say in NASA, "failure is not an option" and that was my thought process which is probably why, a year later, I decided to introduce a new housing service and continue to expand.

To my amazement, my business quickly gained momentum and began to flourish. There was huge demand for what we offered and we were always willing to go the extra mile. Yet, with growth came an overwhelming workload. I was stretched thin, working gruelling twelve- to sixteen-hour days, with young children to care for. The pursuit of business had ensnared me, leaving me with little time to savour the fruits of my labour.

I initially ran the daily operations of my growing enterprise from my kitchen table, where I could stay close to the children, expanding within a year into the confines of two cramped portacabins in my backyard. Within a year the company was employing over 100 people and the chaos was real. It was during one such chaotic day, as a friend visited and I looked around at all the boxes of paperwork and supplies as I scrambled to tidy up, that the realisation struck me like a thunderbolt – The business was taking over and I knew things needed to change.

A glimmer of hope soon emerged with an unexpected gift from my husband, who was working in the USA at the time. He returned with a book, containing a simple message, that would change the course of my life forever – The E-Myth by Michael E Gerber. In the book, Gerber explains that most people starting a business don't understand how to run and scale it. They're very good technically at whatever their skills are, but to run a business successfully demands a whole new set of skills. This made complete sense to me, being trained as a podiatrist with no formal business training.

My favourite line from this book, which I still remind myself every day is, 'If a business isn't giving you more life, it's taking your life away…and if it doesn't give you more freedom, it isn't a business at all.'

I realised then that I didn't have a business at all! So, standing in the face of transformation, the desire for change from the daily grind left no room for uncertainty. It was an irresistible call to action. It was through reading this book I was introduced to the simple but transformative lessons that would reimagine my business thinking. These lessons were instrumental in liberating me from the chains of daily operations and putting me on a whole new journey of strategic growth.

The core philosophy was simple yet profound; work on your business, not in it. With this new-found perspective, I embarked on a path that would forever change the course of my entrepreneurial journey ... a path defined by freedom, fulfilment and the unwavering belief that I could, indeed, craft a life of my own making.

These revelations came not a moment too soon. They opened my eyes to a new way of working. With The E-Myth as my guide, I began to embrace this new philosophy of strategic thinking and development.

The lessons emphasised the importance of delegation and creating systems to streamline operations. To work on your business meant creating structures, departments and processes for everything we did. It encouraged entrepreneurs to share their vision and build and empower a dedicated team to bring that vision to fruition. These concepts became the cornerstone of my approach as I sought to transform my entire business.

Collaboration soon became the key to success. I recognised the value of diverse perspectives and input from various team members. The most innovative solutions often emerged from the collective wisdom of the team. I learned to trust my colleagues and empower them to contribute to our shared vision.

I didn't miss a thing about my old operational role but instead spent time creating structures and teams of great people who share my values to ensure everything was delivered and done; people's lives are always the key focus from the services we provide to the talented teams that deliver them. This new way of thinking has enabled me to build and scale Tarasis Enterprises, (www.tarasis.com) now with several divisions, from health care and housing to renewables and sustainable farming, employing hundreds of people across Ireland.

I have tried and failed at things a hundred times along the way but I look at each one as a an opportunity to learn, just fail fast and move on! Innovation keeps a business alive and just look at every "failure" is innovation in action.

As I navigated this transformative journey, my motivations underwent a profound shift. Following a trip to India in 2011 to look at corporate social responsibility, the desire to use my business to create a better world and to always make a difference in the lives of others emerged as my driving force. My why became clear – to build a legacy of kindness and equality, to leave an indelible mark on the world that I now had the time to focus on. So, along with my colleagues, we set up the Tarasis Foundation which funds two not-for- profits. iCare Charity (www.icarecharity.com) delivers 'acts of kindness' within all our operational regions and each year we do the 'iCare at Christmas' campaign where we deliver thousands of gifts to homeless families every Christmas, and food and fuel vouchers throughout the year to local communities.

The second is Evolve (www.evolvewomen.org), which runs an annual academy teaching women the much-needed skills required to start, grow and scale a business successfully; a way for me to share with others and for them to learn from my mistakes.

Many entrepreneurs are motivated by their passion and freedom to innovate. The skills I've learned along the way have not only allowed me to build a business with a sense of purpose, surrounded by fantastic people and teams, but also brings me the sense of fulfilment and freedom I'd always wanted.

So many entrepreneurs struggle with the day-to-day operations and can't see light at the end of the tunnel or a way forward, but if you believe in the power of examining new ideas, reimagining and rewiring your thinking – something all of us can do – you will find your way.

So my advice to you is to embrace every day as a fresh opportunity for learning, open your mind to new ways of working, developing and trusting in the great people around you – it'll bring you on an adventure with endless possibilities.

To learn more about this author: linkedin.com/in/maireadmackle

www.tarasis.com

www.evolvewomen.org

www.icarecharity.com

www.kingsburywagyu.com

FROM SWITZERLAND TO NEW YORK – FROM PAPERGIRL TO SOLO-ENTREPRENEUR

BY SUSANNE MUELLER, MA

I grew up in Switzerland on the Lake of Thun, with a view of the famous snow-capped mountains Eiger, Mönch and Jungfrau, in the Bernese Oberland. It looks like paradise when I visit now, so why did I leave?

I was in an all-girls high school, where half of us chose to become nurses and the other half secretaries. The school offered a career counsellor service where I underwent a few tests. At barely fourteen years old, the career counsellor seemed like an incredibly old lady with grey hair and a grey dress. She displayed total authority. In hindsight, she was neither warm, charming nor forward-thinking, to say the least. I remember there was a list of jobs from which I could choose. I selected a few vocations, and one was *modistin* (German for hatmaker). I didn't know what that would mean, but I liked the sound of it. When discussing the vocational assessments, the counsellor asked me in a punitive tone, 'Why did you pick that?' I was so intimidated, but I uttered in a soft, trembling voice, 'I don't know but it sounded nice.'

This should have been the exact moment where she asked a few deeper and more mindful questions, perhaps, 'Let's dig deeper for a moment longer. What does it take to become a hatmaker, and why does that sound like something you would choose?' Instead, she concluded, 'Well, your mum is a secretary, and you will be a secretary, too!' Thank you for your creative career advice, old lady!

At the time, it was okay, as I was learning new skills by working in an office, being in a structured environment, going to school two days per week and making some money. These were building blocks for my future career. I am grateful for those formative years as this has brought me to where I am today. Putting money aside gave me the opportunity to spend ten weeks in London where I studied English. Ultimately, I was exposed to the real and global world for the first time, and I LOVED it. This first experience was not the job I would do for the rest of my life and I'm fully aware, now, that I can have more than one career and that building blocks are important. When building a house, I cannot start with the balcony, I must start with the foundation.

As a summer intern job, I was a papergirl and learned a lot in terms of customer service – showing up on time, teamwork and delegation. My sister and some other friends would sometimes go with me. I delegated some deliveries to them as they helped me out at places where there were dogs … since I am mortally afraid of them! On a few occasions, I met the customers and greeted them with a genuine smile. One lady provided me with her fresh produce; I clearly remember her juicy peaches. It was a great learning experience and interesting to know that Warren Buffett, one of the richest men in the world, started out as a paperboy. Start small, start humble; you will learn from everybody.

Fast-forward, I realised my dream of working for an airline. I like to joke that I used to work there when people would *dress up* for flying and when the food they served was delicious. Initially, I worked at the airport in Zürich, in their lost-and-found department. What a great job for learning about other cultures. This was my free cross-cultural awareness training. I did not read books to learn how to communicate with other cultures, I was thrown into the deep end – learning by doing.

After three years working at the airport, I transferred to work in the sales and marketing department in their call centre. This was my hardest job, but also where I developed a deep admiration for anyone who works in a call centre! What a tough job – remember to be nice to them when you call next time! This experience brought me to my subsequent job as a ticket sales agent in New York via a management exchange program. At one point, we had a sales training in Switzerland, with a few managers from various destinations, and the station manager from New York was attending. When the job in New York was advertised I took a risk. I called up the HR department and told them, 'I'd like to apply for the job in New York. I know the station manager there!' Did I really know him? Probably not. I'd said, 'Hi, how are you? Goodbye,' to him. But I used that as my ticket to live and work in New York. It was a gutsy move, but it worked.

In New York City, I was working close to Rockefeller Center on Fifth Avenue – the best place to be. It was around Christmas time when I started, and I enjoyed the early morning strolls around the famous Rockefeller Christmas tree before all the visitors came. I was catching up on diversity and inclusion (DEI), as coming from a homogenous place like Switzerland, New York opened my eyes on many levels. I learned about the good, the bad and the ugly, in the city that never sleeps. For sure, it's extremely competitive, there are a lot of people, nobody is waiting for you and you must be vigilant … all the time … otherwise someone else will take your spot. Working for the airline in New York was filled with cool new experiences.

At the time, I also started to run in Central Park and found another passion. I gave up my beloved skiing for running. Skiing in New York City is not the easiest. Running and being in the fresh air was the next best thing. I joined a running class and built a great circle of friends. I also got to know real New Yorkers – this was not so easy as New York is a very international place. The New York dream came to a halt when they told me to return to Switzerland earlier than anticipated. I was not happy, but a friend I'd made in New York, who worked at the Swiss Mission to the United Nations, called me up ten months later and said, 'Hey, there's a job as a receptionist at the Swiss Mission. If you want to come back to the Big Apple, now's the time.' I decided to go for the interview and got the job on the spot, thanks to her impeccable reference.

A new life began. Leaving the airline was not easy and being a receptionist was not my dream job! But I took on the role and worked my way up to becoming the administrator in charge of all the high-level guests and delegations from Switzerland, assisting with their hotel needs and accreditations at the United Nations. This was almost the same job as I did with the airline.

It brought me back to the customer service mentality I learned as a papergirl. A good reminder: Never forget what you learned at a young age. Further, I took advantage of taking classes at the university and fulfilled my dream of going back to school for my bachelor's degree in psychology, while working full-time. This was a time when I needed to budget well, paying for my own tuition. Running helped me through these tough, but also fun, years.

The running routine helped me to be determined and disciplined. Not only did I become a better and faster runner, and a marathon runner, but I also extended my personal and professional network. This was the best investment. With a group of runners, I also visited places in the USA, Canada and Brazil, while completing a total of twenty-six marathon races globally so far. Having once worked for an airline, the travel bug does not go away.

The time came to make a big decision. Should I stay at my secure job at the Swiss Mission to the United Nations, or should I take a risk and go back to school full-time and take a leap? Little did I know this was the riskiest decision. I quit my secure job and went to school full-time at Columbia University. I worked three days on campus – again, thanks to a running friend who then became my mentor – which paid me US$15 per hour. On the weekends, I did babysitting, again for US$15 per hour, and had a part-time office job with a landscape architect, all while studying full-time for my graduate degree. These were happy times but without much money. I got through school without a scholarship, without a loan or debt, but by having a roommate and being frugal and living modestly.

Then in 2001, September 11 hit. This was my last semester at Columbia University. In December of that year, I would graduate and needed a job, but not just any job, a job that would sponsor my visa to stay in the USA. Not an easy venture. I work well under stress, and I am very resourceful and resilient when it comes to stressful situations, but the time around September 11, 2001, was very difficult – to say the least! There were companies who were not hiring at all, certainly not international candidates who needed sponsorship. Who would hire me? I could only offer psychology and organisational development, without too much experience except for my languages and the experience I had with government officials. It was a hard year ahead of me. I sent out 365 résumés – and got nowhere!

Finally, on a sunny day in November 2002, Nestlé called and extended a job offer. This meant they would sponsor me for my work visa, but the job was outside of New York City. I had to commute an hour and a half each way. I didn't own a car, as owning a car in New York City is a nightmare, so that meant I had to take a bus, a train and another bus to get to work! I was suddenly grateful for all the years when I was lucky to live next-door to school or my workplace. I had no choice! Either I would commute for three hours a day or I'd have to return to Europe. But where would I start back there? I had been in New York for ten years – I was a New Yorker. It was not the glamorous life I would have liked, but it was the life I created. At the same time, I became a running coach and was able to help others become faster and stronger runners. This was another positive aspect of my life in New York.

The job with Nestlé was in HR leading an international team

while the organisation implemented SAP software. My role was to assist experts obtaining their visas and assist with relocation. This was a fun job, not a traditional HR role. It was a similar role to the one at the Swiss Mission to the United Nations. I was working with international HR departments around the world. While there, I took advantage of visiting their offices in Paris, London, Sao Paulo and Switzerland. The face-to-face meetings were invaluable. In Sao Paulo, Brazil, they took me to watch a World Cup soccer game during their lunch hour. Without knowing much of the language, it was a fun experience to get to know and mingle with the locals. Sport always unites. Every time I was travelling to a destination, I would make sure to bring my running shoes and, most of the time, I was able to find a running partner. This bonded us on a different level and the professional tasks became easier.

After a long time patiently waiting, I finally received my green card (which is not really green). It felt like I could now start looking for a new job back in the city without the commute. It was 2008 – the financial crisis! Another crisis I had to over-come, trying to find a new job without success. In 2009, the SAP implementation project ended, meaning my job was being eliminated. 'Your job will be gone by the end of the year – don't take it personally.' This is how my boss started the conversation at 4:30pm in the evening! WHAT? 'Don't take it personally?' Losing a job is very personal. Now what?

This was the worst and best day of my life! I was losing my secure job, my safety net, but also a job that I didn't really want to do for much longer. I was close to burnout. The stress of the long commute had gotten to me. My boss, a thoughtful person, undoubtedly knew ahead of me that my job would be gone. He paid for my coaching education! What a blessing! He also authorised my attendance at the fourth World Appreciative Inquiry conference in Nepal in 2009. This is where my international network expanded exponentially. I felt at ease mingling with other like-minded experts in the field. Appreciative inquiry (AI) is based on positive psychology and uses a strengths-based or affirmative approach. (4D – Discovery, dream, design, destiny). This has helped me reframe challenging moments into opportunities, and ultimately brought me to the mindfulness coaching I am passionate about today.

Now what? The company offered some unemployment assistance programs, but I felt I couldn't jump from one corporate job to the next. Why not volunteer, together with travelling and expanding my network? I learned about the Women's Education Project (WEP) in India. Again, I took a risk: I booked a flight to Hyderabad, India, where I arrived at 4am. There were three men waiting for me with a sign: *Ms. Mueller, WEP.* What an adventure. It was the experience of a lifetime. There, I offered leadership training to young female students. Some of the schools were further away, without public transportation, so they asked if it was okay to go by motorbike as no car was available. I said *yes* without thinking too much. The traffic in India is a bit chaotic, to say the least, and I didn't have a helmet. Some negative thoughts went through my head: *This might be the last day of your life driving on a motorcycle without a helmet; are you crazy?* Then I said to myself, *If you think like that, then it will be your last day. You will be missing out on many great adventures.* It felt like *Eat, Pray, Love* – but much better.

I had a translator for these trainings, and I'd planned it out well, to talk about leadership and soft skills. WRONG – my plan did not work out. The translator didn't know how to translate SOFT SKILLS. I had to switch my 'first-world trained mindset' into a 'storytelling mindset' within no time. Big learning: you must adapt to your audience and meet them where they are!

And did I say, I was sweating profusely as there was no air conditioning! Furthermore, it was a tradition that the guest would sing along. They wanted me to sing a song from my culture! So grateful this was in the time before any social media! I am far from being a singer, let alone a performer. But as a trainer, facilitator or coach, it's about adapting in the moment. Within the blink of an eye, my time in India ended. It was hard for me to say goodbye. I learned so much during my visit. For one thing, I needed very little as I was travelling with one small suitcase, and I enjoyed going with the flow, learning from the locals, adapting, being flexible but having fun! Yes, we did have a lot of fun.

During that time in 2010, I started my weekly blog. I was looking for a catchy name and it was around the time *Eat, Pray, Love* (Elizabeth Gilbert, 2006) became popular. Of course, I couldn't use that title, but then I thought of Einstein's formula $E=MC^2$. So, I picked E=PL3 where E stands for energy where I write about a healthy and happy lifestyle. Adding P for play (or fun) where I can muse about something out of the ordinary. And L3 stands for lifelong learning. Voila, my blog was ready. It started out as a travel blog or journal and today, over a decade later, it has morphed more into a leadership blog. The blog has been one of my passion projects that has also encouraged me to write my two books: *Take it from the Ironwoman* (2017) and *Lipstick Leadership* (2021).

(smuellernyc.blogspot.com)

After five weeks in India, I returned to New York looking for a job! This became a lonely chore. I went to an outplacement office – where I felt out of place! At least I didn't have many overheads and I didn't have to provide for a family! This was a time when I was more social than usual. I felt at ease and opportunities came my way. I was working part-time on a HR project, and then I started teaching, again, through a connection in my network. I was offered the opportunity to teach at New York University in their coaching program. This was an avenue to learn and grow with others by helping them set up their own coaching practice.

But suddenly, the HR project was cancelled, the classes ended and the bank account did not look so rosy anymore. I was still looking for a job. In that outplacement centre, they offered a group for entrepreneurs. I told my advisor: 'I'd like to join them; I want to be an entrepreneur.' At first, she denied my participation since she felt I was not fully committed to being an entrepreneur! *What?* Finally, I convinced her I needed to participate to learn, but on attending I wasn't impressed. I was already a few steps ahead of those wannabe entrepreneurs. I had my business cards; I knew how to network, and I knew how to provide my elevator speech. I was disappointed this counsellor did not consider my entrepreneurial spirit! It felt like deja vu with the old career coaching lady at school in Switzerland. Putting me in a box again – NO, thank you!

That summer, a friend of mine sent me a message: *Do you speak French? Do you know how to coach leaders? Are you available?*

YES, YES and YES. This is when my dream came true. It sounds like I was lucky! No, I have worked very hard towards my goals, I have studied what I was passionate about, I had experience with different cultures, and I was ready and available! This is when many things came to fruition. I learned again from other cultures, I was coaching many leaders, and I was happy! Happiest after many years of struggle and of not working in the field that I had studied.

It's not always easy to go for what you want but it can always be a learning experience. For sure, the journey is more important than the destination. And once we are at a destination – like the end of a marathon race – there is actually no finish line. Life goes on and I must push every single day to get up and motivate myself. When people say I have a good life – I can say YES – but I am also working hard for it. I am proud of what I've achieved, and nobody can take this away from me! Through my marathon and now ironman training, I know how hard it is to motivate myself. I ensure I have a plan, and when you follow a good plan, things become a lot easier. Also remember, there are experts in the field. When training for a big event like the ironman triathlon, it's advisable to have a coach. Every sports team has a coach, many businesspeople have a coach. Why not me? I've learned the hard way, thinking I had to do it all on my own. Sometimes, as a solo entrepreneur there are days where I am the secretary and accountant, as well as managing all the household chores like cooking and cleaning. Being a solo-preneur is not always glamourous.

But, after more than ten years as a solo-entrepreneur, I can't imagine going back into an office or large organisation. Though for some, it might be easier! In an organisation, it can be about job security, having a regular pay cheque and more regular hours. I have been an executive coach and am working globally, however, it's also tricky to find a good balance between work and non-work. Creating work-life success is all about balance. I like that I am successful and proud of what I have achieved alone. I do not have rich parents who were able to connect me with the right people. All of what I have done in New York, I have done for myself. New York can teach you the good, the bad and the ugly sides of life. Living through September 11, 2001, a hurricane (Sandy), numerous snowstorms and the pandemic is no picnic in the park.

The pandemic was hard for me as there was not much work initially, but it allowed me space to develop my podcast, which I had started a few months earlier in August of 2019. I've always wanted to interview interesting people and share their stories with the world, now, more than four hundred episodes later *(Take it from the ironwoman),* I have met many great people and recorded their amazing stories. It's about listening and observing what others do, and I learn from every single encounter.

I always had a dream of having my own company: I have achieved that, so now what? This is a good question. It's not always fun being alone as a solo-entrepreneur. It's about creating a good network of friends and business partners. In an organisation, you make friends, but as a coach, clients rarely become friends. Your network needs to be nurtured and cared for like a plant. Solo-entrepreneurship can be a lonely journey. For me, it's about connecting with others on a deeper level. Sport has helped me, but I also enjoy writing my weekly blog, where I can muse about things on my mind. It's about creating a happy and healthy mindset with good people around you. When you are an entrepreneur, you see opportunities everywhere. It's about finding a way to say YES to what you want to do and being comfortable saying NO to things you don't.

Writing this, and reflecting on my accomplishments, it feels like a journey that will never end. For me it's about getting up every day, being motivated and motivating others. I had the opportunity to be a speaker at a TEDx conference (Running and Life: 5K Formula for Your Success) and I spoke in a few locations around the world – Switzerland, Poland, UK, Hong Kong, Mexico, Brazil, USA. There is no finish line – if you give up then someone else will take your place. This is what I learned in New York City; it's about finding or fighting for that seat on the subway every morning, but also giving that seat up to someone who needs it more than you.

Over the past years, I have been a mentor for the Cherie Blair Foundation for women (cherieblairfoundation.org), EDsnaps for STE(A)M students (edsnaps.org), and Stand Beside Them (standbesidethem.org) for US veterans. I have been enjoying mentoring others – I always look back and think, *Wow, wouldn't it have been nice if I had a mentor in my early career life?* Certainly not that old career counsellor who put me in a box! I wished for a person who understood me at a young age. I am wondering what they would have suggested. In today's world, the sky is the limit. I encourage anybody who has an opportunity to say YES before they think of all the shoulds, coulds, woulds. If you think too much, you will never embark on an adventure. One of my role models, Mary Poppins, says: 'Are you ready for an adventure? Don't ask too many questions. Let's go.'

Are you ready? Let's go – good luck and enjoy your journey. Only you know which direction you want to go. There are many paths, but you can also create your own!

To learn more about this author: linkedin.com/in/ susanne-mueller-ma

WE HAVE TO HAVE THE LOWS TO APPRECIATE THE HIGHS

BY SUE SMILER

Born in Birmingham, England, in 1958, with two brothers and two sisters, I have fun and loving memories of my childhood. My parents went into the pub trade when I was ten years old, and we moved into a beautiful old pub, The Old Hare & Hounds. We lived near the Lickey Hills, a walkers' paradise, where local people often came for the day if they couldn't afford holidays. JR Tolkien and his parents lived next door to us in a cottage. I was told the Lickey Hills were his inspiration for *The Hobbit*.

It was such a busy pub. All of us had to work for pocket money, sweeping the car park or cleaning the pub and toilets. Life in the pub was fantastic and we had incredible parties. My twenty-first was a fancy dress for two hundred people. We did a parachute jump that day and I felt glad to be alive after jumping from the plane.

School, though, was different. I had little interest except for geography lessons. I loved learning about different countries, customs and traditions, and yearned to travel the world. After school, I worked in an office with British Leyland for five years, but knew it wasn't for me; I wanted more. When they offered voluntary redundancy, I took the money and left. I travelled to Sydney, Australia, and stayed three months before returning home. With my job gone, I had no idea what I wanted to do for a career.

I needed money to go on holiday with friends, so when the manageress at Cromwell's Casino, who used to drink in my dad's pub, told me there was a job at the casino as a waitress, I decided to take it. Though on my feet a lot, it was great fun; I enjoyed the job, the staff and the customers. And, surprisingly, I earnt a lot of money.

I would often watch the croupiers working and thought it was something I might like to try. Staff were regularly leaving to work abroad and that really interested me. *Maybe I could travel the world as a croupier.*

After four years, I needed a change and a new challenge. I moved to Bournemouth to train as a croupier at The Vic Sporting Club; a fantastic little casino. I loved the training, liked the people and discovered I was good at maths. After six weeks of eight-hour days learning blackjack and roulette, I was able to apply for my gaming licence, a requirement before being able to deal and play the tables in the UK. However, those six weeks of training were really tough. After eight hours a day of training, I had to work an eight-hour shift in the casino waitressing, just to pay my rent and have money for myself – it was sixteen- to eighteen-hour days for those six weeks. One night I was so tired, I thought about quitting, but I clearly remember what I told myself that night:

Sue, if you quit now, you will NEVER have anything in life … you CAN do this. In times of doubt and struggle, you sometimes need to dig deep and be your own best friend.

Rewards come in many ways. All the hard work paid off and the job gave me everything I wanted: excitement at work, people I enjoyed working with and so many laughs. I had found my happy place.

I remember my first night on the table after my gaming licence came through. It was incredible. I was excited and nervous at the same time. It made my adrenalin pump like no other job I had before. I was where I was meant to be. I was already thinking about travel and working abroad, but a croupier must complete two years working in a casino before applying for a job on a cruise ship or anywhere overseas.

When rent doubled, I moved back to Birmingham to live with my parents and secured a job at the Midland Wheel Casino. It was a great casino to work in and I was happy there. One day I received a phone call from a close friend. She was working on St Vincent, an island in the Caribbean, and suggested I go there as they needed another croupier. I didn't really want to leave as I was so happy at the time, but Mum encouraged me to give it a try. 'Go for six months … you never know where this could lead.' My mum was so wise and wonderful, knowing I needed the extra push to put me on the path to a life I had dreamed of and countries I longed to see. Sometimes we all need a push or extra support to encourage us to jump into the unknown and take the opportunities life offers us.

I flew to St Vincent, and knowing I was going over to work with one of my closest friends made it easier. When I landed,

I had a weird feeling, like I'd lived there before and had come home! I loved the Caribbean and working in the casino. We had so many laughs and adventures.

Life there was … unbelievable. The casino had two swimming pools, three tennis courts and was situated in a valley that was so beautiful, with hummingbirds galore, fresh coconut water every day, a hammock on our balcony overlooking the river and palm trees all around. It truly was paradise. I did miss my friends and family though, especially my mum, but I couldn't afford to fly home as our wages were not great. But it's never been all about the money for me. We had amazing quality of life living on a beautiful island in the Caribbean.

It was two years before I saw my mum, friends and family again. My sister's children had grown and the youngest didn't even know who I was. I vowed I would never leave it that long again.

Flying back to St Vincent, I met a guy who told me he was going to meet his uncle Harold and sail with him in the Caribbean. They came to the casino to visit me and my friend, Arlene, and the next day, on their invitation, we sailed with them to Mustique and back, having lunch on the boat.

Months later, Harold asked us to go sailing with him to South America. This was the next adventure I was seeking. I persuaded Arlene to come too.

We packed enough food for two weeks. We were sailing to Margarita just off Venezuela, known as the pearl of the Caribbean, twenty-five miles from the mainland. The trip took longer than expected. The sea was rough, and being a flat-bottomed boat, it pounded the ocean, instead of gliding through it. In Margarita, we enquired about the cost to fly back to St Vincent. It was a lot of money – too much for us! So back on the boat we went.

We were on the boat for Christmas and New Year, which was hard, but we made the most of it. The boat experience was too much for us both at times but making each other laugh helped. Although it was hard, I learnt a lot about myself on that trip.

We finally made it safely back to St Vincent and realised we both quite enjoyed sailing – now that we'd found our sea legs and had learnt more about managing a boat. We agreed to another trip to sail to Martinique and back.

We had many adventures in St Vincent. The casino didn't rely on tourists, as there was only one cruise ship visit per year, so it was mostly locals playing the tables. We ran a school to train local croupier staff, and if the casino wasn't busy, we helped in the restaurant. We made some good friends there and people liked both me and Arlene. My advice is always to do more than what is expected of you … it comes back to you tenfold, in my experience.

Arlene met a wonderful man, who became her husband, and went to live in Antigua. There was a lot more of the world I wanted to see, and I ended up travelling alone for a few years and working on cruise ships. I made many amazing and crazy friends.

I loved it and worked on many ships. One of my favourites was in the Far East. In 1993, Vietnam, China, Malaysia, Burma, Hong Kong and Jakarta were nothing like they are today. I was living my dream. I was so glad I pushed myself into going alone. One benefit of travelling alone is that more people approach you and talk to you. When my six-month cruise contract finished in the Far East, I got my mum to fly out and we spent a month in Indonesia together.

I also did two six-month contracts in Alaska, which was amazing. The scenery is incredible. I got Mum on the ship with me and took her on every excursion possible. I remembered her encouraging me when I first left to go to St Vincent. My beautiful, funny, kind and loving mother knew, before I did, that she would have some great adventures with me.

Life is what you make it, and you have to grab the opportunities that come your way with both hands. I was on such a high travelling to all those countries and loving my job in the casino with the happy passengers on their holidays. On a sea day, we would work long shifts (often sixteen hours), though as staff, we still managed to get together for a few drinks. It was always so much fun. But ... there is only so long anyone can party and work like that, and in the year 2000, I left the ships.

I went back to Birmingham and decided to learn reflexology. I'd had many treatments while I was travelling, and it fascinated me. Upon reflection, it is one of the best things I've done. I discovered many people who came to me for treatments, would cry and get upset, so I did a counselling course to help me deal with this on a more professional level. That was such a special course. I learned a great deal about myself too. I really didn't like school, but later in life, I am truly enjoying studying. I also went to university every weekend for two years, to learn hypnotherapy. I became a qualified hypnotherapist for therapeutic outcomes. I started as a mobile therapist and loved it. How my life changed! It's incredible how we can adapt to a new way of life.

I loved that I was making a difference to people's lives and health and how much better they felt after a reflexology session. Once, I was doing reflexology on a friend of mine and touched a part of her foot when she screamed and asked me to stop. I couldn't get her off my mind, so the next day I called and told her I was taking her to the doctor, who advised us to go straight to hospital. She was diagnosed with a brain tumour. I just knew something wasn't right. The tumour was removed, and she is well now. I have seen so many amazing things with reflexology.

I didn't realise how hard I'd been pushing myself, and at one point, having worked 120 hours in a week, I suddenly collapsed. My lower back had gone into spasm. My legs wouldn't work with my brain, and I was in so much pain, I cried for a week. I was assessed by a wonderful lady who works with the Welsh rugby team, who told me I was pushing my body too hard. I needed to start listening to my body and take time out. I played hypnotherapy tapes every morning and every night before I went to sleep. It was incredible. I went from *WHY ME?* to *WHY NOT ME?* in a week. Thankfully, I recovered and can walk again.

I advise many people who are suffering from anxiety, fear of flying, panic attacks and more to try hypnotherapy. First find a voice you like and then listen, using headphones, as it internalises it. Try listening, morning and night, and notice the changes in you. Perhaps I was meant to go through what I did so I can help others and realise how incredible hypnotherapy is. I truly believe everything happens for a reason in life – good or bad. Though we don't always realise it at the time.

I think I have always been a 'carer'. I helped my grandmother look after my grandfather when he was poorly, and on another occasion, I went straight home from a cruise ship when I got a call to say my dad was terminally ill. I stayed with my mum and helped her take him to chemotherapy.

When my mum got breast cancer, I also went and stayed with her. She was amazing and so brave. She had her breast removed and recovered. Her sense of humour helped her through. Four years later, she got liver cancer and I stayed with her again. I stayed in the hospital with her, next to her bed, for ten weeks. That was the hardest journey of my life. I never cried in front of her, and I tried to make her smile every day. Losing my mum nearly broke me. It took two years for me to get myself back. I don't think you ever 'get over it,' you just learn to live with it. My mum used to say, 'Sue, life is precious,' and she was right.

Even though I'd had plenty of life experience, you need qualifications to work for a care company. So, I did the course and secured a job with a care agency in Ireland. I now realise how lucky I am after caring for so many wonderful people with different illnesses and disabilities – dementia, MND, blindness, Parkinson's, to name a few. All the wonderful people I have had the pleasure to care for have taught me something, that everyone I care for, I treat them like they are family. It's the only way I know, with patience and empathy. My grandmother would say, 'Sue, I don't feel any different than when I was nineteen … people just treat me differently.' I learned from this and always treat elderly people as equals. I use my reflexology and massage on many people I care for, along with my people skills, counselling and humour. Care work can be hard and emotionally draining, but it is so rewarding to help others. I love being in the caring profession and genuinely care for the people I look after.

While working as a carer, I would sometimes work a few fun casino nights at a local hotel, and I was approached by a friend who asked me to consider managing a B&B on the ocean. I had a look and we agreed on a three-month trial. Three months turned into five years. We worked well together and, most importantly, we had fun.

The B&B was challenging at times. I had to deal with many things, like a lady who had a heart attack in the dining room and a man who fell down the stairs having had a bleed on the brain. However, after experiencing armed robberies while in the casino in St Vincent, I was prepared and never scared in any situation.

All my different vocations were now working together in this beautiful B&B on the ocean. I had my therapy room upstairs and was still doing the odd shift as a care worker. I have been so lucky in life and found that this B&B was my dream job. I loved everything about it. My boss made the B&B so inviting, leveraging his years of hospitality experience.

Sadly, my home and that job had to come to an end. The B&B building was leased, and the owners wanted it back. I cried but am grateful for the wonderful five years I had there. Life can be scary at times, and I am again in uncharted waters. I thought I was going to die when I faced two gale force nine storms on Harold's boat, but I got through that, and I will get through this.

I have been lucky throughout my life with my varied and exciting jobs and the amazing people I have met along the way. I count my blessings every day. My only advice: do what makes you happy. If in doubt, try something different and don't worry too much. The journey of your life will unfold just as it's meant to!

REWIRE

'Fear kills more dreams than failure ever will.'
SUZY KASSEM

WHAT'S STOPPING YOU?

BY TARA BEATTIE

Hindsight is 20/20 vision, they say, but in my case, I'm not so sure. I remember being in school and knowing I wanted to work for myself, but really had no idea at what. I naively thought I needed to be in some form of medicine to achieve that, which was never going to be the route for me! I didn't suit school very well and definitely didn't suit college. Nevertheless, it was instilled in me that I should have a degree, even if I never used it. So, I studied science at UCD, not really settling or thriving. I did, however, have a natural ability for maths and so majored in statistics. Needless to say, I have never formally used my degree. Though, it did give me a good understanding of my ability to get through even the least enjoyable tasks!

I've always believed you can be whatever you want to be – you can always restart and reinvent yourself. My first experience at this was in secondary school when, after fifth year, I realised the level of work I was doing was never going to get me into college. I asked my parents if I could have a do-over!! They complied and I repeated my fifth year at a new school. I went from being one of the students who missed class, underachieving in exams, to being thought of as a nerd and very diligent! My oldest school friends still laugh at this anomaly.

My next reimagination of my life was in 1993 when the Donnelly Visa was launched – a visa allowing access to work legally in the US, via lottery. I applied for the seven members of my family, believing they all wanted to and could reinvent themselves, but just needed the opportunity. All seven of us were awarded the visa – my poor parents nearly died!

One of my sisters planned to go to NYC. I had a good starter job at Dell in Bray as a customer care associate but the thought of really starting my career in the US was hugely exciting. I decided to go two months before my sister to get set up. I went with a friend, and we found an apartment in Queens. She started stockbroker training, while I got a job with a family business in Brooklyn which manufactured components for rockets! I loved the idea of this. My job was a bit of everything; some elements I liked and others I didn't. I worked with the owner's daughter and her team. It was a very strict working environment, but the team I worked with were generous with their time to help me learn. I even learned to code; something I had been interested in since I was twelve when the first personal computers were launched – Dragon 32 and Commodore 64.

This job had me excited for the future, as every three months they brought me into the office for a review and increased my salary. In the twelve months I was there my salary increased by 50%!

However, this reinvention was not to last. Just before I left to go to America on my Donnelly visa, I had started to date a special guy. He did not have a visa and was not coming to the States. So, after our twelve-month long-distance relationship, I chose to come home and see what would happen. He is now my husband!

On return to Ireland, I thought I would try a job I knew I didn't have experience for – sales. I applied for a job with a computer components company as a sales consultant. They offered me a position as quality specialist and I thought, *Okay, that's fate,* and took the job. I loved the company and again learned so much there. I put myself forward for every job or task going. I hung out with the IT manager under the stairs, pulling cables or writing little computer programs to automate several tasks. I spent time with the accountant and took over the job of creating their price book; this gave me a massive education into Excel. I hung out with the purchasing manager and saw how he negotiated prices and contracts. I also managed the returns and the quality management system – implementing ISO 9000 and getting accredited with the NSAI.

All was going well until they decided I needed a designated boss and that it was not to be the IT manager, the accountant or the purchasing manager. It was a new hire for whom I had little respect, as I felt he didn't really do much work. I asked the operations director to make someone else my boss but to no avail. There's a saying: 'People don't leave jobs, they leave people.' So, I updated my CV and applied for a quality management position at Intel. It was another computer components company, and it was big. I secured the job and found it wasn't very challenging. I tried to get involved in other areas of the business, like I had done in previous companies, but it was more difficult in this large corporation to help out in other departments.

Shortly after starting this job, I got engaged. It was a good time to have an easy job, as I had a wedding to plan and a house to buy. A year after joining Intel, I married and soon after that started dreaming with Brian (my husband) about him opening a restaurant. He was a chef with experience in serious fine dining restaurants in Dublin and beyond. For both of us, it seemed natural he'd open his own restaurant. It was the summer of 1998. The accountant from my previous job was starting a software consulting business and asked if I would be interested in joining as a computer consultant for an ERP product in which I had previous experience. I jumped at the chance. Everyone thought I was crazy leaving a powerhouse like Intel for a startup. I was excited by the idea especially as he was renting an office on St Stephen's Green, Dublin. I was twenty-seven, had a house in town and now an office with a parking space. I think when you're starting out in work and are young, you have no fear. I have always thought that if you choose to do something, just do it. If it works, you will reap the rewards, and if it doesn't, you will learn from it and grow. Leaving Intel didn't seem like a big deal for me.

About a month after I started this job, Brian heard of a restaurant space becoming available. We discussed it. This was a special space as he had worked there twice before for two different chef owners – L'Ecrivian and Peacock Alley. These were renowned restaurants in Dublin at the time and had made their names in this little premises. Before we could think twice, he handed in his notice and secured the lease. We decided to call it Mange Tout – partly because it means 'Eat All', partly because it was French and, unbeknownst to me, Brian loved *Only Fools and Horses,* so part nod to Delboy!

This was five months into our marriage. We borrowed, €6,000 from each of our parents and set about getting the place ready. We painted it ourselves. I got welts on my hands from covering fifty-two chairs in two days. I was working full-time but worked in the restaurant in the evenings and weekends. Within our first six months we were listed in all the guidebooks, including the Michelin guidebook. We had been reviewed by all the critics and were thriving. We repaid our parents and I had to give up my day job as it was too difficult to do it all.

All was going well, however, we were victims of our own success and the Celtic Tiger. We struggled with staff and did a lot of the work ourselves. We were in the restaurant from 8am until 1am most Fridays and Saturdays and then from 8am to 10pm Tuesday until Thursday. Looking back now with 20/20 vision – we were burnt-out and, unbeknownst to me, I was pregnant. One day, on a break between lunch and dinner, we sat on a bench in St Stephen's Green and discussed where we were and how we were feeling. We both felt we would have a better quality of life if we closed the restaurant and went back to work for other people. So, we returned to the restaurant for dinner service and met the team one by one, paid them and told them we were closing. That was it. Deep down we must have known we were only taking a break, as we kept the company and name open, just not trading.

A month after closing the restaurant, we found out I was pregnant. This was a little unexpected but made sense to how tired I had been in the restaurant. This was the start of a really challenging few months for us, as not only were we not working, but we found out another month later that our baby was very sick and would most likely not survive after birth. So, without any distraction, we just had to live with the pregnancy. When people got excited seeing my bump, my heart broke and I couldn't tell them what we were going through. On 7 October 2000, our son was born and, soon after, passed away.

I am not sure I have ever properly dealt with this or come to terms with it, but I have learned to live with it. I had to get out of the house, to get a job to distract me, to get my mind working again and to get some positivity and focus. I applied for various positions and was successful in getting a role as business excellence executive for Allianz Ireland. I had no idea what this was but just wanted to do something. Brian went back to work with one of his previous bosses.

Soon after I started this role – very soon – I found out I was pregnant again. I was terrified. Not only about the pregnancy, but also about telling my boss – I was a month into the job. I worked hard to prove to him and the company that they didn't make a mistake in hiring me. I worked three and a half years in the role and had two more sons while there. In my second year, however, we had the bug again and wanted to go back into running our own business. We built a little kitchen on the side of my husband's family farm using some of the money from the sale of our house in town. Brian reinvented Mange Tout as The Caterers, and I helped while I worked or while on maternity leave. After two years, I couldn't continue to do two jobs; I was exhausted. I had a chat with Brian, and he agreed I hand in my notice. Three weeks later, we found out I was pregnant again – I should have guessed! Our daughter, and last child, was born in March 2005.

The Caterers was doing nicely, but now we had to feed three children, maintain a bigger house and pay for child care so we both could work. We needed our business to be successful. We had to push for business growth. I started to look outside the work we were focused upon and research what other companies like ours were doing. I noticed that the ones which appeared successful were catering companies but also ran cafe operations or had catering contracts with government bodies. This was 2007. I observed technical directors and heads of state attending government dinners in Farmleigh and Dublin Castle and knew we needed to cater these events to raise our profile and shake up the current offering. I called every venue to find out how to cater for these events. It wasn't easy – there was a 'list'. I tried and tried to get on this list but was informed we needed to tender. In 2011, I saw a tender for a cafe in Castletown House. Brian and I grew up near the venue and knew it well – we used to walk the grounds when we were younger. We naively tendered, and luck was with us. We won the contract.

After about three months of running the cafe, we realised it was not a busy site and needed a serious turn around. It had a bad reputation locally and there was a lot of bureaucracy around any change or improvement we wanted to make. We put our heads down, listened to our customers, reacted to their feedback and gave them the best cafe experience around. We grew that business by 30% year on year. At the same time, in the absence of getting on the 'list', we catered government dinners during the EU presidency. We were making a name for ourselves.

By 2015, we realised we were good at running cafes and decided to go for other similar tenders. We had begun to make an impression on the event companies. Our catering business grew, as did our cafe business. We finally got on the 'list' in 2016 and catered state dinners.

Our reputation was one of quality. So much so, that by 2019 we had one hundred staff, eight cafes, exclusivity on two high-profile venues, as well as our event catering business. Our children by now were planning to go to college. None of them were interested in getting into the family business, so we started to plan our exit strategy. We had worked hard to grow the business to the level we had, and in tandem grew the management team, laying the foundation to have a strong business to sell within two years. This was the first time we had a proper plan, a road map and a definite goal.

However, as we all know, all plans made in 2019 were changed for everyone by March 2020. We had closed all our businesses by 14 March. In parallel, our eldest son was receiving offers from colleges in the USA. We were devastated for our business and what had happened to our plan but excited for him and what the future looked like. Our son accepted an offer for MIT. He decided he would take a gap year in the hope that he could attend the college in person the following year. Brian and I had time to think and discuss our plans together during daily 2km permitted walks. We talked to our son about a project that had been on our minds for years; to create a software tool for professional kitchens to help them manage costs and waste, as well as allergen and calorie information. We had created and used it internally for our own business but dreamed of it as a stand-alone entity and something we could sell to other businesses. With the help of our son, we used the quiet time of COVID to create our digital recipe platform – Prepsheets.

We secured funding from Enterprise Ireland and in parallel reopened most of our cafes. We again looked at our business and tried to get a buyer, however, it looked a lot different than in 2019. Post-COVID, hospitality was struggling with rising costs, changing legislation and staff shortages. We knew it would take us three to five years to rebuild to pre-COVID levels which would affect the scalability of Prepsheets. We had to make a decision. Would we rebuild and let Prepsheets go, or would we close and focus on Prepsheets? Our children had no interest in the catering/cafe business. We were burnt-out from it and really felt no excitement to committing to another five years. We were, however, very excited about the challenge of Prepsheets. In November 2022, we decided to close Mange Tout, our business since 1998, for the third and last time.

We told all our landlords, our team and our suppliers and closed everything on 23 December 2022. After just over twenty-four years of being part of our family, Mange Tout was gone.

Here we are, starting again. Creating a new business, but this time with a focus on our lifestyle. We don't intend to work the hours we have previously. Our children are not in Ireland, so we want to travel and spend time with them. Our parents are still alive but getting less able, so we want to be there for them. We ourselves want to achieve personal goals such as fitness, social and knowledge, which we never had time for, or maybe didn't make time for, whilst running our businesses.

Going back one more time to hindsight being 20/20 vision, as a twenty-two-year-old starting out, I never realised I was so adaptable, so open to change and so able. I had no fear then and, even now, we have invested significantly into Prepsheets. Would I change anything? Possibly, but then we may not have achieved what we did, and maybe our children would not have achieved what they have already.

Now I look forward with excitement and openness to change, to learn and to continue to explore and grow. I encourage you to do the same.

To learn more about this author: prepsheets.com

HAPPY WITH MY CHOICES

BY LILY CORZO

Born in California, while my Mexican father and French mother were students at the University of California, Los Angeles, I was raised in both Mexico and Europe, regularly going back and forth throughout my childhood, with my native languages being Spanish and French.

My family was not in the military or the diplomatic service, we just liked living in different places. At seven years old, my parents looked at a map of Western Europe and saw that Munich was in the middle; a few months later, my parents, my brother and I moved from Mexico City to Munich with four suitcases. We were there in time for the 1972 Olympic Games and lived there for about two years.

When I was nine, we returned to Mexico City where my youngest brother was born, and where I resumed ballet lessons. My grandmother had signed me up for ballet classes when I was four, and as we had not learned left and right at that time, we wore pink socks on the right foot and white ones on the left. The teacher would indicate which foot to use with the corresponding colour and, to this day, I associate pink with right! Ballet was a big part of my life in my childhood, and I practised four afternoons a week and at home in the evenings.

When I was about to enter the ninth grade, my parents moved to Boston with my youngest brother, while my other brother and I went to Nice, France, so we could complete our schooling under the French system, and I could attend ballet classes at the Opéra de Nice. My paternal grandparents moved with us – the Mexican ones who only spoke a little French!

In the ninth grade, school became a lot more serious. I was going to school, then ballet class, and then home ... to a lot of homework, often going to bed at 1am. At some point, I thought about my future as a ballet dancer. I realised that even if I was an extremely good dancer, my career would be over by the time I was thirty. Whereas, if I focused on school, I would have more opportunities academically. At fourteen, I made what was probably the first difficult decision I'd made in my life ... I stopped dancing.

We moved back to Mexico City for another two years, after which I finished high school in Switzerland. I obtained a bachelor's degree in economics from the University of Chicago in the mid-eighties, graduated from University of California, Davis Law School, in the early nineties and was admitted to practise law in California.

I knew a large American law firm would not be a good fit for me as I enjoyed contact with clients, so I joined a small firm in San Francisco. The firm was new, and I participated in figuring out what we could do in addition to the 'regular' real estate law and litigation services we provided. I went to court frequently and soon realised I didn't want to be a litigator, as I preferred to communicate in writing. What I did enjoy was wearing skirt-and-jacket business suits in happy colours, such as red, amongst the ocean of gray- and black-clad lawyers. I developed my own eclectic general practice – as an example, I had a divorce action where the wife was in a coma and her adult children were involved in her care and made decisions for her. After a couple of years of practice, I decided I wanted to live in Europe again.

I sold my belongings and my practice, and in 1995 moved to Berlin, Germany, where I had no friends or family. I signed up for a two-month long intensive language course at the Goethe-Institut, as although I had learned German as a child when living in Munich, I had quickly forgotten it when I started learning English.

To ensure I actually learned the language, I teamed up with three classmates with whom I had no language in common: a Korean woman, a Greek woman and a Bulgarian man. After two months, I went to the Humboldt-Universität in Berlin and asked the contracts professor if I could sit in during his lectures, so I could learn German *legalese*. In exchange, I gave a few lectures to the class, their favourite being about the OJ Simpson case, which was being prosecuted during that time.

Once I felt I was making progress in German, I started applying to German law firms with offices in Berlin, as I had fallen in love with the city, which seemed to change every day.

During several interviews, I was regularly told there were no jobs for American attorneys, except in Frankfurt, or that I had only been invited to meet with the partners because they were *curious* about me. But I wanted to stay in Berlin. It took a few months, and finally I did get a job offer as a 'foreign lawyer' at a firm named Gleiss Lutz Hootz Hirsch Rechstanwälte. It was hard to say all that out loud!

I worked mainly with the partners in the Berlin office, but occasionally worked in the Stuttgart and Brussels offices. I focused on mergers and acquisitions, which were mostly American, British or French clients buying companies in Germany. For the last two years, I worked primarily with one partner who understood that being a 'foreign lawyer' did not prevent me from being a *lawyer*. At the time, many attorneys in the firm believed my value was only in my knowledge of languages and not in the legal work. My partner and I made an excellent team and closed many deals together. I learned a lot about how to present issues to clients, how to propose possible solutions and how to handle them. He included me in meetings and took the time to answer my questions. In return, I was available to work basically twenty-four seven and always took on any task or project he asked me to help with.

My other focus was work that entailed returning East German properties to heirs of the former owners — usually Jewish people who had been forced to sell their properties during the Nazi regime. I enjoyed looking up the records, handwritten in German, and figuring out the story behind the ownership of the property. I also learned about the Jewish families involved and kept notes for each case on personal information I obtained from the records I reviewed. I sent a summary to the heirs in a separate envelope, with a note explaining how I thought they might want to know more about their family. Some of the information was difficult to process, but the heirs told me it helped to know about their ancestors. These family members lived all around the world, including Israel, France and the US.

After four years at the firm, I knew I had learned all I could there, and that it was time to move on. I wanted to return to Los Angeles, where my immediate family lived. Several contacts directed me to a few companies as being a good fit for an 'international attorney' fluent in four languages.

In 1999, I was invited to join one of the largest global investment firms managing US-based mutual funds and other funds. These funds invest in and outside of the US. I focused on global legal and compliance issues. During almost twenty years there, I worked in the legal department as in-house senior counsel and vice president, wearing various hats.

I negotiated hundreds of agreements: sale and purchase, non-disclosure and subscription. I reviewed documents for participation in private placements and IPOs for investments for companies outside of the US. The investments ranged from US$20 to US$500 million each.

I supervised over forty law firms around the world who advised my company on various corporate and investing matters, coordinating many regulatory inquiries and examinations. I started my day in London and ended it in Hong Kong but was based in Los Angeles. I had early morning calls with Europe and very late-night calls with Asia.

Then, in December of 2017, I was diagnosed with stage two triple-negative breast cancer. Since my late thirties, I had been religious about having a mammogram every year, and that is how my cancer was discovered. I took medical leave from work for nine months to focus on beating it. I was fortunate to be treated at Cedars Sinai in Los Angeles by an amazing team of doctors. Thanks to Dr McArthur and Dr Shiao, I participated in a clinical trial for immunology treatment. I was lucky to be the first patient in the trial, which involved three rounds of chemotherapy, three needle biopsies (not fun at all) and targeted radiation. After the first round of chemo, my tumor had shrunk by 30% and my doctors and I were very happy. After the clinical trial, I went through the standard of care treatment and had eight rounds of chemo, spaced at every other week.

During this time, I was not feeling well and sometimes downright very bad. I spent a lot of time alone and had the opportunity to think about my life and what was important to me. I realised that over the previous thirty or so years, I had increasingly focused my life on my work and colleagues, and less on my own wellbeing. I took the time to spend 'quality time' with my son, whom I had adopted as a single mom when he was one year old. Although he was (and is) my priority, I felt I was not giving him as much attention and time as I thought he deserved.

I noticed that my colleagues, who I thought were friends, were in fact just colleagues, as only a handful kept in touch during my illness. My work-life balance was completely out of whack … and I was responsible for that. When I was not at a doctor's visit or in treatment, I was exclusively at home. This meant I was there when my son came home from school. He would come into my bedroom, hang out with me and tell me about his day. I still treasure those moments. At twelve years old, he was interested in the changes in my appearance, mostly my hair falling out. When that started, I allowed him to pull my hair out, which was actually great fun for both of us. I wanted to normalise what we were going through. We had many conversations, and he was not scared for me, since the cancer had been caught early enough and the expectation was that the treatment would cure it.

After eight months of chemo and breast surgery to remove the tumor, as well as radiation treatments, I went back to work. I felt out of sync with what was going on. I didn't feel part of the group anymore. My colleagues, although happy to see me again, were completely absorbed in their work, with many seeming incredibly stressed out. I was not excited to be there, and my projects felt flat. I no longer had any enthusiasm for my work.

I left my position soon after and, as I had savings, decided to take some time off to figure out what I wanted to do next. I had to recentre myself after so many years of corporate life. I wanted to spend more time with my son.

I felt a huge sense of relief on leaving my employment, like a heavy weight had been lifted from my shoulders. I slept better. The stress in my neck and shoulders disappeared. I took big, deep breaths and felt free and optimistic about the future.

About eighteen months after I left my employment in California, I moved to the East Coast with my son, where he started high school. I had visited many times, but never lived there. It was a big move, particularly as it was at the beginning of the COVID pandemic.

I spent time brainstorming with family and close friends, identifying goals and working through different ideas. I knew that coaching and helping young people was something I loved to do. After some research, I found the right non-profit that matched my goals, and I volunteered. While working in Los Angeles, I served on the board (chair of the board and then as interim executive director) of an organisation that helped children with learning and physical differences receive the education they are entitled to in public schools. I realised then that education continues to make a big difference. Many of my extended family are educators, and as a result, education has always been important to me.

Deciding to volunteer at Court Appointed Special Advocates (CASA) gave me an opportunity to work with youth and immigrants. I joined the CASA chapter serving Delaware and West Chester Counties near Philadelphia in Pennsylvania, as it was close to home. CASA works with children who are in the foster care system. Their mission is to empower community volunteers to connect with and champion children and youth involved in the child welfare system, advocating for equity, resources, stability and permanency. There was also a need for volunteers who could speak Spanish.

I attended training to be a volunteer advocate, which consists of a comprehensive thirty-five-hour course and grounds the volunteer in the court and child protection systems, early childhood through adolescent development, cultural diversity and CASA-relevant issues. I also signed up for classes on how to support children in the foster care system and about the traumas they suffer, so I could understand how to better help them. It's been proven that children in foster care, who have CASA advocates, are more likely to finish high school.

I enjoy working with youth and their biological and foster families. I find myself explaining the foster care system to biological parents who are back in villages in Guatemala. The cultural differences are immense, and I can bridge them, so they make sense for all involved. The work is varied and involves being creative and finding solutions. It's very satisfying to help youth find their way in a new country, with different rules and help them to navigate and overcome conflicts.

When I tell people that I volunteer at CASA, they say it's a wonderful thing. My family and close friends have always been very supportive. Some people are surprised I left the corporate world behind. Some comment that one should not leave a job without having first secured a new one. My response is that my perspective on my life is very different to the one I had before cancer.

My relationships changed when I left my company. I did not stay in touch with most of the people with whom I worked. I now have a compact number of good friends and I prefer it this way. I have more time for family, friends, myself and things I enjoy doing. I have made new acquaintances where I live who have a different outlook on life.

Fortunately, I was saving money the entire time I was working, so I had a good nest egg and am able to live off my savings. I made a budget and reduced expenses. I've also been consulting to earn a little money, and I'm looking for other profit opportunities to balance out my life.

My corporate lifestyle often involved going out for meals, but I now find myself cooking dinner every night and enjoying it more and more. It's soothing and fun to figure out what to make and to eat healthy. Fortunately, my son likes to eat all kinds of foods.

I'm also part of a group of cancer survivors who meet for a couple of hours every month to paint or draw, although I'm not particularly good at it! I have been experimenting with watercolours and pastels and am enjoying chatting with the women in my group. I used to sculpt with clay twenty years ago and I am slowly gearing myself back to do that. I enjoy writing and now have time to write short stories, like I did in my early twenties.

My advice to someone considering a new chapter in their life would be to give themselves time to explore and figure out what feels good to them. It helps to have people who support your decisions and who you can bounce ideas off. Spend time with people who are doing what you are interested in and, if possible, take classes or attend seminars to learn more.

I am happy with my choices and wouldn't do anything differently. I am five years cancer free. These days, it's so easy to get out of bed in the morning as I enjoy my life!

To learn more about this author: linkedin.com/in/ lily-corzo-2613ab38

THE OTHER SIDE OF THE OPERATING TABLE

BY PATRICIA EADIE FRCSI(PLAST)

For as long as I can remember I wanted to be a doctor. I still have an old schoolbook from when I was nine years old and on the cover I'd scribbled, I want to *give people X-rays*. I worked hard in school and secured a place at medical university in Cork. Classes were much smaller in those days – about seventy in total and many of us remain close today. We've had regular reunions over the years. The most recent one, our fortieth, was in 2021 and managed to just escape severe COVID restrictions. It's been interesting to see the changes in people over the years, but somehow when we get together, old mannerisms re-emerge.

Completing my medical training in 1981, I considered learning some surgery and obstetrics, and I also wanted to offer my skills as a volunteer in an underdeveloped country. During my final summer as a medical student, my elective placement was in Eldama Ravine in Kenya. This certainly influenced my early career, as while there, I was given way more responsibility than I would have had in Ireland. The small missionary hospital had just one doctor, who cared for all the patients with a myriad of different problems. I would go out on the *bush clinics*, treating patients who were too far from hospital. I also got to help with the administration of anaesthesia, under the supervision of the doctor. In my naivety, I thought a couple of years of training would equip me to manage a hospital myself!

I started on a surgical career back in Ireland, which in 1982, essentially meant going from one six-month senior house officer job to another. I rapidly realised how much there was to learn and was advised I should get a qualification in surgery. Along the way I met another surgeon, whom I married, and life changed! Essentially, I trained in plastic surgery and did a lot of travelling, gaining knowledge and experience in Ireland, the US, Australia and the UK. In 1994, I returned to Ireland as a consultant plastic surgeon at a major teaching hospital.

Surgical training is a tough life. The work is very demanding with long hours. There's a lot to learn, both from a skills point of view and book knowledge. Learning how to approach patients and to care for yourself are also important to master, though a lot of this is through experience. There are also exams to pass – my final being in 1992 at the grand old age of thirty-four. As I lived in many different parts of Ireland and abroad, it was difficult to keep up with hobbies and sports. For many years these were on the backburner. Stability in terms of location came in 1994, and once I'd settled back to life in Ireland, it was easier to rekindle old interests.

Sailing had been a part of my life since I was a teenager, which I continued while in college and working in Cork. However, during my training, an occasional trip in someone else's boat was the best I could manage.

Back in Dublin, my husband and I bought our first boat, *Scaramouche*. It was a 31ft Nicolson; a classic boat with a good seaworthiness pedigree. It took us around Ireland, to Scotland and Spain. We loved our floating caravan. It was such a pleasure to pack up the boat and head off on our holidays – no airports and minimal hassle! Work was busy but very fulfilling, and time flew by. My husband was also incredibly busy, and we gradually disconnected from each other. In 2000, we parted ways after sixteen years of marriage. Hindsight is a great thing and, of course, there are things we both could have done differently, but perhaps it was for the best as we've found other life partners who make us happy. We are still on good terms and keep in touch occasionally. I have never been one to lose friends and value greatly all my connections, both close and casual.

Ending a marriage or long-term relationship is heartbreaking, no matter how good or bad it was. A whole new adjustment to living alone is required, on a daily basis and when putting longer-term plans together. As there was room in my house, I rented out a room to another woman, which brought company and laughs in the evenings. I have always been a dog lover and was glad that Trampas, our beautiful golden retriever stayed with me. At least somebody was always happy to see me!

My work has been consistently busy – long days and regular on-call shifts – but incredibly fulfilling. When I started, I was very much the 'new kid on the block', but gradually over the years, I've been able to concentrate on areas where I had a specific interest and training. I've always had incredibly supportive colleagues which strengthened our unit, attracting good trainees from home and abroad. Teaching is such an integral part of medical work. It has been a pleasure to have worked alongside them and see so many of them develop and take up their own posts. As a fully trained surgeon, I've spent short periods of time in both African and Asian countries, teaching local surgeons some techniques that would help their patients.

For many years, sailing took up much of my spare time. I was a member of a yacht club and enjoyed competing in the local races and participating in other competitions such as the Sovereigns Cup run by Kinsale Yacht club. By the mid-2000s, I owned a boat with another guy, which we raced with some modest success.

Towards the end of that decade, I was involved in a new relationship with someone I'd met through cycling. He had little interest in sailing and my boat partner had three small children. I was increasingly finding boat maintenance a chore, and shortly after an experience with two very inexperienced crew, we put the boat on the market. I actually had the second happiest day of a boat owner's life – the first being when you buy your first boat!

Over several years, I'd mentioned to my colleagues that I'd be interested in job-sharing if the opportunity arose. With contracts the way they were at the time, this was not easy and would have been difficult to attract a new person on that basis. However, in 2013 one of my colleagues wanted to take a year to do some specific research, so we discussed the question of job-sharing to facilitate this. With some discussion with the hospitals, it was eventually facilitated on a temporary basis, and it worked well. It enabled us to employ another surgeon on a full-time basis and gave me some time for myself.

With my free time, I set a goal for myself for the year: to learn how to swim properly. I had learnt to swim as a child, but wasn't a strong swimmer, so getting to the end of a 25m pool without being completely out of breath was a struggle. I enrolled in lessons and then joined the master's swim class at the local gym. This improved my swimming significantly over a few months, so much so that I began to think about completing a triathlon. My somewhat-misguided thinking was that I could now swim (or so I thought!), I could certainly cycle and, sure, anyone can run or else walk.

In 2014, I was ready for my first triathlon. I entered the Dublin City Triathlon (DCT) which was scheduled for mid-August. Somewhere along the line, I heard that in June, the town of Athy was holding a try a tri, with a shorter swim distance of 250m. I decided to go for it, which was both exciting and scary. I had thought my swimming was okay, but open-water swimming in a race situation is a different matter. Thankfully, I went to the race on my own, so there are no photographic records of my pathetic attempt to swim 250m downstream in the river Barrow. My ability to breathe doing the front crawl seemed to disappear, so I resorted to the backstroke and I'm sure I was swimming around in circles. I did finally get out of the water and completed the race, but it was an eye-opener. Later in the summer, I did make a better attempt at DCT, with a river swim, which took some getting used to.

The job-sharing came to an end in 2014, but having tasted a life with less clinical work commitments, both my colleague and I applied for reduced hours on a permanent basis. On the back of this, we were able to recruit a new, young, enthusiastic colleague – a win not just for us, but the hospitals and the patients as well.

I was now able to work a comfortable thirty-five hours per week, plus a few travel commitments for exams and meetings.

Over the next few years, I embraced the triathlon journey. I joined Piranha Triathlon Club and enjoyed the support, fun and excellent training opportunities afforded by being a club member. Going to races with others was much more fun, especially as my swimming had improved!

I lived on the Northside for most of my years spent in Dublin, which I enjoyed. As a culchie (slang for a person from a rural area), I had no allegiance to either the north or south. My partner, however, was of a different opinion and liked to cycle in Wicklow (south) at the weekends. Where we lived didn't really suit him, so I promised that once I turned sixty, I would cut back on my private practice, and we would move Southside. That also made me reflect on how much longer I wanted to work in the public health service.

My sixtieth birthday seemed to come along quickly, and once the celebrations were done, it was time to find a new house – on the south side! Our vague plan was that this would be our forever home, adaptable for any changing circumstances we might face as we aged. We agreed on the area we would like to live and looked at many houses. Much of the time I would do a 'recce', and if I didn't like them, there was no point in my partner seeing them. I was definitely the more fussy one. I put my house on the market and during the process of selling, we found what we wanted. Not completely future proof, as it has a lot of steps and needed major renovations, but we are both healthy and my partner's mother lived into her nineties in a house with steep stairs up to the only bathroom. My partner reckons that regularly trekking up and down the stairs kept her strong! We moved across the Liffey in March 2019, another step along the way to winding down from work for me.

Around that time, I seriously began to consider a date to retire from public practice. Having downsized the house, I was now mortgage free which made the decision easier. Thoughts that went through my head were based on financial planning and pension, but also how much I would miss the work I had loved for many years. What on earth would I do all day? How could I continue to contribute in a useful way? Did I want to embark on further education?

The financial planning aspect was relatively easy as there are experts for that, and I was guaranteed a good public service pension. From my private practice, I had always invested what I could afford in a tax-efficient way. It was all explained to me a couple of times but, to be honest, it would go out of my head quickly. I had been using a financial planning company for many years and trusted them implicitly. I would advise anyone to employ a reputable firm. It may cost a bit, but if it's not done correctly, you can end up paying more tax or be liable for fines to the revenue.

I can genuinely say all I ever wanted was to be a doctor. I feel fortunate that I was able to work at what I loved and along the way meet so many interesting people, both patients and colleagues. One particular aspect I loved was my paediatric practice, and I will fondly remember many of the children I treated; their ability to just get on with getting better, dealing with the differences they were born with and their generosity of spirit.

I knew I would miss many aspects of my practice but at the

same time working in the HSE was becoming more bureaucratic. Theatre lists were regularly cancelled or curtailed for different reasons which became more and more frustrating. There are huge pressures on clinical staff in our health service across the board. My decision to leave the HSE a couple of years before the 'normal' retirement age was fuelled by this frustration. It gradually became obvious that I was losing my appetite for the 'battle'.

I had a chance meeting with the professor of anatomy at one of the medical schools, who was seeking a new surgical demonstrator to teach the medical students. As a part-time position, this immediately appealed to me, allowing me to continue contact with students and pass on some of my knowledge. I applied and was successful, starting about two months after 'retiring'. This was in 2020, so the usual practice of the students doing the dissection was not possible due to the requirement for social distancing during COVID. The demonstrators were now doing the dissections and the students came to look at them the next day. This allowed me to maintain my surgical skills to a certain extent and in the areas of the body that I was not generally operating on, I had to refresh myself significantly. I just needed to stay one day ahead of the students, but as I plan to do this for some years the learning curve is very useful.

I also continue to work one day per week in clinical practice. I now confine myself to a limited area, with most procedures being minor, but it allows me to continue with patient contact and uphold my skills.

In the area of further education, I was not inclined to return to college and start a new degree. I decided to take up bridge instead and enrolled in classes. About three months in, the first

COVID lockdown began, so the classes stopped abruptly. Our teacher was not interested in teaching online, so I continued to teach myself with books and online resources. Since then, I've been playing regularly online with my cousin and her partner, and thankfully I now have a bridge partner. She is a bit more experienced than me, but it seems to work well. We have good evenings and not-so-good ones when we lose most games! I love playing cards and the mental stimulation of bridge is presumably good for me.

My interest in triathlons and, now, marathons (!) continues. I love the discipline of daily training both on my own and in the company of club mates and I hope that this will continue to keep me healthy into the years ahead.

I've also been trained for a helpline and do three to four shifts per month. This has exposed me to a group of like-minded people and new friends. It's often challenging in a completely new way. I do hope that it is of benefit to those I listen to and sit beside. It has challenged me to explore some personal aspects of life and I do feel better able to cope with questions in my own life.

Currently I am happy, fulfilled and love life. I do not regret in any way my change in direction over the last couple of years. I hope that by reading this it may help others to examine and possibly change their own life and consider if there may be a better way.

AS LUCK WOULD HAVE IT

BY KATE E

In the mid-1990s, the recession in Ireland prompted me to apply for an Australian working visa and head to the southern hemisphere. My Irish employers were not keeping accountants after their contract was finished, so most of us 'newly qualified' headed to the USA, Australia or the Cayman Islands. I had always been up for a challenge. My mother was an air hostess, and she filled our childhood with many fascinating travel stories that encouraged me to seek out these interesting places. During college, I worked a summer in the US on a J1 visa, so I had some experience of working abroad already. A new start in a different country down under did not really phase me.

The Australians welcomed me with open arms, which made the move much easier. I was lucky the reputation of Irish accountants in Sydney was positive. Those who had gone before me made a good impression. In Ireland, as a female trainee, it was hard to gain acceptance as being equally competent amongst my male counterparts. The only way to prove myself was to keep passing my exams all the way up. Eventually, as we had turned for the final stretch, they noticed I was still with them, and so my work was done. In Sydney, the recruitment agents felt the Irish were bright, hardworking candidates and gender was irrelevant. Sydney was the real start of my working life and it put me on an interesting journey.

Circumstances can force change in your life whether you like it or not, but having first the mindset to embrace the change, and secondly the financial support to sustain it, is for me the key. It also keeps life interesting. When you are not born wealthy, the financial support really comes down to getting a good education from the outset. My father implored of us to get that education – 'that piece of paper'. You can always fall back on a good education if times get difficult or change is needed.

In Australia, as Dad had promised, with education, I had great opportunities. I was able to expand my knowledge and gained a variety of experience with different businesses, work cultures and technology systems. I remained for five years and really enjoyed the outdoor lifestyle and people. Being an English-speaking accountant, who was also under thirty, allowed me to apply for Australian residency. If I had been over thirty, I may not have qualified under their points system. It is a good thing to travel early in life, even if just for that reason. Later, with the permanent residency status, I was able to apply for dual citizenship and an Australian passport. One thing had led to another. All these years later, my children have Australian passports too. This will allow for opportunities to work there in the future which I think, looking back now, was a smart decision and is something people don't always consider at the time.

While in Australia, we travelled a lot within the country

itself. It has a unique and varied landscape with huge distances in-between. As we made our way back to Ireland we ventured through New Zealand, Canada and the USA. It was another great opportunity to do something different, while we had time and no family commitments. Unfortunately, you often don't get to repeat these big trips when you have children in tow.

I had just turned thirty when we returned to Ireland in early 1999. It was disappointing to find not much had changed amongst the Irish recruitment agencies. My work experience was mainly in financial services, and they presented me with no real opportunity to change industries or sectors. However, being back on familiar territory in the IFSC in Dublin did help me to assimilate back into Irish life.

Our first daughter arrived in 2000, a millennium baby. Back then maternity leave was a mere fourteen weeks and I returned to work before I knew I'd been off. Our daughter was attending a creche full-time from three months old. After spending a year racing from the city by DART (Dublin Area Rapid Transport), tagging with my husband, swapping cars and car seats, coping with constant baby illnesses and work stresses, with a merger in the middle, I decided to call it quits and leave my finance role. My career had to change again due to circumstances. My departure was not without its stresses also. My then female boss was unsympathetic to the pressure I was under, and unsupportive of my situation of trying to hold onto a career while raising a child. I was disappointed; all I had worked for seemed in vain. In the same breath, I was also relieved as my own health had come under huge strain through lack of sleep and unrealistic work pressures. It was time to rectify this.

During my time off, I started a book club with some friends. Book clubs were gaining huge popularity with Oprah leading the trend in the US. At our club, a friend told us about her mother who was a pharmacist but who, at age forty, had gone to Africa for a few years working for a charity. Their dad had looked after them back in Ireland. This mother suggested we should take the time to reinvent ourselves every decade. I really liked this concept. None of us should feel we have to remain in the same career all our lives.

So, over the next decade, I was lucky to have two more children. My mothering career continued in earnest. This career was the most rewarding for me, but unfortunately feels the least valued. There is very little support given financially from the government or emotionally from the health sector. I believe this is short-sighted, when we have a responsible job to raise the next generation of Irish people. The future lawmakers, politicians, voters. Back when I was trying to juggle a career and raising a child, the creche was open from 7:45am to 6pm. This didn't even give me enough time to commute to the city to work. My daughter was the first child arriving in the morning and the last child collected. There were no after-school facilities, and no options with employers to work part-time. A childminder may have worked out better for us, but they also need time off and sick leave. There have been improvements made in the last twenty years, but we still have a long way to go. The Scandinavians seem to have a much more equitable model.

One day, while working out at the gym, I reflected on what I might consider for my next decade. I recalled my high school leaving certificate. I was young and naive at the time, just seventeen. Academically, I was lucky I was good at math and science and had applied for business and science courses. Business courses needed more leaving certificate points then, and that is how I ended up studying commerce, which led to accountancy. When I think back, my interest in business was not as strong as my interest in science. Really it had stopped at the numbers part! I wasn't interested in whether a company's EPS was growing. Instead, I enjoyed math calcs and found science fascinating. Another decade of my life beckoned; I decided to re-educate myself in fitness and health.

Initially, I studied part-time courses. I still needed to balance minding our children, but I felt rejuvenated and purposeful, loving keeping fit at the same time. It felt like a win-win situation. Again, I was lucky my husband continued to work and that we managed financially without my income. We were also no longer paying creche fees, which was helpful. After a while, I got some part-time work as a strength and conditioning coach, which meant I was making some contribution. The weekend courses I covered over two years were fitness and personal training and, later, nutrition. This whole area should be part of the school learning process. There were so many skills for life taught in these courses. After these courses, I took the plunge and returned to study a full-time sports science degree at UCD. I loved it. I understand how lucky I was to be able to do this with children. A good friend was a childminder, and she did the school pick-ups in the afternoons. I had to juggle all aspects of my life and certainly became good at time management. Every minute counted!

During my third year at UCD, reality struck. My hopes were dashed by the career advisory office when they bluntly told me that as a newly qualified sports scientist, I would be starting on the bottom rung of the ladder, and as my children would still be dependent on me for another ten years, chances of a full-time career in this area were slim. Their advice – it was better for me to return to work in an accounting environment. Back to square one!

Good luck came my way again, though, and through my children's own involvement in sport, I heard of a part-time role involving a large sports event. I was able to combine my accounting and project management experience with my sports knowledge and secured the role. It was another win-win situation. I learned so much in that job. It brought me quickly up to speed with current workplace technologies, digital marketing and negotiations. It was busy and frequently required an 'all hands-on deck' approach, but I gained huge experience as an 'oldie' returning to an office environment.

In my late forties, personal circumstances again intervened. My younger brother became very unwell and more flexibility was needed in my life in order to 'drop everything and go'. I finished working with the sporting event after nearly six years. Once again, I relied on my accounting background and took up a stress-free accounts job. I was lucky this was where my life was at when the COVID pandemic struck. I was already working from home with flexible hours, so the structure of my day did not change dramatically. It allowed me to cope well with the pandemic uncertainties and be available to those who needed me.

Since then, work practices have certainly changed rapidly. Circumstances forced changes. The way we work is more flexible with everything accessible from your laptop, digital signatures are widely used, and most meetings take place via online platforms. Working from home is more commonplace, but I still believe it's important to physically leave your home and switch into your work environment elsewhere. Being out of home can make us feel part of something bigger and can only improve our mental health too. With that in mind, for my fifties, my plan is to keep up my lifelong learning by studying courses that complement a part-time working role. Hopefully both can be done from an office pod away from my house! I intend to continue with some voluntary board roles while still making time for things I enjoy like travel, tennis and golf. Joining clubs helps us immerse ourselves more in the community which they say is where our future socialising will be. I'm more conscious now of keeping mentally stimulated and physically active to remain healthy going forward. And I'm excited to discover what the next decade will bring.

REIMAGING MY LIFE, AGAIN & AGAIN

BY AMY FRIEDMAN

I still vividly remember the very moment I first understood my *life's purpose*. I was thirteen, lying under my bed, eavesdropping on my parents and grandparents in the den below through a heating vent. My grandmother, who grew up in Poland, had lost her entire family in the Holocaust. She had emigrated to the US with my grandfather in the 1920s, when she was just seventeen, but her whole family stayed in Poland and none escaped extermination by the Nazis. By the time I knew her, in the mid-1950s, in addition to having lost her parents and siblings, she had also endured months of uncertainty when her youngest son, my father, was captured by the Germans and became a Jewish prisoner of war in Germany. All these losses rendered her clinically depressed and ultimately silent. That night, as I lay under my bed, I heard my father, mother and grandfather yelling at her. Not a word came from her mouth.

I loved my grandmother, and I looked like her. That night as I listened to my parents yell at her, I wanted to yell back at them.

And so, I climbed out from under the bed, sat down at my desk and wrote my first short story, in the first person: the words I wished my grandmother would say. From that moment on, my passion was clear. I wanted to be a writer, to give voice to ideas and experiences too often left unsaid or sugar-coated.

That same year I began to submit stories and collect rejections. It took me another seventeen years before I published a single word, but in the meantime, I studied creative writing at Barnard College under a master, with a small group of women, most of whom became highly successful, well-known writers. A few years later, I earned a Masters Degree in Creative Writing. While still an undergraduate, I came to understand that to be a writer meant I had to write, but making a living was going to require me to do anything else I could to support that career.

I waitressed. I drove a taxi (briefly, in New York City). I worked in a day care centre. In graduate school, I pretended I knew how to teach undergraduates how to write (mimicking my own teachers). With my MA in hand, I continued to waitress but also learned the ins and outs of publishing by landing entry-level jobs in various publishing houses. I became first a competent, then a good, then a stellar editor, but I was always loathe to give too much attention to editing others' work because it took away from my writing time and attention.

And then, when I was thirty-two, I fell accidentally into a writer's dream job: a small newspaper in Ontario, Canada, hired me to write a weekly newspaper column. I had moved to Canada for a man, but I stayed for the job, and that job led to published books and eventually to the idea to create another newspaper column, this one for children. Another stroke of luck;

that children's column became syndicated worldwide, and so, at the age of thirty-seven, I finally felt as if I'd 'made it'. People everywhere were reading what I wrote and, no longer having to mimic other writers, I was also hired to teach. I figured I was on my way to fame and maybe even fortune. I knew a few writers who made a living.

In the meantime, friends and siblings who worked as lawyers, businesspeople and medical professionals were earning sufficient money to buy houses and have babies, and that didn't seem likely for me. And at thirty-nine, suddenly, unexpectedly and wholly unplanned, my career took a sharp turn.

It was late winter 1992 when I decided to write a series of columns on prisons because I lived in a city surrounded by them and just across the St Lawrence River from the forty-plus prisons and jails dotting New York State. While interviewing people in prison, I fell in love. I married a man who was a prisoner. Suddenly, much of the world perceived me in a whole new light.

Not long after we married, the newspaper where I'd worked for a decade fired me (luckily for my bank account that syndicated column was going strong by then!). Colleges stopped hiring me to teach. My passion for giving voice to ideas and experiences too often left unsaid or sugar-coated, extended to men and women in prison and to their families. I continued to write articles, stories and books (that for a long time became harder to sell). I also became a prisoners' rights activist. I started an organisation to lobby on behalf of prisoners' families, eventually, in 1999, presenting our demands to the Canadian Parliament.

That marriage lasted seven and a half years, but what lasted longer was my love for my ex-husband's daughters, girls I raised from the ages of nine and fourteen, and my passion for giving voice to those whose lives have been impacted by incarceration. I was still a writer. I published more stories. More books. I leaned harder on editing to earn a living. I became a ghostwriter. Eventually I remarried and moved to Los Angeles where my new husband and his young children lived.

My second husband was also a writer and a high school teacher. While I continued to teach and eke out a living as a writer, he and I co-founded a non-profit organisation to support teens with parents and other loved ones in prison. Our non-profit organisation (what I came to prefer to think of as a for-good company) started as just one school club at one high school in Los Angeles. Over the next nine years, I learned how to run a company, training as an executive director, hiring coaches and guides to help me learn. I raised both the organisation's budget and its profile. By 2021 we were serving hundreds of kids each year in nineteen schools in five states, with our budget heading towards a million dollars a year, a growth plan to expand the network to schools across North America and under our belt eight award-winning books – published books that contained writing and artwork by the youth we serve, again giving voice to ideas and experiences too often left unsaid or sugar-coated.

I was heading towards seventy, still full of energy, ideas and passion, more than ever committed to giving voice to those who have always been silenced, but I began too to prepare a succession plan. The bliss of being a writer, editor and teacher was this: I didn't have to retire. I could continue this work, but my succession plan would allow me more time to focus on my own writing – another book or two or three – while continuing to support our organisation as a founding director, part-time, and leading the publishing company we'd founded inside the organisation.

Suddenly, with almost no warning, at the height of COVID, the board of directors fired me; just two weeks before we were to sign our first paid franchise with another non-profit and one year before I planned to step into a part-time position.

They fired me by text on a Friday, in the late afternoon, the day after one of my beloved family members died. In short, a group of young people, who thought they knew what was best for the organisation, took over and left me gasping for breath, out of work, erased out of existence and spending money to sue these people.

I might have been able to forgive them if they'd proven themselves right. If in taking over, they had transformed our organisation into a more meaningful, more powerful, better, brighter, wiser organisation serving thousands more of the one in fourteen American children with a parent who is or has been in prison. But they didn't do that. Instead, they tore through the money I'd raised and within ten months, they were forced to lay off staff and sunset the organisation.

Thankfully, that isn't where this story ends because this reimaging didn't stop with their firing me any more than my writing career stopped when the newspaper fired me because I'd become 'a prisoner's wife'.

Instead, it churned up the fire in my belly. It proved to me again that it's vital to write and vital to give voice to ideas and experiences too often left unsaid or sugar-coated. So, I carried on and created a new publishing project, teamed up with the same non-profit that was going to become our first paid franchise, but whose executive director felt the leadership team at my (former) organisation was impossible to work with.

Today I am a writer and a consultant. I continue to work to give voice to ideas and experiences too often left unsaid or sugar-coated.

I know that this will always be so, and this is the advice I offer anyone planning to reimagine, rewire or retire: Always listen to the voice inside of you. Take the time, spend the energy, find the quiet to hear that voice. Let it guide you to what's next, even if, sometimes, it sounds crazy and even when – because this will happen – other people tell you that you are crazy or wrong or impossible.

One year while I was working with the kids, I learned from one of the teachers about the Japanese art of kintsugi: the art of putting broken pottery pieces back together with glue and gold. The idea is to embrace flaws and imperfections, and in doing so, you will create an even more beautiful, stronger piece of art. As we embrace our own flaws and imperfections, we too become stronger and more beautiful.

To learn more about this author: amyfriedman.net

A STARRING ROLE IN ONE'S LIFE

BY WENDY HAMMERS

For as long as I can remember, I was hungry for creative expression. As a little girl, my parents took me to New York to see an incredible ensemble of actors called the Paper Bag Players. Completely drawn into this enchanted world, after the matinee, I somehow snuck my five-year-old self backstage, wandered out onto it, and thought, *I like the view better from here. This feels like home.*

Little me yearned for connection. My mom remembers strolling through Central Park with me in the baby carriage. While the other moms had quiet, sleeping babies, I would be up, smiling, chatting and waving to all the passers-by. She said I looked like I was running for mayor. Reflecting on these childhood moments, I see now that both experiences were a blueprint for who I was to become.

I fell in love with acting as a child and pursued it for over fifty years. From elementary through to high school, I did plays, took acting and dance classes, then headed to university as a drama major. At NYU, I had the true privilege of studying with the wonderful actor, sit-down monologist and writer Spalding Gray. His class *Fictionalizing the Self* was about taking our life stories and making them stage worthy. Through that process, I learned I was also a writer, and could create content, which led to a forty-plus-year 'accidental' career as a comedian and solo performing artist.

Working with Spalding, I developed my first one-woman show, *sweat/pants*, which led to another and then another. Some of my career highlights have been doing these personal plays around the US, sharing my stories and connecting with audiences.

Stand-up comedy grew out of that, and making people laugh is a sweet high. It's like being in a tennis match with the audience, just volleying the energy back and forth. It's a fantastic feeling.

In my early twenties, I followed my heart to Los Angeles, where I began to work as an actor in theatre, television, film and as a comedian. It was there I married another comedian and had the privilege of giving birth to and raising our incredible son, Griffin.

But then, in 2001, three things occurred. My dear friend, Judy Toll, a brilliant comedian, got cancer and died. The devastation of 9/11 happened. And I went through a divorce. At the time, I thought, if I do not create a place for my friends and me to get onstage and tell our stories, our heads will explode. So out of this pain, I created a little community. It was in a children's bookstore on a small street near my house. Writer/performers would get up and tell real, true-life stories. We had folding chairs, I brought cookies and milk, and we would charge $5. If six people showed up, we thought we were a hit – like we'd sold out Carnegie Hall. Out of that, my company, Tasty Words Productions, was born. That was twenty-two years ago and I'm still doing the show; it has become this *huge* thing. Thousands have attended the live shows, and we have a *Tasty Words* podcast. So out of all that pain, I grew. Our community grew.

Now, decades later, in my sixties, I am rewiring. I've taken all the learnings from my life, onstage and off, and am inspired to utilise them in a new way.

I am coming to understand what it looks like to carve out a life that comes from choice. I didn't know my path would take the turns it did, and it's been a long and winding road to arrive at my truest self.

I've been thinking a lot lately about the concept of having agency over one's own life. In your twenties, thirties or forties, the triumvirate of energy, passion and naivete can fuel you. I think by the time you get into your fifties, sixties and upwards, you feel that you've lived to tell the tale; that you've been to hell and back and have something worth sharing.

In 2015, at age fifty-four, I was diagnosed with pancreatic cancer, and my life became about making sure my life continued. I spent a year on that journey. During that time, I had what I like to call 'the great pause'. For many of us, a life-threatening illness, financial distress, family crisis, divorce, break-up or death of a beloved friend can all be a spectacular opportunity to look deeply and intentionally at the landscape of our lives.

Many people who get cancer just want their lives back. I did not feel that way. I wanted a better, different, more conscious life. I had a cancer coach. Yes, that's a thing. Remember, I live in LA! Her name is Marissa Harris. She had been diagnosed with stage four pancreatic cancer. Doctors said, 'We're so sorry to tell you this, but we can't help you.' She replied, 'I'm very sorry to tell you this, but I can't die because I have to dance at my daughter's wedding someday.'

That was twenty-five years ago. Marissa then left her high-powered job on Wall Street, gleaning wisdom from her skill set and transitioning her professional work into coaching cancer patients. The fact that she herself had experienced a pancreatic cancer diagnosis, well, I felt compelled to work with her. I hired her for three months. I'd never done anything like that in my life. It was a time investment and a huge financial investment (for me). Worth every cent.

We did a ton of writing and visualisation assignments about what my life would look like on the other side of cancer. She would regularly say to me, 'What would you *really love* in your life? Like, if you could have anything? What would you really love your life to look like?' I really got to think about that.

I was so busy imagining my better life in the future, I wasn't scared about the present. People don't always believe me when I say that, but I'd decided cancer was going to be my teacher. I wasn't going to miss the lessons. I thought, *It is going to teach me everything it can, and then we will break up.* That is essentially what happened.

Cancer turned out to be a masterclass in self-love.

At first, I thought I'd reclaim my love of acting. I made a deal with myself – return to your acting passion and do that. Give it 100%. If at any point, acting no longer made my heart sing, I could move on. I had an acting teacher, Milton Katselas, who used to say, 'If you're gonna leave the business, leave on a high note. Do one more show – go out with a bang – so you know you decided to walk away and didn't fail.'

After I was pronounced unremarkable (that's what the doctors call it when there's no cancer left to remark on the scan), I had a flurry of creative activity. I did a fabulous play called *Grey Nomad* with The Australian Theatre Company. I was the token American; me and a bunch of Aussies having the time of our lives. And I did a lot of work – eight independent films. It all felt so right.

Just when it felt I was finally in a groove with work and life, in 2017, my amazing mom, Marion, had a massive haemorrhagic stroke, which left her paralysed. She was hospitalised on Thanksgiving in 2020, and because of the stroke, she couldn't be on a ventilator. She left us that December. My dad, Arthur, had died the year before her. Although the death certificate attributed his passing to pancreatic cancer, I believe he died of a broken heart because he didn't know how to save my mom.

So, between losing my parents, and my own brush with mortality, and then, the pandemic (the world's great pause), I was again hungry for creativity. I hadn't worked in a while. I thought, *I'm an actor, I'm supposed to be working.* That's what I wanted the world to see – me as a working actor. It was an ego-driven decision and not a good one. Shortly after I was hired to do a play, I knew it was a mistake. I decided, moving forward from there, to make better professional choices – to choose with discernment.

Many years ago, I used to teach creative writing. During the pandemic, one of my old students contacted me and asked if I was teaching a writing class online. I responded, 'No, but maybe I should be.' I didn't know if there would be an intimacy in writing virtually. I didn't know if I'd like it or be any good at it. So, I decided to teach one class and see how it went. Well, talk about taking pandemic lemons and turning them into lemonade – that single class turned into a writing tribe of sixty students, two full classes a week on Zoom, private in-person and online clients, and six retreats a year in the US and Mexico. In fact, as I write this now, I can hear the glorious waves from the Sea of Cortez a few feet from me.

I could not in my wildest dreams have imagined this would all be possible. Why? Because I was working with an old operating system and was still married to what my life was *supposed* to look like. And meanwhile, I was having so much fun and making a living doing something I felt really good at, working with creatives. But since I was still stuck in an old idea, I'd assumed that teaching was not my real job. That's when I began to notice – I felt so fulfilled.

I went from 'I'm so happy my agent called with an audition' to 'oh NO, my agent called me, and I have an audition'. My gut instincts were showing me the way. I just needed to listen. FYI – I must mention that the pancreas *is* the gut, the intuition. Some even call it 'the third brain'.

There are signs and information around us all the time, but a lot of us are on automatic pilot, not listening to our intuition, perhaps thinking, *I'm* supposed *to be married to this one person for my whole life. I'm expected to have two kids and a 2.5-car garage, and this job, whether it is stifling me or not.* Simultaneously, there is this other thing that feels good in your heart, and makes it sing. *That's the thing to pay attention to.*

But if you're stuck like I was, it's hard to hear the truth as it comes barrelling down the pike. I have to say this because hopefully it'll be helpful to somebody. I was *so* committed to the idea of being an actor than *any other thing I did in my life* – and I did a lot of cool things – got dismissed: 'Oh, that doesn't count. It's not acting.'

In the meantime, I'm travelling and performing and doing stand-up and speaking and getting paid – but none of it mattered.

What I know NOW is what I wanted, above all, was ...

TO BE IN COMMUNITY AND FEEL VIBRATION WITH OTHER HUMANS.

No five-year-old says, 'When I grow up, I want to be a conscious individual who shares their story with people, travels and helps people with cancer and their creative lives.'

I just knew I wanted connection and community. I didn't have any other name for it, so I *assumed* it was acting. I understand now that all creative outlets – acting, writing, teaching – are all just delivery systems for love and connection. That's how I look at it. I am a heart-centred individual, and I'll continue to create ways to connect with humans.

It's not so much that I changed my career, but I got a better understanding of what was really at the core of my wanting – the need to create community and connection. How do I make the world a sweeter, smaller place? There is a phrase, 'Take your pain and turn into a purpose.' I believe that is what has come to pass.

As I transitioned from acting to teaching and now keynote speaking, it occurred to me that after forty years of stepping into the skins of others, the role I enjoy most is the one where I share my truth and star in my own life. Being my authentic self turns out to be the part I am best suited to play.

I encourage you to surround yourself with other people who are committed to growth and evolution, who are not threatened by your change and are growing right alongside you. If people are afraid of change in you, it's because it forces them to look at their own life. Many people aren't making choices. Life happens *to* them. It's easier to focus on somebody else than yourself. It's always easier to point fingers than consider our own plans, visions and destinies.

I believe it is our birthright to be happy, joyous and free. If we don't feel good, there are things that need to be looked at. If it's chemical, and medicine is needed, fine. If you need to be in therapy, do that. Those are things to attend to. But a lot of times it's just what this book is about – really honouring your passion, figuring out what ignites you and following that.

There is a great assignment in Julia Cameron's book *The Artist's Way* called 'The Artist Date', where you take yourself out for two hours. It doesn't matter if you just go to the park and stare at a tree you've never seen before. Then maybe write a poem about it. Just something that's so completely out of your routine; something that allows you to see life in a fresh way.

Here's the thing – someday, I'm going to die. We all are. There's no guarantee of tomorrow for any of us. We only have today, so how do we honour it and make it delicious? What can you do with this day you've been gifted? Can you breathe some more life into it? It is not about waiting until conditions are perfect to take action.

I would like to have known earlier that it would have been *fine* to be a writing teacher, and an actor and a comedian, and a person who loves gardening, and a person who needs to take walks on the beach, and go to yoga, and loves to dance and throw parties. That all those things have value. All these things are important. That's what creates a life. I spent a lot of my life making so many things I was doing wrong, because they didn't match this *one very limited* idea I had of what my life was supposed to look like.

Having a successful acting career is like winning the lottery. They say, in our industry, 10% of all the actors in our union work 90% of the time, which means 90% of the actors only work 10% of the time. I wish I'd known earlier that to have a healthy financial picture, I could do other things to support myself and *feel great* about that. I wish I had understood that I didn't have to be a struggling artist. My ego was like, *Um,* no, *I'm an actor,* which meant I wouldn't allow myself to consider other jobs, and thus worried about whether I could pay my rent, which caused stress and anxiety. I think years and years of that is part of the reason I got sick. At a certain point, my body said, *I need a break, it's too much.*

I want to feel happy. I want to be surrounded by love. I want to do things that bring joy to the world and to myself. Well, I don't need to be a millionaire to achieve any of those things. And I certainly didn't need to be an actor to utilise my voice in a powerful way.

There are people that never lean into their creative lives at all, because they're so committed to being responsible adults. Then later in life, they come to me as creative clients, and they feel they've missed their lives. Then there's people who are the opposite, who decide, *I'm just going to be creative. I'm not going to pay attention to the world or rules or bills or any responsibilities.*

Between these two extremes, there is a middle ground. It's all about creating balance.

You show up for your boss, you show up for your partner, but do you show up for yourself?

One way to grow your true vision of what you want your life to look like is to have an accountability partner. You get on the phone on a Monday morning. The whole call should be no more than ten minutes. You commit three things each and both write them down. The following Monday, you report your progress to each other – and just keep doing it.

Sometimes it is as simple as just taking the action. Telling yourself and the world that you mean business by creating deadlines, respecting them and having your accountability partner as support. Left to my own devices without a deadline, I'm on the couch, with *Law and Order* and chocolate. But with a deadline, I can actually get something done.

Finally, there are some principles that became clear to me during my time with cancer, but honestly, they can be applied to anyone's life. I think of them as my ten tenets. I am including them here and hope you will find them helpful:

1. THE WORTH-IT RULE – When it comes to men, bread and chocolate, there are only two kinds – worth it or not worth it. You can apply this to all the decisions you make – is it worth it or not worth it?

2. THE CLOSER/FURTHER PRINCIPLE – Since being alive and well is my number-one priority, and I hope it is yours – I have come to realise that everything … every interaction, conversation, decision about how I spend my days and whom I choose to spend them with … either brings me

closer to my health or further from it. It's my job to make the choices that take me in the direction of continued health and vibrance.

3. THE HOURGLASS RULE – I love my curvy body. Now that I have been fortunate enough to survive cancer, I can't believe I spent even a *millisecond* hating my body. Our quest for perfectionism is such an insult to those of us who are no longer living on this earth. I am guessing many of them would be grateful to be alive, in your body or mine. To still be above ground. Let me ask you this: If you knew it was the last day of your life, would you spend it wondering whether or not your stomach was flat? And do we ever know when it is our last day? We do not. Cancer taught me that my body is a genius and deserves a standing ovation for keeping me alive.

4. SELF-LOVE RULES – I have been starving for self-love my entire life. I like to think that when the chemo helped rid my body of cancer, it killed off the self-loathing as well. I am no longer willing to weigh my self-esteem on the bathroom scale. I'm not perfect at this, but I am deeply committed to loving and living fully in the body I have right now. Not forty or ten or three pounds from now. NOW. Not when someone else tells me I am lovable. NOW.

5. WHY I LOVE AGING – I know that makes me some sort of unicorn – a woman who played the show biz game in Hollywood for decades and who doesn't lie about my age. I actually *like* getting older. For starters, it's better than the alternative. But I know a lot of people don't feel comfortable telling their age, so I suggest if you're going to lie, lie up. For

example, let's say I tell you I'm sixty-two, you probably think I look pretty good, but if I tell you I'm eighty-two, that's so much more impressive, doncha think? One of the blessings of aging: most of the time, you don't care what people think, and the rest of the time, you don't remember.

6. WHAT WE ARE REALLY AFRAID OF – It's my belief, that as a culture, we are afraid of aging because it reminds us of dying and we are afraid of dying because it reminds us that we're not fully living. Perhaps our focus should be on living, today, fully.

7. COMMUNITY IN RECOVERY – I was blessed with a Grand-Canyon-sized support team. Friends. Family. Rabbis in California. Nuns in New Jersey. Atheists in-between. If you've got atheists praying for you, you've done something right. One can Google cancer support services nearby. There are Facebook groups and online support. There are in-person clinics. One of the things that all the cancer patients I have met have in common is we are better at giving help than receiving it. Cancer forced me to ask for help. I had no choice. People cooked for me and my family. A friend helped me get into the bathtub because I was too weak to do it myself. I accepted help. I allowed myself to receive. I got better.

8. WHY I GOT CANCER – I used to think I was healthy until I got cancer. Now I see that I got cancer *so* I could *get* healthy.

9. I ONLY HAVE TODAY – I know it to be true that my life today is the best it has ever been. I have today and no guarantee of tomorrow. But I know it to be true that I really have this moment. And I'm good with that.

10. UPDATE YOUR OPERATING SYSTEM – If you are making all your life choices based only on your life so far, in my opinion, this is a limiting way to see the world. In my case, my operating system needed an upgrade. I needed to understand there was so much possibility and opportunity available to me that I just couldn't see or know yet. This tenet is about trust. Massive trust in your own intuition and the future blessings the world has in store for you.

The French have an expression – *raison d'être* – which literally means 'reason for being'. In this chapter of my life, with all I have seen and experienced in my sixty-three years, I now believe my raison d'être is to tell my story and share my hope. If my message has been helpful to you, then my journey has been worth it.

To learn more about this author: wendyhammers.com

LIVING FROM THE HEART

BY KATHLEEN HOLLAND

Disillusioned, disengaged and unfulfilled as a marketing executive in 2002, there had to be more to life. Then, one night, inspiration appeared in the strangest of places: a dark nightclub in downtown Toronto. A tall handsome stranger, with the most striking kind eyes and warm smile, told me his story. He was from Senegal and was in Canada to study engineering so he could return to his homeland to share his learnings. I will never forget the moment. The loud music was pulsating around me and wine in my head, but I had clarity like never before; my answer had arrived.

I had an extraordinary feeling *I was meant to go to Africa.* Now, I had never been, and truth be told, never desired to go, but a knowing deep in my heart gave me the certainty and courage to take the leap. This feeling reminded me of another strange experience I'd had ten years earlier, which I had forgotten about, but it all came rushing back at the time. I worked for a large consumer goods company and was transferred to Vancouver from Toronto leaving my friends, family and soon-to-be fiancé. I found myself sitting on Kits Beach staring at the snow-topped mountains behind the city, filled with extreme loneliness and pain, crying out, 'Why am I here?' Tears were streaming down my face … and then I heard a voice in my head. I had never heard a voice like this before, so it was startling. It said, *You are here for a reason, you are here to learn something, to make a difference in the world* … and then it was gone.

I did learn. I learned marketing, strategy and the dynamics of culture from a top Canadian consumer company at the time. Little did I know these two moments would come together, setting me up to reimagine and rewire my life. It did not happen instantly – it took from 2002 to 2005 to fully step into my new role with many synchronicities, disappointments and challenges, but all was worth it when I finally stepped off the plane in December 2005, meeting Nigest from CAWEE, the Centre for African Women's Empowerment Ethiopia, and on the same trip, Zoë Dean-Smith from Gone Rural in Swaziland. I became a marketing and strategy consultant, travelling the continent of Africa identifying and supporting high-design textile, craft and furniture companies looking to export their products globally. Interestingly, these companies actually taught me far more than I shared with them, I ended up establishing a triple bottom-line consulting business in 2008 because of what I learned about managing 'people, planet and profit' from these extraordinary African social entrepreneurs.

By 2024, I had travelled the world, consulting, training, coaching and mentoring women entrepreneurs across forty countries and six continents, in a large part due to my connection with Zoë Dean-Smith mentioned earlier. She has become a connector, a colleague and a dear friend.

Now entering a new phase in my life, I am once again listening to my heart, my inner voice telling me it's time for a new adventure, a new calling has emerged. Never have I felt the world in such a fragile state, with climate, war and institutions failing us, yet at the same time, I feel great hope and possibility, with social consciousness rising. As much as things are breaking down, new opportunities are emerging. I believe this is the *age of possibility* where following your heart into new possibilities is exactly what the world wants and needs us to do. Imagine how different our world would be if we were empowered to make decisions and step into possibility from our heart and not from fear. My new adventure is focusing on inspiring, connecting and supporting women beyond fifty to step into possibility through their heart.

Here are twelve lessons I have learned living from my heart and stepping into new possibility:

1. Possibility is often triggered by a challenge/frustration or traumatic event.
2. It calls us from deep inside (from our heart, from our soul).
3. Uncertainty is always present for the path ahead.
4. It's not a straight line – *(oh so many curves on the path)*.
5. Fear puts up roadblocks (many!).
6. Navigating the barriers expands us (when you can face the fear and do it anyway – that's growth).
7. Letting go of expectations and control, while crazy hard, opens up possibility bigger than we can imagine.
8. Exploring opportunities can reveal possibility (I've had to try many things to test if I'm in the right direction).
9. Taking inspired action (success or failure) leads us to possibility.

10. Possibility inspired by the heart is always moving us to our higher potential.
11. Listening to our heart keeps us in alignment with our true self (our head does not, too much ego).
12. We don't do it alone, trust is foundational (in ourselves, in others to support us and in the universe to guide us).

For all the possibilities I have stepped into, there was a calling for change from my heart and from my soul. Often, I did not have clarity on the possibility, I had to navigate a path of uncertainty to get there, but it was always leading me somewhere. My job was to be open to the messages in my life to move me in the right direction. It has resulted in an incredibly fulfilling life with few regrets, and I look forward to continuing to follow my heart into the infinite possibilities that exist … I just want to make the most of this journey while I'm here!

To learn more about this author: ageofpossibility.com

A WORK IN PROGRESS

BY MARY KELLY

It's funny the things you remember from your childhood. Like people asking, 'What do you want to do when you leave school?' I think everyone was asked that at some point, by an uncle or curious neighbour.

I would have a vague answer of wanting to work with animals, nothing certain, nothing definitive. Having gone to a convent in my local town, if college was not on the cards, we were expected to go into nursing, the bank or the civil service – a job for life and a pension. None of these options appealed to me!

In 1983, jobs were thin on the ground, the unemployment rate was high. The college path was not really an option for me, and home life dictated that getting away was my best option.

Born the youngest of four, my elder siblings had flown the nest by the time I was in my mid-teens. My eldest sister Sheila was working and living in Dublin, the second-eldest sister Anne, had gone travelling and was in America – she has lived there now for forty-five years. I can clearly remember the day she left when I was twelve and I thought I'd never see her again. It turned out, that over the years, I see her more often than I see some neighbours! My brother, the only son, went to boarding school when he was nine, then college in Dublin.

It was decided I go and visit my sister Anne in the States. So, a week after I finished my leaving cert, I was on a plane to America. I'd never been on an aeroplane before, and my sister Sheila handed me my passport with a US visa at the airport! I landed in New York on a one-way ticket (price IR£75) and was hauled into the immigration office and questioned. I was innocent and naive and was very lucky not to be sent back on the next flight! Important lesson learned; at least have the address of where you are going written down.

I arrived at Anne's, who promptly said I would have to get a job. Did I want to work minding children or with horses? My father had worked in the horseracing board in Ireland for his whole working life, and both my sisters had followed into the horse industry. I knew a little about horses and less about looking after children, so took the horse option.

So began my working life. A few months spent in Pennsylvania and home I went again for reasons unknown. It would take me several months flipping hamburgers in a Dublin burger joint to save enough money to go back. This time I went to the country music centre of Kentucky, Louisville. It is also stud farm country and was my home for a year. Then followed three years of working in Ireland, New Zealand and Australia, all on stud farms. I was lucky to be able to work and see some amazing parts of the world. A brief two-month Inter Rail trip around Europe in 1986 and more countries ticked off the list.

My next step happened by accident, or luck, as did most

of my jobs throughout thirty-five years of working. My sister, Sheila, was working for a horse transport company in Ireland and was getting married and moving to the UK, so I took her place. With little knowledge of how the business worked and even less secretarial skills, over the next seven years I became a dab hand at using Tipp-Ex on triplicate sheets! I travelled the length and breadth of Ireland helping to load horses onto planes and ferries. Looking back, it was hard work, but I met great characters and had many laughs. It was in the early days of advances in technology; telex machines, fax machines, enormous mobile phones with no-one to call because no-one else had one! Ahh, good times ...

So, my horse knowledge stood me in good stead; jobs with two of the biggest stud farms in Ireland followed, spanning over twenty years. Such was my luck, I only remember ever doing two interviews in thirty-five years. I just fell into jobs and didn't think much of where it was taking me. I was never really career oriented, progression or advancement was not important to me. I just thought I could keep plugging away, day-in, day-out, and get to retirement age without any fuss.

In early 2018, I had been working for a well-known stud farm for fifteen years and my day-to-day life had become monotonous. There was no longer any joy in my work, so I asked my boss if I could have a few months off to do some travelling and recharge the batteries. He was old-school and believed everyone should work as hard as he had done his whole life and not need time off. He declined. So, at that moment, I had a decision to make. Do I stay and remain unhappy, or do I step away? I weighed up the pros and cons of both options and decided it was time for me to find a new direction. It was a hard decision as I enjoyed the work and people there, but it had come to a natural end. The day I left was a sad day for me, but I had made plans to do some travelling, which I was excited about.

With the benefit of hindsight, it wasn't just work that was the problem. As a woman in her fifties, I had other physical and emotional issues going on, and I'm sure this contributed to my feelings of hopelessness and fatigue.

What the hell do I do now? My initial reaction was that I'd made a huge mistake. Could I get my job back? But did I want my job back? I'm blessed to have many good friends in my life who always supported and encouraged me in whatever I decided to do. One suggested I make the best of the situation and go ahead with my plans to travel and get away. This was my chance to reinvent myself, she advised – and how right she was, but how the hell do I do that? My friends and family could all see I was struggling and were there to support me all the way.

My plan was to take a year out, travel and spend time with family and friends. The first thing I did was plan a trip doing something I had wanted to do for years; three weeks in glorious Thailand working on a wild animal and elephant sanctuary. How lucky was I to be able to do this; waking up to the sound of the baboons and birds and feeding these gentle giants and sun bears, all of whom had endured terrible torture and abuse from human hands. This tiny act of giving back fed my soul and brought my smile back.

As we head into middle age, our parents (if we're blessed to have one or both still with us) may need more care and help. I believe to be able to do this is a privilege, to give back a little for all they have done for us. My mum had health issues for many years and her condition was slowly getting worse. This too was a worry. Hospital and doctor visits were a weekly occurrence which usually fell to me to organise. My siblings and I were lucky enough to be able to be there for our dear mum, until we said goodbye to her at the end of 2019. She taught me a lot in her quiet and unassuming way. How important it is to be thankful, to give back and to always be kind. She understood what it was like to be vulnerable and spent many of her later years helping people overcome and accept their weaknesses.

Over a past number of years, I discovered I have a passion for whiskey. This came about when I was encouraged by a friend to invest in a cask of whiskey. I knew very little about it, but we thought it would be fun and a great conversation topic! I quickly learned I was fascinated about the process of how it is made and the history of whiskey in Ireland. My father would have been proud; he was a confirmed Powers whiskey drinker all his life. So down I went the path of learning all about it. I sold it at Dublin airport and was a guide in a distillery. I then worked in a city centre shop talking about it and selling it. I liked the banter with customers and how much there was to learn about all the nuances of the flavours and processes. Then along came the COVID pandemic. Sadly, the shop was a victim and did not reopen again.

By the way, I sold the cask of whiskey I had invested in, as it was not the best whiskey I had ever tasted, and I decided not to bottle it for myself. But I'm glad I did it as it steered me in a direction that I never would have considered. So don't overlook 'happenstance'.

Happenstance (noun): Chance or a chance situation, especially one producing a good result.

When I look back over those two years, I learned more about myself and my resilience. Living alone meant a lot of time spent by myself at the beginning of the pandemic. It was a time to go back to basics and find joy in the small things. I am fortunate to live close to a great place to walk my beloved dog. Everyone had time to stop and chat (at a safe distance!) and take an interest in one's life. It was also a time where many took stock of what was important in their lives and adjusted accordingly. Sadly, though, it seems most people have once again returned to living life at a frantic pace with no time for the simple joys anymore. What a strange, almost surreal, time to live through.

Be kind, you never know what someone is going through.

I'm officially a middle-aged woman, and there's something that for many years was not spoken about or given a voice – and that is menopause. I didn't take it seriously until I was in the middle of it. The Japanese call this *the second spring of a woman's life*. For me, it was not all a bed of roses. It invaded my sleep and my mood. At times my body and mind seemed like I wasn't in control of it. I sometimes felt I was on the edge of despair. This influenced my life, relationships, friendships … and much more. Thankfully I have come out the other side. Some sail through these years with no issues, while others do not.

If you wait to be happy, you'll always be waiting.

If you know what you want from life, make it happen and go get it. Know that the law of attraction will move mountains to fulfil your dreams if you believe in it enough. If, like me and many others, you haven't found what that is, that's okay too. Because there's nothing wrong with not having it all worked out. Life has a way of showing us what really matters and making it work out the way it was meant to in the end. I am the first to admit, I have never been good at saving for a rainy day. I did have a pension and was able to use some of that to finance my time off. At this point, I will say how important it is be financially astute and to try and save as much as one can for the future. You never know what lies ahead and it's important to be prepared. Seek financial advice and plan accordingly. If you have access to a pension, use it to make sure you have sufficient funds to help you live when you're not working anymore.

Middle age creeps up on us like a stealth bomber. It demands retrospection and makes us aware of the time passing and time remaining. Our mortality salience becomes evident, due to health issues and the passing of parents and friends. This is something that never occurred to me when I was in my twenties and thirties. I was kryptonite back then, nothing could get in my way. I was going to be young forever.

'The things you do for yourself are gone when you are gone, but the things you do for others remain as your legacy.' – Kalu Ndukwe Kalu

I, like many perhaps, feel I want to leave something after I've gone. A legacy. For many, marriage and children give definition to the passing years. Parents watch their children grow and make their own lives. This was not on my path, so other milestones have provided meaning for me, including my charity work, most notably my many trips to South Africa. I feel a great sense of achievement in doing my small part to help change lives, by building houses and schools in townships. To give those who have nothing the chance to live in a secure home and educate their children, so they can break the cycle of poverty and make a good life for themselves.

Time with family and friends is something we can never get back. I have learned it is important to take that time and make memories. Nothing is guaranteed and nothing stays the same. At any age, young or old, it's important to take stock. Learn what's important to you, set goals, desires and dreams. Don't be afraid to do this if you need to, at any or all stages throughout your life.

'Life begins at the end of your comfort zone.' – Neale Donald Walsch

Don't be afraid to try something different. I've tried many things that have pushed me out of my comfort zone. I'm not good at public speaking, so I joined Toastmasters. One of the hardest things to do as an adult is to learn how to swim. I was never taught as a child so grew up with a fear of the sea. I've had lessons and, while I'm not there yet, I now enjoy going into the sea and reaping its benefits. I learned to ride a motorbike in my fifties. I had never as much as sat on the back of one before then! I inherited a love of music from my mum, so I joined a choir after years of thinking I wasn't good enough. Turns out I can hold a note or two and I love it!

Surround yourself with positive people, friendships that work for you. The friends who will always be there to help and encourage. They will also be the ones to keep you grounded.

'We have to get used to the idea that at the most important crossroads in life there are no signs.' – Ernest Hemingway

I'm once again at a crossroads considering my work options. I would like a job where there is interaction with people, as I believe that's important for me. On reflection, I know I don't want to work full-time as I've enjoyed the flexibility of the last few years allowing time with friends out hiking and walking. It would be nice to work part-time and have the best of both worlds. I realise now I want for little and can survive on a lesser income. I'm lucky to have my home with not long to go on my mortgage. As I meander my way through the next decade of reinventing myself, I have faith that I'll be okay. I will bring all I have learned along the way with me. The dream of owning a campervan and seeing our beautiful country, and maybe further afield, will happen some day!

ON REFLECTION

BY KARIN PETRIE

Having experienced a few key forks in the road in my career to date, I have tried to define the approach I've found helpful to carry on my life journey, as I continue to 'reimagine'. I share it with you here:

- Be open, observant and opportunistic. Get dressed. Define your goal.
- Plan your preferred route. Stretch and breathe. Check and check again.
- Assess your needs.
- Always do what you must within a good time.
- Working is a journey of relationships. The constant is you as an individual adapting to your environment.
- Solid steps for optimum balance.
- Bringing others along in a spirit of inclusivity fuels power.
- Focus on your outcome. Move, lengthen or shorten your stride depending on the elements.
- Listen, breathe again. Gather information, share it with those around you.

- Repetition is good as you continuously move closer to your aspiration.
- Forward propulsion.
- Learn. Toe first. The head needs balance!
- With each day you gain experience. It is important to acknowledge the good, the bad and the ugly moments, but it is essential to seize the view, the wins and the surprise.
- Steady round the edge, nearly there. Take a long-term approach. Complete many compact trails. Stop. Review and be objective.
- Contemplate your interactions past and future.
- Rest.
- Record the measurements. Adapt.
- Ready steady GO!

THE POWER OF WRITING DOWN GOALS

BY VAL QUINN

I have worked hard all my life. For pocket money, my brother and I did odd jobs like mowing the lawn or cleaning the Venetian blinds – God, I still remember the paper cuts! My first job outside of the house was at fifteen in Funderland, on a dart stand for IR£1 (old money) an hour; on Christmas holidays I worked eleven hours a day for two weeks straight and stayed on for the next two weekends. With my pay cheque I bought myself my first brand-new bike – a silver Peugeot racer. I was so delighted with myself.

In my first year at college, I worked on the till at H Williams (now SuperValu). For the remaining college years, I made and delivered pizzas.

I wasn't sure what to do when I finished school. My brother is four years older, and in college he studied marketing, but I decided to give myself exposure to many subjects and chose to do a BComm – a three-year degree in University College Dublin (UCD). In 1989, when I finished my degree, Ireland was in a recession with few jobs available for recent graduates, so I applied to do an MBS in general management/marketing, for the first time funded by the European Social Fund, and thus available for free.

I finished my MBS in the summer of 1990, but because Ireland was in recession, I moved to London to start a graduate trainee job. I worked as part of the Sharwood's Indian and Chinese food team, starting in sales, driving around London selling curry powder to Indian nationals. At twenty-two, I had never lived away from home and knew no-one in London. It was very lonely at first. I drove all day, on my own. In those days there were no mobile phones, no sat-nav, and the cost of a flight home was half a month's wages! I settled in and found friends through house sharing. After eighteen months, I joined CPC/Unilever as I decided I wanted to work full-time in marketing.

I cut my marketing-cloth on the great British brands Bovril, Marmite and Ambrosia. Career-orientated and impatient to get ahead, after three years at CPC, I signed up with employment agencies to see where my next gig might be. Being Irish, the recruitment agency asked me to interview for an international role with R&A Bailey, based out of Dublin. After a fun interview, they offered me the job. Four weeks later, I was driving my little white Peugeot 205 back to Dublin, with all my possessions in the back.

I loved my new job with the Baileys Irish Cream brand. After eighteen months, the company restructured which unfortunately meant the role I would have loved to do next no longer existed. At the time, I was playing hockey, and one of my team members worked for Mars/Masterfoods. When she told me there was a marketing vacancy, I applied and was appointed brand manager for Uncle Ben's. For the next seven years, I worked at Mars in several roles in marketing and commercial. The company's structure was flat, so, to progress further in the company, I would have had to move back to England, which I didn't want to do.

One day, chatting with an ex-Baileys colleague, I discovered there was a commercial role available at The Coca-Cola Company (TCCC). Sometimes Ireland feels like a village! She thought I would get on well with the MD there. When we met, we had a great discussion over coffee, and he invited me to a formal interview. He hired me for a newly created role of commercial director at TCCC Ireland.

What followed were years of fulfilling and challenging work. I started at TCCC as commercial director before being promoted three years later to MD/country manager when my boss moved back to Australia. The role was busy, but I loved the exposure I had to all the elements of running a business whilst leading a strong, fun team. Later, when TCCC went through a significant European restructure, all twenty-four of us on the Irish team were affected.

I was asked to become the MD of the Nordics (five countries) based out of Copenhagen. While I seriously considered this opportunity, I didn't accept it. My (then) partner didn't want to relocate, and flights between Copenhagen and Dublin were really infrequent.

During the restructure, I did my best to communicate regularly with the team, ensuring they had as much information as was available, leveraging my external network to connect those seeking opportunities whilst leaving with a redundancy package in their back pockets. Through my TCCC network, I reached out to a senior colleague, explaining my situation. Through those contacts and conversations, I was given an opportunity to interview for a global commercial role based out of Dublin, though involving a lot of travel. I accepted the role and became global customer director; a job I did for the next eight-plus years. Thankfully, all my Irish team secured roles. Through this process, I learned a tremendous amount; my greatest learning, that change, while at first glance may appear scary, can provide opportunities which otherwise may not have existed. I learned about the importance of communication and how critical it is during times of change to provide reassurance and to create new connections and opportunities. You never know what you'll discover and what doors may open as a result.

When I reflect on this period, I recognise it as a fork in the road. I chose a fork which led me down a certain path for the next few years. Sometimes I wonder what would have happened if I'd chosen the other fork – accepting the job in the Nordics. I wonder, but I also know we must not live our lives looking in the rear-view mirror. Sometimes life plays a hand, some of us call that fate, and although I am not fatalistic – that is, I believe we always have a choice and mostly make our own luck – I do sometimes believe things happen for a reason, even if we can't always see the reason at the time.

An example of this is what happened a year after I turned down the Nordics opportunity and accepted the global role. That year, my dad passed away very suddenly. Had I accepted the Nordics role, I would have only been able to visit him once every few months. As it was, although I was travelling for a few days every week, I was Dublin-based and saw my parents every Sunday. For the last year of my dad's life, I got to see him every week, and I'm deeply grateful that the universe intervened to give me that chance.

As a global customer director based out of Dublin, the role required me to travel all around the world meeting local teams, reviewing business plans and their implementation, as well as helping to resolve any challenges that arose. This was a diverse and exciting role, giving me the opportunity to meet lots of new people and experience new cultures, along with exposing me to how business was conducted across more than thirty-two markets globally. After eight years, I grew tired of the travel, 4am wake-up calls and frequent eighteen-hour days. I was exhausted. I began missing friends and family events. The cons of my seemingly glamorous job began to outweigh the pros.

For Christmas holidays in 2018, I booked a week off. Reflecting on how I was feeling, I realised I was feeling absolutely terrible, sleeping just four hours most nights, always tired, forever wishing I could climb back into bed the moment I got out of it. I was two stone (28lbs) heavier than I am today, and I knew I had to do something.

I reflected on when I may have felt tired, unfit and overweight before. I had experienced this once before, many years earlier. That time, my strategy was to start running to deal with the challenges head-on. I had always wanted to run a marathon, to prove to myself I could, so this seemed like a good time to try. In 1999, I knew almost nothing about running. I went to a bookshop and bought a *beginner's guide to running* which offered a plan for first-time marathoners. As I left the shop, I bumped into a friend from college whose sister was running marathons. When she saw the book in my hand, she asked me what I was planning. 'I thought I would do the Dublin marathon.' She smiled and said, 'You won't run a marathon. They're hard and take a lot of time commitment.'

As I walked away, her comment made me even more determined. There's nothing like someone telling you that you can't do something to fire up determination! I learned from this that it's wise to surround yourself with people who fully support your dreams and goals. The naysayers are energy drainers. I also learned to tell as many people as possible about my goals, as they then become accountability partners. I told everyone I could about my plan to run a marathon because I knew that would make me do it – I didn't want the shame of not achieving something I'd told everyone I would do! I completed the marathon that October in four hours forty-two minutes with a big smile on my face.

All those years later, Christmas 2018, I paused to reflect on how I could change to feel better. I wanted to feel energetic again, to feel passionate for the day ahead. I reflected on the highs and lows in my life – when I had felt happiest at work/in my life and when I had felt the opposite. I thought about what had driven me. I used an exercise called *the lifeline exercise*, and I identified what I wanted more of in my future and what I wanted to remove.

Number one, I realised I am happiest in my life when I am fit and healthy. I decided to become physically healthy again, to sleep better and to lose some weight.

At the time, a friend of mine was into triathlons and had joined a club. After talking to her, I decided a triathlon could be good for overall body fitness and toning and would be less likely to cause me an injury than running another marathon. Also, my older brother started running marathons in the early 2000s, and he was REALLY good. I didn't want to be compared to him, sibling rivalry at its best! So, I signed up for the Dun Laoire half ironman (1.9km swim, 90km bike in the Wicklow mountains, followed by a half marathon along the seafront). I would run it in August 2019, which gave me eight months to train.

As I reflect, I realise how important it was for me to decide on my goal, to be crystal clear about it, to break it down into bite-sized chunks and to write down each step I needed to take to reach my goal. Apparently, you can triple your chances of achieving your goals by writing them down, yet only 3% of people do.

One useful framework for planning is 'the GROW' model. Be warned, making a plan, deciding on next steps and starting the process doesn't happen overnight! I spent eight weeks creating my fitness plan, buying a bike and joining the club. Then in February 2019, the hard work of training began. I became more organised with my work life since I had to fit at least one hour of training into most days. At the end of August, when I completed the race, I felt a deep sense of achievement. I felt fitter, had lost some weight and my mindset shifted. I was happier.

My role still had me travelling around the world. And my hours and workload had increased, as people resources were tight. I needed a break. I wanted to have fun again and downtime to re-energise myself. Over the Christmas 2019 break, I reflected on changes I could make. I decided to request a year off work, as a colleague on my team had done previously.

Not long into 2019, I had a one-on-one meeting with my

boss to discuss the team structure. It was the perfect opportunity to ask for a year off. I decided if I could take a year off to train for a full ironman (IM), it would be my ideal personal system reset. It was hard enough fitting in training with work to do the half ironman, and it would be impossible to train for a full IM with all my work travel. I told him what I wanted, 'Who does a half of anything?!' I joked. After discussions with my boss and HR, we agreed I would finish work at the end of October 2019 so I could train for Ironman Barcelona on 3 October 2020. We were busy putting everything into place for the year off – nine months gave us time to find the right person to take my role on an interim basis and to do a detailed handover.

As planned, I stopped work in October 2019, and that weekend, I travelled to Milan to an Italian friend's fiftieth birthday party. Usually, I would not do something so extravagant, but the trip seemed like the perfect way to start my year off. At the start of November, I spent a week in Paris as a coach and global ambassador for Vital Voices 'Women in Leadership' training program. It was an amazing week spent with wonderful and inspiring women. It's unlikely I'd have had the time or opportunity to attend if I'd still been working.

During the winter, I continued to do some light sports training, signing up to a fitness coach for the expertise and guidance needed to prepare me for a full IM without the risk of injury. I spent most of December having long overdue catch ups with friends and preparing for what promised to be an amazing 2020. I signed up for IM Barcelona, booked trips away with friends, bought tickets for music concerts and holidays, all interspersed with the IM training required. This was going to be MY year. A one-off, amazing year, to enjoy life and reset my priorities.

I was due to take my first trip in February. As we were preparing to go, of course, COVID hit. Literally, the week we were due to fly! Everything was cancelled, and the roller-coaster began. One day, in mid-March while on a training cycle, I was finding it hard to keep up, and by that night every bone in my body shook. I was freezing cold. Long story short, I had contracted COVID.

I have never been so sick as during those weeks. I could barely stand. My resting heart rate, normally fifty-two, was 110 beats lying on the couch. I had a raging temperature that lasted ten days. I lost ten pounds despite eating daily – every cloud has a silver lining! It was four weeks before I fully recovered and was able to go for a short run. All the travel I'd arranged was cancelled, leaving me with more credit with Aer Lingus and BA vouchers than one person could ever wish for! I continued to do some light training, but IM Barcelona now seemed uncertain, given COVID restrictions. With the help of some connections, I began pro bono executive coaching, keeping myself busy at home doing jobs I'd rarely had time to do when I was travelling – like cleaning the oven and defrosting the freezer!

At the start of July, I went for an 8km jog and was about a kilometre from home when I saw some floaters in my right eye. The next thing I knew, I felt as if the London Underground map was traveling across my eye – all in bright red. Then *whoosh!* It spread out and I couldn't see a thing. I had gone blind in my right eye! I stopped running immediately. There was no pain, but I put my hand to my eye to keep it closed and walked home as fast as I could, where I called the eye and ear hospital. Due to COVID there were no walk-ins for emergency. I needed an appointment. Though freaking out inside, I tried to keep calm and managed to get an appointment for two hours later.

Due to all the blood within my eye, the doctor couldn't tell what was wrong. Since the surgeon I'd had a year earlier for a retina reinforcement was on holiday, the doctor told me I'd have to await his return. In the meantime, I was to move as little as possible, avoid phone screen time, reading, walking or lifting. I was instructed to sleep upright to help the blood drain.

The following week when the surgeon returned, my eye was the same, so he decided to operate. It was my mum's birthday, 22 July, so I took it as a good omen! Thankfully they were able to wash out my eyeball to discover a torn retina, which they repaired. That afternoon I walked out of the hospital, my sight restored. Science is amazing! I was under strict instructions to never again lift weights at the gym, skydive or use a trampoline. I figure I can live happily without any of those activities in my life! Unfortunately, it also meant that doing the IM in October 2020 was off the agenda.

I worried because my year off was passing fast. Nothing had gone to plan! I tried to make the most of it and practised the art of gratefulness. Having my full sight was always top of my list for being grateful and I reminded myself I was not unique when it came to COVID, with many far worse off than me.

At the end of July, my boss called and asked if I'd like to interview for a role to manage Costa Coffee for Central and Eastern Europe (a brand TCCC had bought eighteen months before). I did the interview by Zoom and secured the job.

So, in October 2020, I started the Costa role. I was extremely busy working on my laptop from the dining room table on regular Zoom calls; the new COVID era of working. I was quickly sucked right back in to working extremely hard, and my training took a back seat as I focused on business demands.

Soon after my return, TCCC announced a global restructure. They said they would roll out the restructure region by region, with varying timing to be announced. They offered a voluntary as well as compulsory redundancy scheme.

At the end of October, I returned to the hospital for a review on my eye operation recovery. Whilst waiting for my appointment, an email came through on my phone informing me that the TCCC voluntary redundancy program for Europe would soon open and I was eligible. A few minutes later, the doctor informed me I had an eye condition in both eyes. An hour after walking into the hospital my old self, I was walking out facing the possibility of a voluntary redundancy package in one hand and in the other, future eye operations and possible blindness!

I began to think long and hard about my future. Having no idea how long I'd have full good eyesight and whether future operations would be successful or not, I decided I would apply for voluntary redundancy and explore other avenues in life, while I still had my sight.

I left the Costa team in March 2021. It was hard to say goodbye.

One morning over breakfast, having recently finished working, I was pondering my options when I was struck with the notion that there must be many people in the same boat as me — either through choices they've made or circumstances cast upon them. I began to think how interesting it would be to capture those stories, and how powerful it could be for others to read them. I realised they could inspire others looking for a change, or for new life experiences. I drafted a book outline whilst drinking a second cup of coffee and thus the idea for this book was born.

A week later, I was having a cuppa with my mum when she sat me down and told me she had something to discuss with me. She had rarely done that, so I knew it wasn't going to be good! That was the day Mum informed me she had been diagnosed with breast cancer. She asked me to attend an appointment with her a few days later.

Throughout that summer, treatment ensued, followed by an operation and, unfortunately, many infections. When not in hospital, Mum stayed at my house so I could take care of her. Most of 2021 passed in a blur of hospital visits and appointments. While I did train for the ironman, giving me a mental break and helping to keep my body fit, other plans remained on hold.

The Barcelona Ironman was confirmed for 3 October 2021. We delayed Mum's radium treatment by a few weeks so she could come with the family, support me and have a fun break. I completed the full ironman in thirteen hours and fifty-eight minutes – it wasn't pretty, but I did it! (If you'd like to read my ironman story, it's on my website tilly.ie)

At the start of December, Mum completed her radium, and we spent two weeks over Christmas and new year in Tenerife for her to rest and recover. The trip helped, and Mum gained strength every day. By early January 2022, she was strong enough to move back home.

During 2021, I was primarily a full-time carer and in training. In early 2022, I yet again had to sit down and consider what

I might like to do with my time. Many people asked me, 'Why not just fully retire?' I pondered this question. After all, if I was careful with money, I could probably live reasonably comfortably until I draw down my pension. However, I feel relatively young (now fifty-five) to be fully retired. I worry that if I don't use my mind productively, I may lose some brain function! I already easily forget things right now! I blame menopause; brain fog has set in! I believe that working in some way will maintain my brain function for longer. After all, the brain is a muscle that needs to be used. Use it or lose it! Plus, since giving up full-time employment, I'd noticed that time passes quickly and the bank balance diminishes even faster!

There is an interesting movement underway called FIRE (financial independence, retire early). It advocates frugality and extreme savings and investment, with the aim for its adherents to retire as early as they choose. There is plenty of information on the web, including some TED talks, one of which spoke loudly to me. The speaker said her aim was not to retire but to have the financial freedom to focus on doing good in the world, on sustainability and on helping the planet. The FIRE content online definitely provides plenty of food for thought.

I often ponder the purpose of life. I have a fear of 'wasting time' and feel I should be doing something. I watched Martin Seligman's Ted Talk on Positive Psychology in which he explains that we have three lives – for true fulfilment and a happier life, we need a meaning in our lives. No doubt what makes a 'meaningful life' is different for us all and I focused on trying to figure out what a 'meaningful life' is for me.

I did not want to work full-time again. I wanted to work a

few days a week to provide a sense of security. When I reflected on what had meaning for me in the past, the coaching and mentoring of others had always brought me joy. Hence, I decided to focus on that as part of my rewiring phase. Ideally, I wanted to work in a hybrid fashion and in more diverse areas than I had in previous years. I like the old-fashioned way of pen and paper to write and capture my thoughts. Using the GROW model, I scribbled on many sheets. I summarised my thoughts on one page capturing my plan for the way forward. These may of course change and evolve over time but included short-term contracts, iNEDs (independent non-executive directorships), business training, executive and life coaching, as well as time for charity/ pro bono work, as this is very important to me.

To formalise my mentoring and coaching experience, I completed a Diploma in Executive and Life Coaching and became a member of the EMCC. More recently, I launched tilly.ie, my own business.

I love my work. I find it internally rewarding. Working for myself provides lots of flexibility, allowing time for catching up with friends, hiking and some sport – of which I have done little since completing the ironman! It is easy to enjoy the company of good friends, good food, a few drinks, the couch and Netflix!

The amount of time rewiring takes should not be underestimated. It is very useful to have people to act as soundboards for your thinking as it evolves. However, if asking someone for advice, make sure to let them know that before you meet. Go prepared with the questions you have so that you can fully leverage and respect the other person's time.

In addition, consider your social media presence. What

message do you want to portray publicly about yourself? Many people start with a LinkedIn profile. I updated mine so that if someone looks me up, they know what to contact me about.

Most days I am optimistic and excited about what may lie ahead. While other days, I am frustrated that I don't seem to achieve as much as I would like. The recent years have been a time of deep reflection on all that has gone before, on all the lessons learned and imagining options for my future.

Rewiring, for me, is a process of evolution. Some of my pillars may come to fruition over time, and some may not. I may replace some and allow space for the universe to bring other opportunities as yet unimagined into my life.

I hope from my sharing, people will find some learnings and perhaps some inspiration. As I reflect on my story, I have come to understand the lessons I have absorbed so far.

In no particular order of importance, these are:

- As one door closes another opens – true for me when I declined the Nordics opportunity to then be offered the global role.
- We can achieve more than we ever imagined possible just by writing down our goals, making 'SMART' action plans, reviewing often and putting a support network in place.
- The importance of planning while acknowledging the power of visualisation and manifestation.
- Things don't always go to plan.
- Sometimes there is a higher plan. We may not understand the reason at the time, but on reflection, it may make total sense and become clear. Often, the next opportunity is bigger and better than what we had hoped for.

- The power of networking and connections. This is how I secured nearly every job throughout my career.
- Focus on sleep; seven to nine hours are required daily.
- The importance of friends.
- The power of new connections as well as old.
- The power of walking/time out/reflection time.
- Insights are gained from putting finances on a spreadsheet.
- When you get a pay rise, save half of each increase ongoing.
- Start a pension and investments early, and if you haven't already, then start now.
- Learn how to negotiate – it can be fun and provide huge benefits and savings.
- Get the support you need – a coach, a mentor – someone who can partner for your success, act as a soundboard, help to avoid pitfalls, offer encouragement when self-doubt sets in. Have accountability partners.
- For true fulfilment we need purpose in our lives (listen to Ted talks by Martin Seligman and others).
- Every situation, no matter how bad, offers a lesson; you just need to look for it.
- The importance of practising the art of 'gratefulness'.
- Sometimes you need to stop or leave something in order to allow space for another thing to enter.
- Start today – there is no ideal time to start a course/a job/a plan.
- Never put off a dream. Who knows what is around the corner.
- And some of my observations …
- An increased awareness of the limited time that we all have.

- How little spare time/fun time people have.
- How stressed out many people are.
- How worried people are about finances.
- How quickly time goes in a day (and how little we often achieve in a day!).
- Without work, self-confidence can quickly diminish.
- Anxiety (at a manageable level) can lead to change which in turn leads to growth.
- Most people one meets for the first time asks, 'What do you do?' – have an answer, any answer, ready!
- The universe has its own plan.
- No-one wants to know what you are doing during the week to enjoy yourself while they are working hard; don't post your fun on social media, and don't call someone who is working for a catch-up chat during their working day.
- Social media/internet is a big time-stealer.
- We must find a way for more laughter in our lives, as we seem to laugh less often as we age.

I am excited to explore and enjoy the adventures that await me. I am keeping an open heart and an open mind. I curate this book with the hope to inspire others to do the same.

Some additional reading and tools:

hbr.org/2023/12/use-strategic-thinking-to-create-the-life-you-want?tpcc=orgsocial_edit&utm_campaign=hbr&utm_medium=social&utm_source=linkedin

'A midlife career change is as good as a rest': on.ft.com/3NMiJOa

To learn more about this author: linkedin.com/in/val-quinn-59338a

MY SQUIGGLY, KALEIDOSCOPE CAREER

BY DR MARIANNE ROUX

'Our deepest fear is that we are powerful beyond measure. It is our light, not our darkness, that most frightens us. We ask ourselves, who am I to be brilliant, gorgeous, talented, fabulous? Actually, who are you not to be? You are a child of God. Your playing small doesn't serve the world.' – *Marianne Williamson*

Born in South Africa, I have lived in Germany, England, Namibia, Australia and now Dublin, Ireland. I live in Ireland with my husband of twenty-six years and our seventeen-year-old daughter. At fifty-three years old, I'm slap-bang in the middle of menopause and all its shenanigans.

Academically, I have a Masters in Organisational Psychology and Human Resources and a PHD in Leadership. My early training was as a journalist and copywriter. Now, I live a portfolio life where I work as an independent management consultant and business school professor, a not-for-profit board member, a writer and a keynote speaker. I also work to help refugees, asylum seekers and those who have been trafficked or sold into slavery. I am passionate about education and job creation. Growing up in South Africa in the middle of apartheid and surrounded by complex, ever-changing environments, it was important to me early on to make a difference and fight for a better world.

I was born into privilege, and although I feel I use it well, I do not know what I could have been capable of under the extreme trauma these people suffered. I admire my dad, who was independent and values-driven in his views as a white male in apartheid South Africa, and who raised me to believe in myself. He always mentors and advises me, sometimes telling me truths I do not want to hear. As a young woman, he believed I could conquer the world and made sure I grabbed every opportunity available to me. We were taught to have our own views and debate challenging issues. My parents believed in travel to grow our perspectives and understanding of the world and in social justice for all. As a result, I have an insatiable sense of adventure, curiosity and independence.

The joy of mixing my African and European heritages, I feel, gives me unique insights. I believe in *ubuntu* – meaning 'I am because you are', indicating that there is a universal bond that connects all of us – it is our humanity towards others.

I believe in the power of leadership in transforming complex situations. I want to create better leaders in the world that create sustainable organisations who care about people and the planet. I am driven by 'learning and growing', 'making a difference' and 'creating connections'.

I don't think I was ever made for a mainstream career journey.

I call my career *a portfolio of learning and travel adventures*. Or perhaps as LA Mainiero calls it, a 'kaleidoscope career'. This is when you rotate different aspects of your life to rearrange your roles and relationships at different times. At the core, it is the ABCs of authenticity, balance and challenge. It is when you examine choices and options to create the best fit based on work interests, demands, constraints and opportunities given your values and purpose. It is rarely a linear career where you apply for jobs. Most roles and opportunities come through networks and relationships. Following a kaleidoscope career means 'being able to move frequently within and across organisational and country boundaries and transition in and out of the workforce in line with personal goals, nonwork demands and changing economic conditions' (Simmons et al, 2022).

When you live your life like this, not everyone understands it. I have had unsolicited advice and raised eyebrows along the way. I've made lots of mistakes, was in over my head many times and may have been perceived as 'hopping between jobs'.

My work life started when I became an aerobics instructor in the 1980s – yes, you have the right image in your head, leg warmers and all – when I was still in high school. I did this for six years to save money for travel while I studied. It was also a great way to stay fit without paying a cent. When I completed high school and had to choose what to study, it wasn't easy. There was no proper career guidance at school, and everyone wanted to become a nurse, doctor, teacher, lawyer or engineer. No-one talked about being a writer or an entrepreneur. My parents, though, discussed all possible opportunities with us and encouraged us to think about different options.

I decided I wanted to be a journalist or copywriter. So, I studied a degree in communications. South African media was still under state control, and I remember the reaction when I took part in a public debate on campus about media freedom. I realised I could not write independently, so I made my first pivot and completed an honours degree in the second major I took, organisational psychology. It was heavy human resource (HR) process, policy and theory based, and I was unsure if I had made the right decision. I was not made for anything detail and administration heavy.

The world became clearer when I backpacked for six months before completing a HR internship in Germany. I worked in leadership development and was exposed to amazing psychologists who were grappling with global leadership and integrating east and west German operations of the company. It was an eye-opener as my country, South Africa, was on the brink of its first democratic election and was about to become part of the global landscape again, whilst driving a process of rebalancing and reconciliation. I understood the power of leadership in transforming complex situations and felt I wanted to create better leaders in the world. I had found my calling!

I returned to South Africa, unsure how to proceed, and my father encouraged me to test out management consulting for its great training, travel opportunities and the possibility to work across several industries. I knew I also had to advance my knowledge, so I completed my Masters in Human Resources and Organisational Psychology part-time over four years, whilst flying around the world and working long hours. But then it was time for a change. I was burnt-out and had also met my husband on one of my trips.

I got married in 1996 and decided to take a role in an organisation to experience the client side of consulting and travel less in the first few years of being married (travelling less didn't happen!). I started as the head of change and then the head of human resources for a food retailer. I was only twenty-nine years old, and it was a challenging role. I had to retrench 40% of the workforce and work with the new executive team to turn the ailing business around. But we did it, and I learnt more in four years than I could ever imagine. From building a strategy, to reorganising, reskilling and creating high-performing teams, I got a full remit of transformation. I also had to tackle the challenge of affirmative action and quotas. I worked on leadership development programs across the whole company, and with my chair, with groups of South Africans in the community that had to learn to trust each other and work together.

I found I was able to throw myself into situations where I did not have all the skills and experience, but that I was brave and could learn fast. After the excitement of turning around the business, I then had to run a 'business as usual' HR function, so I got bored. I have never been good at maintaining the status quo. Give me a complex, transformational challenge, and I'm all there.

I knew I loved leadership development, and I knew I loved complex, transformational work. I also knew I loved variety, adventure, learning and making an impact. This ongoing reflection helped me to create my own future. I wrote on a page what I wanted to do and not do. A picture emerged. A friend recommended *The Seed Handbook* for me to work through, and it helped me clarify. I defined my purpose, values and unique value proposition and wrote a business plan. I discussed it with my banker. I was going to run my own business.

At this time, one of the business schools asked me to teach the turnaround case study of my previous job and eventually I became an associate lecturer and program director for the executive development unit for part of my time. Through this work, I was able to grow my network and visibility and gained many wonderful long-term clients this way.

I signed varied retainers which provided guaranteed income, allowing me time to build the business. They included working with the South African cricket team and coaching partners at a law firm in emotional intelligence. For seven years I had a great adventure lecturing (executives and MBA participants) and consulting and working with an incredible group of associates, mostly women, on leadership development, people strategy and organisation transformation and redesign. I mentored young people and developed entrepreneurs in our townships with the wonderful Pat Pillai and his team.

During this time, we took care of a family member, aged sixteen, and became instant parents. It was a steep learning curve. At the age of thirty-five, I had my own daughter. Parenting has brought out a whole different side of me. It forced me to balance things and to make time for family and for play.

Then my life was threatened in a crime incident in 2008 and everything came crashing down. I struggled to recover from the trauma and fear. With a three-year-old in tow, my husband and I decided it was time to emigrate. We considered several options, and Australia emerged as our best one.

Moving countries is hard and very different to travelling for work and fun. I was keen on running my own business and continuing teaching at business schools, but I had no network, and no recruiter understood my portfolio life and kaleidoscope career. They wanted to know whether I was a HR director OR a business school professor OR a management consultant. No-one knew the companies or business schools I had worked with. I was advised to start on a lower salary in a more junior role and work my way up.

So, I did what was easiest and went back to consulting for a few years. I worked for two of the firms on a level lower than I had been operating at for the previous ten years, but I built my network and my résumé. The family had to make several adjustments. Our daughter adjusted to being in day care from 7am to 6pm every single day.

Once I had worked back in the two consulting firms, I decided to take the head of people and culture role at Cricket Australia for a few years. People could not understand this choice. How can I go from working with large multinational companies to working in sport? They warned me about the politics, which I learned to navigate. I got to work with the 2015 World Cup team, facilitate the integration of Australian Cricket and women's cricket, and toured and worked with the men's team.

After this, I had gained the experience and network I needed, so it was time to head back out on my own globally. I sat down again and formulated a plan. I started my consulting firm and my PHD at the same time. I got a great accounting team and an even greater executive assistant. I let people know I was open for business. And they hired me for work.

That was eight years ago. And what a journey it has been – I have done amazing work in leadership development, HR transformation and strategy and have worked in Europe, the UK, the USA, China, India, Saudi Arabia, South Africa and Nigeria.

In the meantime, I kicked off a board career and have served as a director on three not-for-profit boards. I helped build schools in Africa, develop social entrepreneurs around the world and work in the healing and recovery of those saved from slavery and human trafficking. It has been life-changing. It gives one so much perspective and made me feel as if I was making an impact again.

The freedom of working for myself and making my own choices was liberating, but the stress of fluctuating incomes not so much! Especially when COVID hit! For three months all my work was postponed or cancelled, but I had a great opportunity to spend amazing quality time with my family and exercising every day. The excitement of travel and long hours and wanting to save the world sometimes came at a cost to my own health and family. COVID was a gift that created better balance in my life and made us reflect as a family of what we wanted to do next.

Post-COVID, I was working in an Australian time zone with global clients, on never-ending Zoom sessions, all hours of the day and night. I was thoroughly exhausted. There were things bothering me about Australia at the time that I could not reconcile. I was criticised for working too hard and travelling too much and was regularly asked who took care of my daughter when I travelled. I was concerned about the lack of progress for indigenous people and asylum seekers' rights and also environmental issues.

We concluded we wanted to move to Europe. The challenge was we had South African and Australian passports. How did we get the right to work and live in Europe? My husband got a job offer in Dublin, Ireland, with his company, which gave him a critical skills visa. So, we set off on a new adventure.

Our second full immigration process was happening! One might think it would be easier than the first but try moving countries during COVID! At the same time, I had a little crisis of confidence when I saw what rent and living costs were like. I applied for a few roles and every time I was interviewed, it just didn't feel right. I knew I could earn better and enjoy what I do more on my own. It was time to be brave and bold again.

This is where relationships are so important. My network came through for me and my global clients stuck with me. I am happy to report I am busy as ever. I completed my PHD, am writing my next book and teaching at several business schools. I am earning more than any role I applied for and still have my independence. I've learned that it's okay to be scared but to take the chance anyway. I live in a country that is beautiful, welcoming and humane and where people are generous. It has been such a joy to move to Ireland.

I love being an entrepreneur and having a portfolio life. It is fantastic and it is frightening. No-one tells you what to do. You can shape the business exactly the way you want. You can choose what you want to do, who you want to work with and how much you want to work. However, I work harder than I ever did for anyone else. When I started my business, my father said to me, 'Good luck with the new boss, she's a slavedriver!' It can also be very lonely – alone on flights, alone in hotels, alone in my home office. Work is not constant. It is often too little or too much. You must have the faith that things will be okay in years like that. Money fluctuates. You need a great accountant and financial adviser. And a great executive assistant. I have all of those and cannot live without them.

For me it has always been critical to be independent financially, to protect my income, stay out of debt and ensure I have enough money to see out my life comfortably. I believe we should all be financially literate and informed. I do not want to be dependent on anyone financially as there are so many unforeseen events in people's lives.

I always make sure my income covers my ongoing expenses and that I save some earnings for the times my income fluctuates. When I started out, I made sure I had six months of savings to give myself time to build up my business. We have paid off our mortgage and have no debt. We saved for our daughter's education.

Working for myself comes with financial risk, so I have income protection cover and serious illness cover. Many entrepreneurs I speak to do not have this in place. I also have life insurance and private medical insurance. These are non-negotiable for me. Having said that, I do not constantly worry about the money because I believe if you love what you do, work hard, continually skill yourself and have good relationships, the money will flow. And it does.

The decision-making process is important. I listen to my own voice and to those of my personal board. I know my purpose, passions, strengths and values, and I make my decisions accordingly. I have long-term goals and move towards them with each decision I make. Yes, sometimes I must take detours, but I always focus back on the long-term goal.

If I feel discomfort, I do not react, I respond. I talk to people I trust about it. I gather more information and I live with whatever decision I made with the information and understanding I had at the time of making it. That is the best I can do. I do not always get it right, but I am okay with that. That is how we learn.

One of the most common questions people ask me is where I get time to do everything I do. I believe in focus, discipline and being indestructible. I do not get sidelined by pings, dings and rings. I have learnt to have good and healthy boundaries with people. In fact, I do not think about time, I think about what is important to me and where my focus and energy is. I am very disciplined with my time and have daily practices that help me. Every day I spend a moment thinking about the two or three most important things I need to get done that day and the two or three people I must connect with. I make sure I have a clear day every week to do deep work like research and writing without distractions.

I only check my emails and social media three times a day. Not everything needs an immediate response. I do NOT wear a watch that shows my emails or phone calls. I believe there is nothing worse than someone who constantly looks at their watch or phone while you are with them. Respect their time with you – be fully present. I read every night for an hour before bed – half an hour is poetry or a novel and half an hour is a business book. If I am tired, I will watch a Netflix movie or a documentary. These rituals keep me moving forward and help me be productive.

My practices in a nutshell:

- I focus my time and energy on what is important and what will achieve my long-term goal.
- I spend time reflecting on whether what I do is aligned with my purpose, values, strengths and passions. I check what is working and not working, planning experiments and shifts to pivot.

- I never stop building relationships and asking for help – I have a group of associates in an ecosystem I work with and people I catch up with regularly. I network and attend events and conferences. I carefully accept LinkedIn invitations and link to people I meet or hear about.

- I make sure I have a personal board – mentors, sponsors, coaches and friends – that give me honest feedback and urge me on – ones who are happy for my success, but also honest about my blind spots. Do not have anyone on your personal board that does not support you fully or sucks the joy and energy out of you.

- I learn and experiment continuously – you have a skills backpack you carry with you that has a certain worth. If your skills become obsolete, you are no longer relevant. I read fifty-two books a year and complete at least one new course. I attend one or two conferences a year. I try out what I learn to see what works and what doesn't.

- I build my brand – not in a cringy way but by posting and writing about topical issues. I try to be useful to people.

- I exercise and take time off. I spend time with my family. To achieve this, we get help with cleaning and ironing as we want to be able to spend quality time together.

- I could not do anything without the right partner. He loves me, supports me and partners with me. He has never questioned my decisions and has patiently lived with my squiggly career and constant need for adventure.

I have a great capacity to work on and achieve many things, but I wish I had learnt earlier in life to take on less, pace myself more and be more patient. I broke my foot in Nigeria and continued working there and in Saudi Arabia for three weeks before going home. I ended up needing three surgeries to walk again. My body lets me know when I take on too much. I was diagnosed with rheumatoid arthritis at twenty-nine and have been managing pain and inflammation since. One can be too gritty. I must take care of myself, my health and my family as my absolute priority.

I do not see myself ever 'retiring' fully – I think I would go mad. But more importantly, I would drive my husband mad. I love running my company and teaching executives and will continue to do so. I am writing another book, and I am looking to get back on a not-for-profit board. I also want to broaden my life and interests, as our daughter goes to university and off into the big wide world.

Although I will continue working, we are planning on buying a property in France in the next five years with my husband making a pivot out of the corporate world. We want to run a gite business and venture into growing food. We are learning French, and my husband will soon be doing short courses to build new skills. I might add *Pilates instructor* and *wine master* to my skills backpack. And maybe I will write a non-fiction book. Why not?

I do not believe we were just made to do one thing in our lives. We can be anything we want to be with courage, focus, hard work and learning new things.

To learn more about this author: linkedin.com/company/ roux-consulting

LESSONS LEARNT & NO REGRETS

BY SUSAN WILSON

At a recent dinner party, I was asked to sum up my life in one word. Unfortunately, or fortunately, I was sober when I was asked, as I am sure if I'd had a few drinks under my belt, it would have been easier. Other guests seemed to find this straightforward. I struggled.

After some thought, I came up with 'segmented'. To fully explain this would take more than one chapter, but in a nutshell, my life has had various, almost separate, stages which have led me to where I am today. What overarched all these stages was my employment in what we like to call here in Ireland 'the bank'.

I successfully negotiated my leaving certificate and completed a posh commercial course. Now it appeared I had the limited options of a young Irish woman in the 1980s: Guinness, nursing or 'the bank'. Thanks to my course, I could type and do shorthand. I have been thankful all my life for the ability to touch-type, but never once have I used the shorthand. In school, when I raised the option of studying law with my career's guidance teacher, I was quickly told it wasn't an option for me – to this day I'm unsure if this was my academic ability or a gender issue. I was fairly confident my idea of joining the guards was never going to be a runner with my parents ... as 'what would the neighbours think?'

I joined 'the bank' at seventeen. Getting into 'the bank' was a time of great joy for my parents. With a good pensionable job, they could tick me off their list. And as the baby of the family, their work was done. Little did they know I would be back home with them at twenty-five with a four-year-old and a broken marriage. I still vividly remember the interview; I'm not sure what I said to get the job, but my lovely white wool jacket, Farrah Fawcett hair flicks and kilt skirt with a large pin, may have swung it.

One of my strongest childhood memories was visiting my uncle who, as branch manager, lived over the business. I remember walking through the bank lobby and seeing what seemed to me the huge desks and teller stations. Maybe this is where I got my interest in banking.

I left the bank more than thirty-five years later. I had many roles, worked my way up to a reasonably senior position and made a few lifelong friends. I worked in head office and in branches. I worked in, and led, small and large teams.

I was never overly ambitious. I have always rated happiness above all else and to enjoy work was probably my key goal. I almost certainly achieved this until the end, when 'the bank' lost its soul and, in my opinion, stopped caring for their staff as a key resource.

I took a voluntary redundancy package after three extremely

stressful years working in mortgage arrears. While there was a strong sense of achievement when you ensured someone could stay in their home, the unmanageable workload, sky-high stress levels, strict government oversight and emotionally bereft leaders made the decision to leave seemingly easy. At a management meeting, the head of section when discussing the high levels of staff out on stress leave stated, 'We have to expect casualties – collateral damage.' That was the final straw for me.

On the day of my departure, I couldn't get through my leaving speech – I broke down. Why was I so upset? I had a good few euro in the bank and another job to go to in a few months. Nearly all my friends had left or were leaving. When I walked out the door for the last time, I didn't feel a sense of relief or freedom, I just felt sad at a journey that had ended too soon.

On reflection, I think it was because 'the bank' was always there, giving me challenging and boring jobs, good and bad managers, lifelong and transient friends and most importantly a sense of belonging. I was in 'the bank'. When people asked me what I did, I was proud to say I worked there (until the banking crisis – then I was a hairdresser!). I was set free and no longer had the comforting structures around me.

I know now, I wasn't ready to leave, but it was still the right decision.

So, did I reimagine my career? Honestly, no. I had planned to take six months off, but *man plans, and God laughs*. Within a few weeks, I was working again in an HR consultancy business. I had worked in frontline roles, but this was completely different.

I had the opportunity to work part-time without going through too many hoops, in an area I felt would somewhat suit my skill set and with limited responsibility. This is another example of my lack of ambition, but at a later stage in life, I didn't want too many responsibilities. I also didn't want to manage staff again. After years of doing this and completing hundreds of performance reviews, I had done my time. I was good with staff, but it can be draining.

In my new role, I was working with clients rather than customers, and this is a key difference. You can only advise, not manage or directly implement changes, and I found this difficult in the early days. I also found the autonomy a challenge. In 'the bank', we had rules – your lending discretion, your till to balance, your central bank guidelines. Your work underwent quality assurance and there was always someone more senior than you, however high up the ladder you were. In the real world, you made your own decisions and didn't have to refer or get a second sign-off. I was now alone to make mistakes and successes.

However, my fear of being *useless* and totally institutionalised did not materialise. I did learn quickly that all those years in various roles had made me capable of more than I realised. I seemed to naturally know 'stuff', and once you know Microsoft Office, you can work any system. After working with and managing so many staff I knew how to read people and adapt my style to theirs. I didn't need to be a genius to develop solutions to clients' problems as my long experience covered that. I had strong communication skills, old-fashioned ability to write reports and make presentations. I had 'the bank' to thank for all the direct and indirect training. I reused what I knew in a new scenario and continued to learn.

I then went back to college, and through IBEC, got my HR

qualification. I enjoyed this so much; the weekly college class of people of all ages, from different walks of life, all eager to learn and share experiences. Proudly, I walked up to the podium at my graduation – better late than never!

The one factor which made this job complicated was that one of the owners of the company was my romantic partner. I was apprehensive about this being an issue, and if I'm to be totally honest, it was. Like most marriages, after time, we had limited interest in each other's jobs. There's nothing wrong with this, as many people's jobs are boring to others. We had agreed to avoid working together with clients as much as possible, but this wasn't always feasible. We did work well together, and our skills were complimentary, but, and it's a big *but*, I didn't like being told what to do by my partner, and he didn't like the way I did things a lot of the time. After a few major disagreements, we finally reached an understanding, but it was never easy. Strange that so many people meet in work, but rarely continue to work together. I believe this is a good thing!

I worked in the consultancy for four years, going from part-time to full-time. I enjoyed it by and large, but it was never 'the bank'. The company closed down and finally I saw retirement in my sights.

So, have I retired? No – I've rewired. I retained several clients from the consultancy and work a few hours a week, mostly when I want to. I do the jobs I like. I learned that I hate admin and love interacting with people, be it interviewing or advising. I have earned the luxury of doing what I want and turning down the work I don't want to do.

Working a few hours a week is interesting. It becomes harder to do less, in my experience. All the years of getting up early (not easy when you're not a morning person) and putting in long hours is quickly forgotten, and an early start becomes hard when you are out of the habit. A relatively simple task can get put off because it's the only work *thing* I have to do. It's easy to lose confidence, as you have the time to second-guess your work. You can rewrite and check and check again, for no reason other than you can.

For a long time, I have believed that the only person who can make you happy is yourself. This is also true of work. I've worked with many people who regularly complained about how unhappy they were in their job but never did anything about it. I helped them write CVs and they never sent them anywhere. They went for promotions and, when unsuccessful, didn't seek feedback. You have to own it or put up with it. You will never be happy if you are negative. Not everyone can do a job they love, but you can learn to enjoy some aspects – the people, the location, the task itself.

So – what are the lessons I've learnt in over forty years of employment?

1. Have a firm handshake – nothing is worse than a limp fish and creates a terrible first impression.
2. First impressions are important – make eye contact, show interest, remember names and use them.
3. Keep secrets – you tell one person – you tell the world.
4. Give everyone a second chance – not a third.
5. Be loyal – and strive to gain loyalty from your staff.
6. Have time to listen to people's problems but let them come up with the solutions.

7. Be brave but don't be stupid.
8. Proven experience can sometimes be more important than book smarts.
9. Never underestimate yourself, but don't be overconfident.
10. Delegate as appropriate – you can't do everything.
11. The old ways aren't always the best – embrace the new.
12. Change can be scary but always worth it. Just go for it!

RETIRE

'It's the rudest word in the dictionary, "retire".
And "old" is another one. I don't allow that in my
house. And being called "vintage". I don't want
any of those old words. I like "enthusiastic".'
– Dame Judi Dench

HOW MUCH DOES IT COST TO RETIRE IN DIFFERENT COUNTRIES?

We're sure this is a question most people want to know. Will you be able to maintain your current lifestyle when you finally quit for good?

The latest retirement confidence survey[1] states that 70% of workers expect to continue to work for money during retirement.

The NetCredit study for 2023[2] looked at what it would cost for a US citizen to comfortably retire in a variety of countries. They used Numbeo's cost of living data to calculate the figures (in USD) during the period between retirement (sixty-one years) and life expectancy (76.15 years).

Key findings of this study over a fifteen-year period were;

- The most expensive country to retire is Singapore, costing $1,118,375.43
- The cheapest place to retire is Pakistan, at $158,410.13.
- For US citizens living at home, the average cost is

1   ebri.org/docs/default-source/rcs/2022-rcs/2022-rcs-summary-report.pdf?s-fvrsn=a7cb3b2f_12
2   netcredit.com/blog/cost-of-retirement/

$702,330.47.

Here's some further data listing the *minimum* recommendations for various countries:

Ireland: €22,000 per annum (€330,000 over fifteen years)[3]

UK: £23,300 per annum (£349,500 over fifteen years)[4]

Australia: AUD$27,902 per annum ($418,530 over fifteen years)[5]

Canada: CAD$31,400 per annum ($471,000 over fifteen years)[6]

---

3   globalcitizensolutions.com/retiring-in-ireland/

4   theguardian.com/money/2023/apr/15/uk-pensions-how-much-retire-cost-of-living-inflation-income

5   amp.com.au/insights-hub/retirement/retirement-basics/retirement-money-needs

6   moneysense.ca/save/retirement/whats-the-average-monthly-retirement-income-in-canada

RETIREMENTALITY

BY RICHARD COLLINS

Retirement is an unnatural phase in the modern life course. It is inserted between work and death. It can be seen as intrusive and invented by a past society, for a purpose that no longer applies to modern society.

Is it really intrusive though? It could be seen as a life event that can be manipulated in your favour to live a more purposeful life. A number you can aspire to beat.

As an employee, retirement may be the ultimate life goal. Work hard for 2,600 weekly pay packets to retire with a pensionable salary and hope to outlive the money. Strategic financial planning is needed for this to happen as defined benefit schemes and annuities can take the romance out of retirement drawdown and intergenerational wealth transfer. For me, employees should not merge pensions from previous employments. Instead, isolating each deferred pension allows for a staggered drawdown of each pot which complements cashflow management, capital preservation, tax-free drawdown management and intergenerational wealth transfer.

Retirement may seem like a far-off event that you can't even imagine, however, in my point of view, retirement is no longer an endpoint but a phase of life that can span decades. One can engineer multiple 'retirements'. Unlike previous generations who worked for one company for many years, today's retirees are more likely to have multiple careers, and may continue working well into their seventies or eighties. This means that planning for retirement should be top of mind for those who wish to retire early. We call this a tactical retirement plan and strategic drawdown.

A blended approach of tactical pension drawdown from careers as an employee and then employer/self-employed, means the hamster wheel of trading time for pay packets becomes less relevant, as your passive income and long-term money silos can be hacked to mitigate the need for full work weeks. Aim for your passive income to be greater than earned income. When this happens, the relevance of earned and dependant income is dissolved at the intersection of financial and lifestyle independence.

One of the key aspects of retirement planning is to focus on personal fulfilment. While it's easy to imagine retirement as a time of leisure, golf and travel, it is important to remember it is also a time to pursue new interests, take on meaningful projects and give back to the community. By seeking out what truly fulfils you and makes you happy, you will be more likely to enjoy a fulfilling retirement.

Financial planning is crucial for early retirement. While saving money for retirement is important, it's equally vital to invest wisely to ensure a steady income stream during retirement. There never is a 'right time' to start saving. Why? LIFE

HAPPENS! Instead, break your lifestyle and financial goals into short-, medium- and long-term silos.

Starting early and taking risks can enable significant wealth creation, and a well-structured, diversified retirement plan can help you achieve your goals. For me, I love cashflowing assets rather than investments in the stock market. I like to bank the profit by buying property in my pension that produces income, regardless of the direction of movement in the stock market. In Ireland, the rent is tax free, and the capital growth is tax free when I do this. Dependent on your geography, you may need to review the guidelines on this.

Retirementality should not just focus on pension relief though.

I propose a new way of thinking about retirement and suggest people should focus on living a 'life of significance' instead of striving for traditional retirement goals. This puts a greater emphasis on personal fulfilment, a sense of purpose and work that is rewarding.

Retirement doesn't have to mean the end of work altogether. It should mean a movement to re-engineer financial independence to retire early, by utilising traditional retirement think with a modern twist of financial planning. At Walfrid Private (my business), we call this retirementality.

It's time to change attitudes towards aging. We argue that society needs to move away from the idea that retirement means becoming unproductive or resting. Instead, we need to see the value and unique skills that older adults bring to the table. Early retirement opens a long stretch of life that can be shaped to the individual's preference. The way we achieve this is through meticulous lifestyle financial planning. We utilise traditional pension relief with modern think around business reliefs.

Pension relief in Ireland provides up to €200,000 tax free and is available from sixty. If retirementality is present, the new-age thinkers will see retirement as a way of taking tax-free money from a business rather than the commencement of decades of sleeping in, pipes and slippers. Review and assess the reliefs in the country you live. The reliefs positioned alongside the possibility of retiring in tax-efficient jurisdictions means one can essentially afford to retire many years earlier because less tax will be paid on your pension capital. Portugal, for example, allows those who register for the Non-Habitual Residency program to pay just 10% tax on pension benefits. Less tax means more money for you! However, even this tax draw to Portugal has changed since first draft of this piece as the Government in Portugal have altered the non habitual residency programme. This further compounds that financial planning with safety nets and alternative strategies are mandatory throughout one's career.

LEARN MORE
- walfridprivate.ie
- thewealthsummit.ie
- Foundersboard.ie
- richardcollins.ie

Safety nets should always be the focus. People face many risks with their retirement accounts. Here are some examples:

PRE-RETIREMENT

- Investment risk. Stay true to your comfort threshold to risk, your attitude towards the volatility of your investments.
- Capital risk. Don't compromise what you can't afford to lose.
- Structural positioning. There are opportunity costs to holding pensions in certain structures.
- Underfunding of defined benefit schemes. You might not get what you expect. Pensioners in payment get preferential treatment.
- Legislation shift.

POST-RETIREMENT

- 'Bomb-out risk'. This is when the rate of income drawdown exceeds the rate of return in an ARF.
- Investment risk.
- Annuity risk.
- Changes in legislation.
- Legacy control.

In conclusion, early retirement planning is a complex and evolving process that requires a unique and creative approach. By adopting a 'retirementality' mindset that places personal fulfilment, financial planning, access to tax-efficient money and work in a wider context, you can find a new, more fulfilling way to approach retirement or the work-optional stage of life. The above does not constitute financial advice, we recommend going to a financial advisor for that. However, remember, in retirement, every day is a Saturday, and you tend to spend more in the early days. Act and spend wisely!

To learn more about this author: walfridprivate.ie

HAVE YOU BEEN LOOKING FORWARD TO RETIREMENT?

BY CATHY DERKSEN

Have you been looking forward to retirement? Counting the months and days until you can start a new reality? If you are in your fifties or sixties, chances are you've spent your life with a game plan that told you to work hard and save a lot of money for forty years so you can retire comfortably. So many of us have been living life with these plans in our head, but many of us have spent very little time really thinking about what those years will look like.

When retirement age was originally set around sixty-five, it was done at a time when the average person would only live for five to ten years in retirement. In those days, it might have made sense to limit your plans for those years to golf, garden, travel and spend time with the grandkids. In our current situation, people need to plan to live into their nineties! That means you could be spending twenty to thirty years in that stage of life. This is one of the reasons why the old model of retirement may not be a good fit for many of us.

Let's reflect. Is sixty the new forty? In our sixties it has become common for us to remain outgoing and energetic. We are not ready to slow down to fit the old model. This could be the time to follow your passions and create an impact in the world.

Many of us have spent time with our financial planner, putting numbers on a page for decades, as we save and plan for retirement. This is all very important, but the piece that is missing for many people is a vision of what retirement will look like. The numbers on the page are often built around a vague idea of what finances could be needed. Imagine if those numbers were tied to a real vision you were planning for, not just a list of travel destinations, golf and home renovations, but a bigger vision of what you really want the next couple of decades to look like.

Don't let yourself push toward retirement with only a plan to get away from your job. Instead, consider moving toward retirement with a plan for the next chapter of your life. Yes, you will probably want to move away from the nine-to-five routine. And yes, it will be a good idea to plan for a few weeks to relax and adjust, just like you should for any major transition in life. But after this time of transition recovery, plan to step into activities that energise and inspire you.

Many studies have shown that our fifties, sixties, seventies and often into our eighties, we are in a prime time in our life to take on something big. Start a business doing something you love. Write a book. Mentor the next generation. Go back to university. Take on a leadership role in your community. What is the legacy you want to leave behind? How do you want to be remembered?

Another important factor to consider is your quality of life and longevity. We know our mental and physical health are both tied to factors such as quality social interactions, feeling a sense of value and the ability to contribute to our world. Staying in the habit of lifelong learning keeps our brains energised and healthy. Staying connected with a community and building your network to add new relationships is very valuable too. Looking around us now, we have a global community at our fingertips. Reach out and connect with people who will join you along the way in your journey through these amazing years of life.

As you plan for, and move into, your next chapter of life, call it retirement or by any other name, ensure you are allowing yourself to really dream and create a life that energises and inspires you. Do all the financial planning pieces with a clear vision of what you are working toward. Look for opportunities to try new things and expand your circle of influence. Build in time to relax, enjoy family and look after yourself, while you are using your lifetime of skills, experience and wisdom to step into your vision for the future.

Through the following chapters and reading others' stories in the retirement space, there could be inspiration awaiting you.

To learn more about this author: linkedin.com/in/ cathyderkseninspiredtenacity

EYEING UP RETIREMENT!

BY OLIVIA CONNOLLY

I've worked as an optometrist for almost twenty years, meeting people of all ages and from all socio-economic backgrounds. Almost everyone needs help focusing up close as they approach the fifth decade of life, and it's not uncommon to meet with people frequently as they get older. Over the years, I've observed many people mature into older age and often wondered why the journey varies so dramatically from one to another.

Frequently, I would learn of someone's passing within a few short years of their retirement from employed work. Given that the prevailing expectation is for one to work hard to a point where they can relax into a blissful retirement, this news would always appear a little sad and unfair – 'he won the lottery and died the next day', kind of mood music.

Conversely, others would bound into the clinic with an almost unrecognisable glow and new lease of life after retirement. 'I don't know how I ever had time to go to work,' was the general sentiment expressed in one way or another. I like to think of them as 'the doers'. These folk had many characteristics in common. Invariably, they were all members of some type of club and had family or community responsibilities where people were depending on them. For example, they might have been members of a golf club where they played with friends on a regular basis and enjoyed a group lunch afterwards. They regularly looked after grandchildren or had charity work commitments. These people had plenty to live for, they valued themselves and were valued by others.

Interestingly, I can't say I remember much talk about their previous incarnation as a banker, a teacher, a lawyer or whatever role they embodied. Which begs the question; how can a role you have identified with for such a significant portion of your life become so redundant? Could it be that this manufactured sense of self, that we all have, is much less dense and more pliable in some than others? And perhaps in some, it is much less entangled with our job title and the position in society we think it affords us?

It's all about the story we tell ourselves, about ourselves and what happens to that story on retirement.

For example, John is a school principal. He tells himself, *I'm the principal of a school. I'm responsible for the wellbeing and education of the children. The livelihoods of the teachers depend on me. The health of the community/social cohesion depends on me graduating well-rounded students. My role is very important. I'm very important.*

John takes early retirement and someone at a party asks, 'What do you do?' How does John answer that question when his title is gone? Who am I beyond the story I've been telling myself for so long? Am I important anymore? I suspect this is one of those stark moments where life prompts you to get to know yourself beyond 'the story'. This is the point in *The Matrix* where the blue and red pill are on offer! In the real world, so to speak, I'm guessing many of 'the doers' opted for the blue pill. They weren't too attached to the story they told themselves about their career, and many found new things to do, new identities, new stories in their roles as 'captain of the golf club', caring grandparent, Eucharistic minister etc. They expanded roles they played while working. They found purpose in the everyday. I wonder if those who pass soon after retirement think their purpose and value is intrinsically linked to their job.

There is also another cohort of people who don't ever transition from paid employment to retirement. People for whom there is no sharp transition from being 'a something' to being finished at being 'a something'. Many of these people owned their own business and continued to work in some capacity or other, well into very senior years. Their work is their life, but not in the way we think of someone being consumed by a job and living a two-dimensional life, living every day as a means to an end, praying for the day their pension will kick in and they can start living. Instead, these people continue to use their hands and brains in service to others. An example might be the local florist who is there to mark life's milestones, the bicycle repair guy who helps you continue the journey, the unpaid carer whose work is intrinsically woven into the fabric of their existence. People who are deeply ingrained in the community, an essential cog in the big machine. I recall an appointment with a vibrant woman in her eighties. She advised me she needed to see the labels on medicine bottles more clearly because she was a carer for an 'elderly lady'.

Curiously I enquired as to the age of the lady being cared for. Ninety-two was the response!

I'm reminded of a quote from Kahlil Gibran: 'When you work you are a flute through whose heart the whispering of the hours turns to music. To love life through labour is to be intimate with life's innermost secret. All work is empty save when there is love, for work is love made visible.'

How many of us can say our work is 'love made visible'? And if this was the case, would you ever want to retire?

There has been considerable focus in recent years on why areas of the world have higher concentrations of centenarians than others. *Live to 100* and *Blue Zones* on Netflix are fascinating documentaries that explore longevity. For years, I have been listening to the well-meaning warnings about instigating a pension fund, else face a grim retirement. While watching the centurions, however, I was struck by the lack of pensions. Many of these people lived in poorer areas of the world, where to live was to work and to work was to live. There was no separation. These people were vibrant and performed their daily tasks with purpose and presence.

So much of human endeavour is spent developing labour-saving devices, mechanising our world, creating wealth for people so that they can retire early. Our mindset towards work has changed dramatically and appears to be correlated with our ability to accumulate wealth. Creating a large pension fund allows us to dream and gives us the option of pursuing a life of self-centred indulgence, but it comes at a cost. In the words of Eugene Delacroix, 'We work not only to produce but to give value to time.'

MY JOURNEY TOWARDS LIBERATION

BY LIZ BARRY

I have never considered 'retirement' as an acceptable concept. For me, this sense of a possible and unconstrained time in my life has always been a reality and an aim; the prize being a period of absolute liberation.

While I accept we still need to use the word 'retirement' while discussing the world of pensions, we have now moved on from the 'old-world' idea of retirement being the short and sedentary bridge between the end of work and the graveyard. We now live vibrantly long and healthy lives, which far exceed those envisaged by the original developers of the status.

Personally, I always envisaged an early retirement for myself and actively financially arranged my career in order to achieve it, sometimes taking a serious short-term financial restraint in order to achieve the long-term goal. It's not that I thought I would be spending this part of my life unoccupied and on a beach, more than that, I knew if I was lucky enough, I could choose what work I want to do, or, indeed, not to do, and the work I enjoy and the aspects of it which I feel I can best contribute to.

The prospect of being able to treat what work I have now chosen to do as a form of hobby is exhilarating, because I'm still involved in the aviation lease and finance sector which I know so well, and still at board level, but I have the gift of social contact with people I not only like but also esteem, and have the ability to support them during challenges, some of which I have seen before but also vice-versa. My greatest help here has been referrals from industry friends, advisers and team members; something which I can never be grateful enough for.

As I write this, I am into my third year of liberation, and while I admit I may not be doing quite as much sport and socialising or travel as I had initially envisioned, such factors being impacted by COVID, I have learned to love many 'small' spaces in my current life, which my previous demanding career and home life as a working mother never allowed. The gift of being able to walk and appreciate the outdoors, or be the garden, in all weathers because I can now make the time, is one of them. The great joy of making new friendships with people outside of my school, college and work group has been uplifting and stimulating.

If possible, I do recommend taking a long overseas trip to mark the immediate time between ending one busy life and starting another. Additionally, it supplies an easy response to those endless questions about plans for the 'afterlife' from colleagues. Lining up a course you always wanted to do and having the focus of lectures and/ or exams to give an initial structure to the new life is also a good idea.

This absence from the old world of work allows your brain the downtime to organically choose to follow a new lifestyle and hobbies or revert to a different form of that previous work, on your own terms. You may in fact actually choose to agree with yourself that you enjoy the work itself, if not the restraints of working within an organisation.

Also, pragmatically, if you are coming from working for a company rather than yourself, you will need time to arrange your new income stream, pension entitlements, taxes, investments, health care and the nightmare of an unsupported access to IT. This area can be especially challenging, so it's good to be able to network with people who have walked the path before you and found solutions or consultants to support them.

The one surprise I've found is how fast the day goes, and I do wonder how I ever managed the life I led for so very many years – little sleep, the gym at dawn, long hours at work with operational management at board level, deal closings and home management. However, I enjoyed so many aspects of that life, the only change I would make would be to have left that world three years earlier. Now I watch my grown daughters map much of my previous lifestyle but can only hope they too will have a liberated lifestyle at some stage.

If you wonder how I developed this life pattern, it's because I was very close to my grandparents who had worked in the Far East and the mandatory retirement in the tropics was at the age of fifty! As a child I observed my grandfather leading a good and full lifestyle until he passed at eighty-five. I recognised then, that he had been living his liberated life for more years than he had worked. An appealing concept to me even then!

To learn more about this author: linkedin.com/in/ liz-barry-05128010

COMING FULL CIRCLE

BY CLAIRE CUFFE

At fifty-five years old, I'm coming full circle on a journey I began many years ago. When I left school, my working life began in the craft sector, which I adored, but left after twenty years for various reasons. I am now returning back to what I love, in a very different way.

I was always *that* child who made the craft project on *Blue Peter* and *Play School,* looking for empty washing up liquid-bottles and cardboard cores of toilet rolls, wishing I had double-sided sticky tape. At twelve years old, a friend and I started Saturday pottery classes. Although neither of my parents were involved in the arts, they very much encouraged my artistic interests. I did lots of extracurricular art classes during my teens, as well as studying art in school. I finished secondary school in 1985 and did a general craft course for a year, designed to give students a taste of different disciplines – weaving, batik, metalwork, jewellery, pottery, printing. I chose to specialise in pottery. I loved the immediate nature of clay; how it picks up the slightest impression you make on it, its earthiness, its malleability. All of this made me fall in love with the medium, and I immersed myself in it. At the time, I saw it as a lifestyle rather than just a career.

I went on to study ceramic design at Limerick School of Art from 1986-1989. There, I gained a solid foundation in the different aspects of ceramic design and production. The area I was drawn to straightaway was creating objects on the potter's wheel. At that time, making domestic pottery, mugs, plates, teapots etc. was considered a bit basic in the art school environment. It wasn't considered *creative enough*, but it was what I loved to do. I was encouraged instead to use the potter's wheel to create decorative one-off pieces. I did enjoy this, but really, I just wanted to make domestic pottery.

While working for a potter in Galway, after I left art school, I heard of a new Craft Council of Ireland course opening in County Kilkenny to train college graduates in the art of production pottery. This is the art of creating large quantities of domestic pottery, accurately and quickly. It was exactly what I was looking for, and in 1991, I was one of the lucky twelve to get a place on the course. We were taught how to create all sorts of shapes and sizes of pottery objects and to repeat the shapes over and over again, all the time gathering confidence, speed and proficiency. The aim was to train us to be *production potters* producing high volumes of work for established potters or to set up our own pottery business. I took to the training course like a duck to water. I loved nothing better than producing lines and lines of identical items. I simply loved it – the challenge, the rhythm, the repetition. I found it therapeutic and comforting and I would happily do it all day. That year was, hands down, the best experience in all the years I spent in pottery. It gave me the skills, at last, to do exactly what I wanted to do.

In 1992, I was offered a place on another Crafts Council of Ireland course, designed to give craftspeople a twelve-month opportunity to develop their own craft product and set up their own businesses. We were paid a weekly allowance, given our own workspace, access to mentors and full use of all facilities and equipment. It was an amazing opportunity to hone my skills, develop my own range and learn the necessary skills to run a business without the burden of trying to make a living at the same time. I concentrated on developing a domestic range of pottery to my own design and finish. We exhibited in various trade shows, exposing us to buyers and getting feedback on our products. It was a challenging year, and by the end of it, I felt a few years' experience working for other potters would be best for me. It felt too much of a challenge to set up my own business at the time. I returned home to Dublin in 1993 and worked for an established potter for a few happy years, before deciding to set up my own business in 1997.

My partner, an art teacher, and I built a small studio in our garden, and I worked from there for about two years. I found it very lonely working all day on my own, it really didn't suit me. I then got the opportunity through Fingal County Council to open a workshop in the grounds of nearby Malahide Castle. There were other small craft businesses there and it was an ideal situation having other craft workers around me, as well as the public coming in to watch us create our work and buy our products.

The first few years of my own pottery business were enjoyable and exciting, but being self-employed was hard work, as there is so much more to do than just making pottery. Accounts, marketing, packing orders, sales, etc. all took time, and I didn't enjoy those aspects. My partner helped out where possible but was teaching full-time. Our long-term aim was that they would be able to give up teaching and we would both be involved together in the pottery full-time. We gradually realised this was not going to be financially possible, as profit margins were tight. I was barely paying myself a living wage and the only way we could change that was to grow and take on staff. I didn't have the appetite for that. Borrowing money and taking risks was not something I wanted; it was never in my plan to be an employer. With pottery, as with all handmade crafts, anything made by hand is very labour intensive. The raw materials may be cheap, but if I was to charge *properly* for my time on each item, no-one would want to buy them. People expect to pay a certain price for a handmade mug or bowl, regardless of the amount of time it took to make it.

Over my seven years of self-employment, I became disillusioned with my life as a potter. I needed to find something that paid me enough to have a reasonable standard of living, and pottery was never going to give me that. I wanted to be able to do the normal things my friends and people of my age were doing: taking on a mortgage, owning a car, going on holidays.

With a heavy heart, I closed my pottery business in 2003 and took a job with Camden Pottery in Dublin, giving me time to consider what I wanted to do going forward. By then in my late thirties, I struggled to decide on what to do next. Whatever I chose, I couldn't afford to give up work entirely to retrain in something new, and I wanted to do something I would enjoy. It was a tall order and a hard balance to get right.

I met with a career advisor, doing various aptitude tests which highlighted my strengths and weaknesses. I eventually settled on retraining as a legal secretary; a very big change from pottery, but I needed that change. During the retraining period, I worked part-time as a potter and did some night shifts in a local wine shop, while doing my course part-time.

It took about fourteen months to make the transition. All at once, there were many changes happening in my life. My relationship of ten years ended and life turned upside-down for a while. It was a dark and difficult time, while I constantly questioned my decision to retrain. Now, I know it was absolutely the right thing to do. I needed to become financially independent, and moving away from pottery was the only way to do that.

I began my first job as a legal secretary in early 2007. It was a world away from life as a potter in every possible way, but that in itself was exciting and just what I needed. By the end of that year, I was in the process of buying my first house, had secured a mortgage and was even at the start of a new relationship. I enjoyed this new world of work I had stepped into. I liked the black-and-white nature of law. I liked the accuracy and certainty. Having felt so unanchored, this career change gave me the security I needed.

Everything settled down for me and I was happy, but there was still a little voice telling me that while this career served its purpose in many practical ways, it didn't really 'feed the soul'. Over time, I realised there was something missing. By then, in my early forties, I had twenty-five years of working life left and knew the 'law' wasn't what I wanted to do for the next two and a half decades.

I remained in the legal profession for six years and began looking at my options again. What was I interested in and what could I do for the final part of my working life? I contacted my careers advisor again. My situation was different this time. I had married, had financial stability and a lot more options open to me. My natural leaning is always towards the creative and I came out of the career advice process deciding to retrain as a hairdresser. Funnily enough, it was something that had been in the back of my mind for a long time. I felt it would move me back to a more creative and social lifestyle, with plenty of opportunities. I thought I would enjoy this hands-on type of work.

I researched all the available courses in Ireland. I visited hairdressing schools to talk to students and tutors and spent a day or two observing. I decided on Robert Chambers School in Dublin and began a sixteen-month full-time course in July 2012. We were a group of ten – two of us aged forty-five, while everyone else was mid-twenties or younger. It took some adjusting, but I got used to it. The course was full-on and for the most part very enjoyable. I don't know why, but I went through a crisis of confidence towards the end of the course and experienced some anxiety about finishing it. When I qualified, I quickly got a job in a salon close to home but struggled to feel confident and happy. My boss was challenging to work for, and I constantly questioned my decision to become a hairdresser.

A friend suggested I look at different areas within the hair industry. She had trichotillomania (compulsive hair-pulling) and had visited various wig outfitters. She felt I would be suited to that kind of work. The idea appealed to me, and I looked into it, contacting various wig shops. Only one replied, offering to meet me. When we met, the owner was open to me shadowing her for a day, which was a great experience. She said she would have a job vacancy in a few months as she was expanding the business, so when the time came, I applied and was offered the job to begin in Roches Hair Solutions in October 2014.

Working in the hair loss industry is extremely interesting. There are many areas of expertise, with a lot to learn, plus it is an industry constantly developing and changing. In my job as a hair loss advisor, I worked mainly with two types of clients: cancer patients who had hair loss through chemotherapy and clients with hair loss through other means, such as alopecia, health conditions and genetics. With cancer patients, the hair loss was mostly 'total', where they required a wig which looked as close as possible to their existing hair. For hair loss through alopecia, for example, hair pieces were often more suitable to cover the problem area and blend in with their own hair. I needed to be a hairdresser to do this job, but it was very different to working in a regular salon.

Every client had different needs. The challenge was to assure them they were in safe hands. Typically, a first-time client would be extremely emotional. To put them at ease, so they could hopefully face their hair loss with less anxiety and fear, I wanted to ensure their first fitting was a really good match for their own hair. It was my job to choose the right style, colour, texture and density of wig or hair piece, along with cutting a fringe or putting in some layering; that was where my hairdressing skills came in. It was a great moment when the client finally looked in the mirror with their new wig on and saw themselves looking back. You could see their confidence returning straightaway. What appealed to me most was being able to help people through a difficult time, though it was often emotional for me too!

In my six years working as a hair loss advisor, I found my job both rewarding and difficult in equal measure. I worked four days a week for my first two years, reducing to three days a week for the following four years.

In late 2020, I was in the fortunate position of being able to choose to retire, as my wife and I were in a financial position to do so, at age fifty-nine and fifty-four respectively. If the job taught me anything, it was that life can change in a second! We can't presume we will have time to do all the things we want to do in the future. We were fortunate to be in a good financial position and wanted to take the opportunity to spend more time together, rather than wait until we were at a more 'usual' age to retire.

Our plan was to buy a campervan and travel, for several months at a time, over the coming years. COVID put a halt on 2021, but in early 2022 we finally bought an old campervan. We spent a few months getting it fixed up and travelled around Ireland during the summer and autumn, getting familiar and confident with how everything worked. Look out Europe, here we come!

With my life now coming full circle, I am re-embracing the craft aspect of my life and am loving tapping into my creativity. The most important difference now is there is no pressure to earn a living from it. I have complete freedom to pursue what I love to do and that is a wonderful feeling!

I love to draw and am taking classes, with plenty of time to practise at home. I volunteer at our local theatre and enjoy all that has to offer in terms of the arts and getting to know people in my local community. I do classes in a nearby print studio, trying different methods of printing and effects, and have discovered this is something I have a talent for. I have gathered basic equipment and materials, producing several prints at home as gifts for family and friends. This is a craft with so many possibilities and I'm excited to explore it. I've always loved to cook and now have time to engage with that, to the detriment of my waistline … I love to try new recipes and now have the time to do it, with willing 'guinea pigs' to test it! It is two years since I stopped working and, can honestly say, I am so happy. I fill each day with great ease and sometimes find it difficult to fit everything in. I am excited about the future and wake each morning looking forward to the day ahead of me.

WRITE THE NEXT CHAPTER

BY BRIAN CHRISTOPHER GIDDENS

I took a circuitous route on the way to my primary professional career, so it's fitting that post-retirement has me embarking on a completely different path. In this chapter, I'll share my professional journey, my transition into retirement and a brand-new life as a writer of fiction and poetry, providing some insights into what I learned along the way.

As I write this, I find it surprising it's been just eighteen months since I retired as an administrator with a major academic medical centre in Seattle. My work involved overseeing multiple patient and family support programs (social work and care coordination, interpreter services, housing, patient/family financial grants, bereavement services), as well as utilisation management programs for two hospitals. During my tenure, my budgets and responsibilities continually expanded, as did the number of programs and staff I managed. In addition, I taught a master's level course annually for over twenty years, most recently at the highly ranked University of Washington School of Social Work.

My retirement was delayed for nearly a year due to COVID. As we all know, the pandemic thrust health care into chaos, as systems had to be developed to manage the virus and its consequences. As an administrator, I wanted to be present, to help reassure staff and assist with the development of new processes of care. COVID presented many challenges, but I was glad to be onsite and actively helping. Many good things came of the pandemic. We moved much more quickly on concepts such as telehealth, programs for employee wellness and retention and redefining organisational priorities.

Once the vaccine became available and we began to return to normal operations, it seemed like the right time to leave. I was in a good place professionally, my programs were led by strong managers, goals were being met and I felt respected and appreciated. It had been a 'good run'.

When I first enrolled in university, like many other eighteen-year-olds, I had no idea what I would do for a living. There were no role models in my family when it came to higher education. Though my siblings were hardworking and gainfully employed, I was the first to graduate from college. I explored several majors, including communications (a journalist?), drama (an actor?), and finally settled on political science. I had no desire to be a politician or an academic, but I had more credits in that major than anything else and wanted to graduate within four years.

By the time I graduated, I shifted back to pursuing acting. I had performed in community theatre and school productions since I was a teen and thought that if I didn't at least try to make it professionally, I would always wonder what might have happened. So, I packed up my Volkswagen Bug and drove from

Seattle to Los Angeles. I had no job or place to live, but I did have a stack of head shots, for what I hoped would get me a slew of auditions and meetings with agents. Soon I was waiting tables in Beverly Hills, living in a cockroach-infested apartment in North Hollywood, taking acting classes and hoping to get 'discovered'.

Venturing out from the safety of my hometown and having to independently find my way was a life experience I never regretted. But the more time spent in that environment, the more I realised I just wasn't that dedicated. What I wanted was to be a *movie star*, not necessarily an actor. Being committed to the acting profession required a willingness to wait tables for as long as it took to get an acting job. Or doing workshops for nothing and trying to fit in paying jobs around performances. That is, if you won the audition. I worked with several fellow waiters, some approaching their forties, who were still waiting for their 'big break'.

But I discovered more than the realisation that I didn't want to be an aging waiter/actor; I wanted something more meaningful, less superficial. I have nothing but respect for actors, but much of that business requires a focus on how you look, who you know and being in the right place at the right time. Maybe it was my political science background, but I wanted to do something that made a difference.

Back to Seattle I went, finding a job with planned parenthood, becoming the first male pregnancy counsellor in the state. I had volunteered for a crisis line in college and always enjoyed helping others, and now was being paid to do the same type of work. But because the pay was so low, I had to find yet another waiter job to pay my bills. It was clear that if I was to continue in this work, I needed to go back to school for a master's degree.

Thus was my path to social work. And that route launched me into mental health practice, which led to working with geriatric patients and then the world of long-term care and health care. By the time I moved to my last position, I had worked up the ladder at another major hospital system, gaining valuable administrative experience, then rerouted to serving as part of the director team for a community-based HIV/AIDS program during the height of the AIDS pandemic. Finally, I went back into general health care in the multi-hospital system, where I stayed for twenty-three years until my retirement.

I was in my early sixties and could have continued in my role for several more years, so why did I want to retire? There were several factors, more pertaining to quality of life than any clear idea of wanting to do *something else*. At various times during my career, I was dissatisfied, as I'm sure is the norm for any working professional. Even the best of jobs can seem uninspiring at times. Some of the dissatisfaction was due to boredom, sometimes I felt a lack of appreciation and other times there were new opportunities beckoning. Over time in health care, I felt the pressures grow, not just for me, but for health care workers and administrators in general.

As my professional responsibilities grew, in sync with the increasingly challenging health care field, work became harder. Staff were stressed, requiring more problem-solving and, at times, difficult encounters to correct negative behaviours. I was often on pager twenty-four seven, and as many have experienced in the last decade, the line between work and non-work time became diffused. I checked messages constantly, from first thing in the morning to before turning off the lights at night, whether it was a weekday or a weekend.

My quality of life had significantly diminished. At the same time, I was increasingly aware of the limitations of time. I knew of two people, in my last few years of working, who died suddenly; both were my age. I became aware of others in my world who were experiencing health issues and seeing their retirement dreams not come to fruition.

The concern about finances was also present, almost illogically so. As part of a long-term marriage between two professionals, there was enough saved to fund an early retirement. I was making more than I had ever dreamed of, but the idea of walking away from that created anxiety. My husband retired three years before I did, and prior to that time I began to review our expenses more carefully. We went to a financial planner, but even with assurance of a professional, it felt like a major step to go from making and saving money, to taking withdrawals from our savings.

It was at one of the financial planning sessions that the reason for retiring became all the more apparent. We were looking at 'end dates' – when we would no longer be drawing down the savings, *because we would likely be dead.* That process suddenly made the remaining years seem quite finite. The average life expectancy for an American male in 2019 was just under seventy-nine years. If I retired at the end of my sixty-second year, that meant I had sixteen years left. And who knew how much of that time I would remain healthy? I didn't necessarily know what retirement would look like, but I did know I wanted to have time to enjoy it.

The lead-up to retirement was hectic. After twenty-three years, there is a lot to pass on, whether or not people end up finding it useful. Hours were spent reviewing digital information, including thousands of saved emails, most of which could be deleted. It was bittersweet realising that what had once seemed so important to save, no longer meant much. It was a humbling reminder of how transitory our work can be.

I still remember that wonderful feeling, on my first Monday of retirement, waking up knowing I had no meetings that day, nothing to worry about and no responsibilities except to myself and my family. It's hard to express just how freeing that was. I no longer had to constantly be strategising or preparing.

So, once that feeling of immense relief passed over me, how did I approach the transition? I have always been someone who is very organised, creating lists of 'to-dos' for each day, and longer ones for the week and beyond. Thus, I created a new list for things to do upon retirement. I subtitled that list in big block letters, *ONLY DO WHAT YOU WANT TO DO.* As simple as that sounds, it has been an important mantra for me. Making such a significant transition in life is a great opportunity to reconsider how one is spending their time. There were people I had grown apart from over the years that I realised I no longer wanted to spend time with. There were volunteer activities I had participated in that didn't offer the same appeal anymore.

Of course, it's impossible to cut out everything. I'm not going to ignore a friend in need or absolve myself of any social responsibility. But by starting with my mantra, I was able to resist filling up the calendar with activities I didn't want to waste my time doing. It was that 'finite' concept that time was more valuable than ever. It allowed me to start thinking about what I did want to do. One of those activities was returning to a love of writing.

From an early age I enjoyed writing poetry and short stories. Over twenty years ago, in one of those phases where I was questioning whether I wanted to stay in my field, I took a nine-month evening course in fiction writing, starting some short stories and drafting a novel. But work was less demanding then. In my case, I found writing required consistent quiet time and, with work commitments, there just wasn't enough time in the day for me to sit down and focus on writing.

To help me get started this time around, I signed up for a writing class. One of the positives from COVID was the advent of more online learning opportunities, and I was able to join a respected program through Stanford University. My class involved daily exercises, which required both carving out consistent writing time and practising writing in a variety of genres.

The class was a great learning experience. I was able to spend time with others who enjoyed writing, and the exercises initiated some ideas for additional writing projects. The writing time expanded into a few hours each morning, as I worked on assignments from the class but also on my own growing list of ideas. The class was the first of several I have taken, covering a variety of writing topics.

Included in the classes were learnings about the publication process. When friends and family asked what I hoped to accomplish with my revived interest in writing, my first response was to say I just enjoyed writing and wanted to keep creating stories and improving my skills. But I found a carryover from my professional life was a need for external validation, and for me, that meant having my work published. Writing is a bit like acting. Who or what gets chosen is a very subjective process, and there

CREATE YOUR BEST LIFE

are more actors and writers than avenues for their work to be seen. Still, I felt I couldn't really call myself a writer until I was published.

In my prior professional life, promotions and pay increases served to tell me I was valued. For me, and perhaps for others, I saw a neediness in that quest for validation that continued to a lesser degree post-retirement. It is likely the reason some new retirees go back to work, move to consulting or fall headfirst into depression.

Writing was not meant to be a replacement for that sense of validation, but I do have to watch myself. I tell myself I'm in this for the writing, not to be a famous author. But I certainly have moments of doubt as to whether I'm *any good* at writing. This is where the classes are helpful. They allow me to receive feedback.

I wrote a few short stories within a few months of my retirement and discovered an online tool, called Submittable, a portal that offers listings of publications accepting stories or poems. I jumped at the chance to send out my work. I would finish a new piece, send it out to a few journals, and wait. Initially, I was confident my work was going to be accepted. Instead, I waited a long time, through many rejections.

I corresponded with one journal editor after he had rejected my work a second time, stating I didn't feel I could call myself a writer until I was published. I told him that some nights I woke up with something in my head that just had to be written down. He kindly responded that if I got up in the middle of the night to write, I was a writer, regardless of whether I am published. I took that to heart. Yet, still, I was tired of being rejected and decided to create my own book of photo-haikus I had been posting on

Instagram, to give out to friends and family as a holiday gift. Fortunately, before I completed the book, about six months after I first started submitting, one of my short stories was accepted by a small journal. I could finally call myself a writer.

I took several other steps to cement this new interest. I met with other friends and acquaintances who liked to write, forging a small community of writers. I started a separate email account to manage my writing-related communications, in a sense creating a new persona, changing my name to include my middle name. I began writing poetry, also taking classes to better learn that craft. I grew my Instagram account by posting more often, but only my photo-haikus. I started writing a novel, based on a first chapter I wrote many years ago.

While this new writing life is different from my role as an administrator, there are skills I can apply to my new work. One of these is my organisational ability.

On the advice of another writer, I created two Excel spreadsheets to track my submissions, one for my poems and one for my stories. Just like any other profession, there is a business side to creative work. I needed to track who I sent my work to, when it was acknowledged as being 'in process' for review, and when I got a final answer as to whether the work was accepted or rejected. This allowed me to not duplicate submissions, and to assess the average turnaround time for various publications.

I also continued carving out time for writing. I avoided scheduling other commitments on weekday mornings. I had a set physical space for working and developed a routine where I would review my 'to-dos', then dive into whatever project I was prioritising for the day. This reminded me of a work habit I had, when I would purposely arrive early before any scheduled meetings to review my lists before starting the day. There was a familiarity and comfort in retaining this long-held habit, helping me to centre my day and remember my purpose.

Even though I have integrated some of my former work habits into my new retirement routine, my life is much different than before. There is no longer a focus on deadlines, for example. I still differentiate between weekdays and weekends and try not to do my writing on the weekend. The dowager countess in *Downton Abbey*, so marvellously played by Maggie Smith, asked the question, 'What is a weekend?' but I've yet to get to that point.

This new life is not just about writing. My husband and I, always avid travellers, are now exploring much more frequently, with multiple trips planned far into next year. Another 'to-do' for me was enhancing and growing my friendships with others, so I consciously initiate lunches with new and old friends on a regular basis, and we have more time for hosting events at home. When the demands of work were present, I wanted to go home and not have to socialise. I needed to recharge on the weekends, focusing on quiet activities such as gardening or cooking. Now, because I have so little stress, I can expand myself outward, which certainly helps to enrich my life.

Even though I am less than two years into it, I have made some key discoveries about myself and this major transition we call retirement. One of the most important, is the realisation that 'it's not just about me'. For those readers in relationships, moving from the work world to retirement is not just a transition for the retiree, but also for the spouse or partner. My husband imagined my retirement differently than how it has turned out.

He had hoped for much more spontaneity in our days and more time together.

But I enthusiastically jumped into my writing, creating a world that was different than my spouse had envisioned. We had to come to terms with that through better communication, clarification of goals and compromise. I was aware of the potential conflict. As more time was focused on my classes and writing time, I created parameters. I tried not to write on weekends or while we were traveling. I made sure afternoons were free for other things, and if something else was suggested, such as a one-day car trip or a hike, I would plan not to write on those days. But as I began writing more and seeing some success, there were concerns my writing could become a full-time job.

What I discovered was that as my excitement grew, and this work became more integrated into my life, there was a perceived threat the writing would shadow out our relationship. Anyone who has been in relationships knows they are dynamic. As people change, so does the partnership. Changing dynamics help to keep a relationship fresh, but they can also be a challenge, especially if the changes are pertaining to just one person in the partnership. Increasing check-ins, clarifying goals and compromising as to schedules and availability can help to manage change. Sharing the joys and difficulties of new developments is also important, so the other person can share in the ownership of the change.

Another key discovery was the realisation I was adopting a new persona, in a sense. As mentioned, for my writing, I began to include my middle name, for the first time as an adult. I labelled myself as a writer and introduce myself as such in certain situations. For years, I had called myself a social worker or health care administrator; now I was someone new. I was surprised by the psychological impact of this new persona. It felt more than just a change in name, but also a symbol of a major life change.

This new persona was reinforced by the reactions of others. When I first was published, I sent out the notice to a wide swath of people … friends, former colleagues, family. As an introvert, I don't often share much about myself, so the news that I was suddenly published, exacerbated the surprise. I have to say, it has been fun to surprise people. I certainly have surprised myself and hope to keep doing so.

A third key discovery is the significant change in lifestyle over-all, from the old workday routine. No more waking up before 5:30am to start my day. No more sleepless nights worrying about some project or HR issue. No putting on a tie and a suit jacket. No more rushing through a sandwich at my desk while scrolling through emails.

Instead, there are a lot more walks with my husband and the dog. There are trips being taken, without having to fit them into available vacation days. I 'exercise' less, but move more, keep up the garden, complete house projects and get outside as much as possible. I spend much more time with my husband and friends. We host more, without worrying about the time it takes to set up and take down after a dinner party. We don't necessarily get up or go to bed too much later, but if we have something that makes us short on sleep, we don't fret about it. The pluses are plentiful with retirement. The cons negligible.

In terms of my new writing career, I have published five works so far, both short stories and poetry, and have several more look-ing for a home. I have completed a novel, and the first full draft is now with some volunteer readers for feedback. My writing goals continue to be to develop as a writer and have my work published, increasingly in venues that reach more readers.

I also want to keep on working on the shared goals I have with my partner. Seeing more of the world. Spontaneously going out for a movie. Strengthening our friendships, which seem to become all the more important as we age. And of course, staying as healthy as possible so that my 'end date' can be delayed for a long time to come.

To learn more about this author: brianchristophergiddens.com

PLAN? WHAT PLAN?

BY MARIE GRIFFIN

Apart from subliminal catholic repression, my childhood growing up in the sixties in Ireland's rural North Cork was idyllic. Surrounded by rich agricultural green fields, my parents purchased a site on a hill overlooking one of the tributaries of the great Blackwater River and built their forever home there. They then proceeded to bring two strapping boys and two stroppy girls into the world!

Typical of small country schools, my primary school class was made up of three boys and five girls – yes, a sum total of eight of us. And the stroppiest of those eight? Yes, perhaps me! My mother was one of the three teachers in the school, so for a period of three whole years, I had the misfortune of being one of her pupils! In my adult years, my mother would have said the misfortune was all hers! She was Mammy in the car going to school, and inside the school gate, she was Mrs Griffin. I hated that; I think she probably did too. But we both survived.

As my father was a manager in North Cork Co-Operative (he was nicknamed 'the pen pusher' by the local farming community he served), I lamented being one of only a few kids in the playground who didn't live on a farm, so I spent most of my spare time on our neighbour's farm. Looking after the animals was never hard work to me. Throughout our childhood, hard work was instilled into us all by our parents. I was the happiest schoolgirl in the whole of Ireland when my father eventually bought a farm.

My love for farming, and animals in particular, grew over the years which prompted my aspiration to qualify as an agricultural advisor. In the late 1970s, the scholarship structures prohibited girls from accessing limited agricultural college places. So, despite numerous applications, meetings and interviews, my prospects were thwarted from the start. Without graduating with a certificate from that college, I could not apply for the university program. My second career choice was to join the Gardai; I think a career in the Irish police force would have suited my stroppy nature well! While I'm pretty sure I would have passed all the fitness tests, I didn't meet the then minimum height criteria. At barely 5'2", I was a whole three inches short of the 5'5" minimum requirement for women. Thwarted again.

With plan A and plan B no longer options, I literally had no plan C. I stumbled onto, and completed, my business studies course in a Cork college, without any plans or ideas for next steps. Early eighties Ireland offered little prospects and huge levels of emigration. However, I secured a permanent administrative job in the city, bought a car and started to enjoy all the benefits of city life. For me, that didn't mean drinking and partying, it meant training and total dedication to my second love after animals – sport. Playing at local, club and county levels for many years, the pinnacle of my sporting career was in 1985, aged twenty-three, lining out for the senior ladies Cork County Gaelic football team, as well as wearing the green soccer jersey for Ireland. Sadly, Flower Lodge in Cork against the decidedly stronger English team, was not a good outcome for the Irish.

A week later, I was on a flight to New York City. Nowhere to live, no job, no working visa and no idea where to start ... but there the adventure began.

With nothing to lose, the naive fearlessness of youth on my side and the anonymity of New York offering me the opportunity to be whatever I wanted to be, I knocked on doors ... any doors ... all doors. UNICEF employed me for a day until they determined my holiday visa entry date to the US exceeded their allowable margin for legal status application. So, this stroppy twenty-something-year-old headed down Wall Street. Via an employment agency (who 'manipulated my visa status'), I landed myself a job with a large underwriting corporate, headquartered on the fourteenth floor of the World Trade Centre. Six months later, on a cold December Friday morning, HR summoned me to their offices and offered to put me on their trainee underwriter program. I just thought – *God Bless America, the land of opportunity!* Delighted with myself, I said yes. Long story short, sadly, because of my precarious visa status, I had to leave the building that day!

But the agency had a new job for me Monday morning with a small mid-town Jewish accountancy firm. It felt like the United Nations in that small office – a combination of African-American, Korean, Israeli Jews and one Irish. And I loved it. With their encouragement, I undertook New York state tax exams ... and subsequently passed. But my legal status caught up with me again, prohibiting my graduation. I was loving life in New York and its diversity. I had so many friends there, playing many sports and was able to explore other parts of the US. However, being an illegal alien was beginning to wear more than a little thin.

I didn't have a plan when I arrived in London in the late 1980s, but Ireland still offered few job options. As an Irish national, I was able to legally work in Britain. A huge plus! Turns out London wasn't a difficult place to find a job and London Dockland's new driverless light railway got me to work each day. Buying a garden flat in Barnet wasn't a plan either, but I quickly realised paying rent was cost prohibitive; it made sense to buy. Or at least it made sense until eight months later. Margaret Thatcher's government decided to take the heat out of the over-heating UK property market by pushing mortgage interest rates prohibitively high. Those of us on variable rates suffered badly. Interest rates went from 10% to 15% in around nine months, pushing me and many others over the edge. Property prices duly collapsed, and mortgage defaulters went out in protest. So, I rented out my flat and somehow got my job back in New York (I know!) for another year plus and financed my London mortgage deficit from the United States.

Ireland still wasn't the land of opportunity when I moved back in 1991. I was determined to move 'home' to Cork, but the only job I was offered was a seven-month contract in Dublin's Coopers & Lybrand. I don't know how it happened, but time rolled on, and my seven months contract turned into seven years. That's how Dublin accidentally became my home and offered me other job opportunities including seven years with Aon's captive management arm. At Aon, I put myself front and centre of the company's inaugural conference management project to globally champion Dublin's captive management industry. By then in my mid-thirties, I didn't know it at the time, but that was the beginning of my retirement journey!

Managing an international two-day conference was never part of any plan for me (I never did have a plan, did I?), but I soon immersed myself in developing the program content, sourcing industry speakers from around the globe, devising and selling sponsorship packages … and all the rest. The more the sponsors, association directors, delegates and speakers demanded of me, the more I thrived. This stroppy Corkonian had found her niche!

Owned by one of my former employers, I ran Event Management International for five years from 2005. I expanded into other industry associations in the financial services sector, the Celtic tiger was roaring in Ireland by then and business was booming. Until it all came tumbling down … 2008 wasn't too bad, 2009 was horrible and 2010 wasn't any better. Conference income collapsed. Selling sponsorship packages to cash-strapped corporate banks and asset managers was an impossible mission. Reinsurers and fintechs reigned in on all discretionary spend. Corporates across the globe asked employees to stay behind the desk, firefighting against the financial collapse impacting the global financial markets crash.

When the Celtic tiger was roaring, I took on BES investment opportunities amongst others. I was founder investor in an event management portal. When that flopped in the crash, my investment flopped with it. A retail stock management portal startup I'd invested in limped along. No buy-out was in sight, so I expected no return on investment (ROI) there any time soon. I remortgaged my house to pay my share of the debts we had incurred before winding up a serviced offices venture I was involved in.

I'd never planned to be an entrepreneur and start up my own business but ... desperate strokes for desperate folks. I knew I could make an event management company viable if I could reduce the overheads. So, in May 2010, aged forty-eight, Summit Focus was born. It felt like a huge leap of faith. I had to believe in myself all over again. I had to convince industry associations, sponsors and delegates alike that all would be as before. I set to work, growing and developing a new conference management company, but this time I was the 100% owner.

Despite a slow start during 2011, 2012 and 2013, the hard work started to pay off from 2014/2015 onwards. After 2016, Ireland became the location of choice for many firms leaving London for Brexit-related reasons. By 2018, I was capitalising on these mobilisations and business was booming for Summit Focus. By then, I was married, had buried one of my parents and was looking at my own life and mortality. What might the next chapter of my life look like?

Deciding with my spouse that we wanted to enjoy a life with more freedom, we thought about the financial implications of retiring early, as well as dreaming about how we might spend our time. A camper purchase was high on the list, an opportunity to hit the open road across Europe and see where it might take us. I set my sights on more time with family and friends, more hiking, more mountains and more head space that had, up to then, been focused on running the business. With growing enthusiasm and cashflow projections out of the way, I set about cashing in on my (eventual!) entrepreneurial success.

Preparations for selling the business began. Step one, the housekeeping. Client contracts had to be airtight, company accounts and company secretarial had to be in order and ready for due diligence processes. Next step, identify potential buyers. Surprisingly, I ended up with a rather long list of both national and international organisations. However, on more careful scrutiny, I ended up with quite a short list of more realistic targets. I had to cautiously approach these targets while navigating the tricky challenge of keeping it secret! I didn't want to spook my clients. As I was inexperienced in the art of selling a business, I had no idea how to prepare a memorandum of information for the company. I engaged the services of an experienced UK-based former PWC colleague. I made the initial target approach, talked through the proposition and future prospects and she did the negotiations on my behalf.

By late 2019, I had a buyer, purchase details agreed, due diligence completed and I was feeling very excited. However, the buyer withdrew just before Christmas. Disheartened but undeterred, I ventured on the road again with other potential prospects. Of course, I had to continue to run the business and keep it successful. By early 2020, I again had a buyer on the table; more due diligence and processes were underway. In March, COVID had swept its way across Europe, and Ireland went into lockdown along with countries around the globe. Conferences were initially postponed and eventually cancelled. Unsurprisingly, by September that year, the sale fell through … again! It took until December 2021 for a buyer to finally sign on the dotted line. We celebrated Christmas in a big way that year.

I believe I have the best of both worlds. As part of the sale agreement, I have been retained as a consultant for a period of three years. I carried out the handover transition during spring 2022; the UK buyers carry the full responsibility of conference delivery. I have none of the burden but do like that I'm still somewhat involved. It's like a gradual transitioning from full-time working into an eventual full-time retirement. This, I believe, has suited me better than retiring cold turkey.

One of the joys of my semiretirement is that I have flexibility to try new things. I've recently spent two days on a movie set in Wicklow with British actress Leslie Mansfield in the leading role of *Moonflower Murders*. No, I haven't decided to start a new career as an actress! I was one of the movie extras! In addition, I was recently 'a bag lady' for a week on a South West Ireland tour with a Canadian hiking group! My friend is a tour guide, and the full minibus couldn't fit both the visitors and their bags too, so I drove a van with their bags. I hope to take up many other varied invitations and opportunities as they arise.

My spouse has now retired also. We bought a sixteen-year-old campervan and hit the road in March 2023 for our first three-month adventure across Spain, south of France and northern Italy, before crossing back to Ireland through the middle of France. The trip has given us the appetite to do many more such journeys in the years to come. This year's planned three-month camper trip will be southern Germany – Bavaria and the Black Forest. We can now spend more time with family and friends, and I've been able to sign up for my first week-long hiking holiday too.

I will never know how my life might have turned out if I'd been able to follow the path I initially wanted to choose. But in the end, I can only assume for me, as I assume for all, where we end up must have been our destiny all along. We just didn't know it. Let's enjoy the journey.

To learn more about this author: linkedin.com/in/ mariegriffin

A DRIVE FOR FINANCIAL INDEPENDENCE

BY ANONYMOUS

My parents only ever seemed to argue about money. I don't remember this causing me upset or concern, but it did leave a lasting impression. My mother was a stay-at-home mum and my father's salary didn't go a long way with four hungry and energetic kids. We were a happy middle-class family but the only discord I observed was about spending those hard-earned punts – we need to 'spend less on the weekly shopping', 'leave the immersion on for a shorter time' and 'spend less time in the shower', 'go on shorter vacation breaks'. It was the reality of living in Ireland in the 1970s and 1980s, but I was determined to never let money dictate my enjoyment of life. This was without doubt an opinion I formed during the innocence of youth, but one which formed the basis for how I would live my twenties and thirties.

My focus here is the importance of financial independence in enabling choices during retirement or rewiring your life. Money is necessary to allow a flexibility in your life at that next stage. The lifestyle and opportunities now available to me and my family are due to how I approached the 'necessary evil' that is money. This is a story of my journey; certainly unconventional, often disorganised, frequently without a goal, but enjoyable nonetheless and full of experience with great memories.

I wasn't fixated on money or material wealth, but from an early age, I wanted to experience life to the fullest, albeit with limited money. My first challenge arrived when I was sixteen years old and informed my parents I wanted to do an interrail train tour of Europe during the summer. They quickly retorted that they would not agree, as I was too young and, regardless, didn't have sufficient money to travel in Europe for a month. I questioned if I would be permitted to travel if I raised enough money. I remember them laughing out loud and reiterating there would be no way I could raise that amount of money. Challenge accepted! A few months later, I had enough. I sold vegetables from my garden to the neighbours, worked any odd jobs I could find and sold my beloved bike. I raised £400 for forty days travelling around Europe. I slept on trains and in train stations, lost a stone in weight that I didn't need to lose but lived my best life. I was hooked on experiencing life.

As with most young people, I had no plan for my life. I didn't know what career to pursue or where I wanted to live. I presumed I would get married, and I wanted to have children.

I went to a public school in a medium-sized town. The quality of teaching was poor, and the school was rough. I was one of the minorities who went to university. I completed a degree in economics and faced the working world at a brutal time. The impending recession prompted a masters to be completed, as the unemployment rate for graduates reached 50%. There was little chance of a job in Ireland or in Europe in those depressing times. I did not apply for any jobs during the 'milk-round' of that year. I came to the conclusion that my education was more theoretical than practical and that it was a good time to accumulate additional job skills. I departed for Germany under the European-funded exchange scheme, COMET, allowing me to learn German and do a basic business/accounting course. I had very little money and slept on a couch for a year, but I loved the experience of travelling, living and learning in a new country.

I eventually obtained an internship with a manufacturing company in northern Germany and thus started my career. I moved from manufacturing to finance and worked for three different finance companies over the next twenty years. I really enjoyed working with smart people and the intellectual challenge of the job, however, I wished to continue to travel and experience more of the world. When the opportunity arose within the company, I was always the one to put my hand up to relocate to another location in the world – often before I was informed of the destination! I worked all over Europe, North America, Asia and Australia during this time. At times, my promotion prospects could have been better if I'd remained in a stable role, and indeed, the new job in a different location was often less secure over the medium term. However, I had resolved that there was always a 'Plan B' – if things didn't work out, I would leave my job, drop everything and travel to find a job with another company elsewhere. Several times this option came close to being actioned.

During this time, I adopted the mindset to work hard and seek to accumulate wealth, rather than spend money frivolously. All the while, I continued to travel extensively and experience the richness of life. I married and we had three wonderful children together. Thankfully my wife wanted to travel too. She engaged in a career she wanted, and one that also allowed her to travel and switch locations – working remotely.

In my early forties, I had reached a point whereby I could significantly change the path of my future career and life. While working in finance had been good to me, I was adamant I no longer wanted to work for someone else. I had continually saved and invested money, so I knew this new change of lifestyle would not involve money-related stress for the family. This life change was not a result of a sudden realisation, it was part of a long-term plan to exit a 'regular' job and eventually embark on a different life. I simply wanted to do more things I enjoy doing, with people I like, with the inherent freedom and flexibility to do it. Many people suggest following a passion when first looking for a career, I thought it best to engage in what I was good at and follow my passions afterwards.

So, I resigned from my job and exited the mainstream work-force. I still didn't know what I wanted to 'be', but I did know what I wanted as a minimum starting out on this journey:

- Significantly reduced income-focused working hours.
- Significantly increased time with my young family.
- Concentration on activities that focus me and my family on enriching experiences – nature, charity, travel, hobbies and, yes, more travel.

It can be said that some of these goals could also be described as 'values', and maybe that inherently was my thinking.

The key to being able to remove yourself from a steady pensionable nine-to-five career, and instead to live as you wish, is being aware of the state of your financial independence. From my first pay cheque, I would save a portion of my income and invest it in a diversified manner. As a quick example on saving and compounding returns, if as a fifteen-year-old you save, for example €185 every month, at an average investment return of 7%, you will have over a million euros by the time you are sixty-five. If instead you start saving in your fifties, with a view to retire at sixty-five, it will require you to save many thousands a month to achieve the same goal. In better times, I invested more of my income, and some years the investment returns were poor, but the overall sum kept growing. I had simply saved money over my career and budgeted for basic investment returns vs expenses for my required future lifestyle. I knew we could live well in the future on these returns.

I have noticed over my years that many of my peers increased their spending commensurate with an increase in earnings. In fact, in some countries where I worked, it was usual for company graduates to buy their first car for an amount of money equal to their gross annual salary! Many people with good salaries believe their income will continue, ad infinitum, and spend accordingly but end up with no savings. Frequently, I heard the refrain from my peers that they needed to treat themselves with an expensive holiday to relieve the stress of life and work. They wanted to be pampered. Maybe I just had the view that I would treat myself in the future to a less stressed life and career. Or maybe, an expensive two-week holiday doesn't really fix inherent problems elsewhere in your life. Not that I denied myself or my family anything for us to live well, but I avoided buying material goods that tended to depreciate significantly in value or spend large amounts of money on short-term experiences. Our family travelled frequently, and it was not to the five-star resorts but sometimes to a homestay, agricultural tourism or backpacking. Our thinking was that the children would benefit and be more grounded from the experience.

Of course, on leaving my nine-to-five, I missed the social contact of my previous working life. I enjoyed interacting with people whether it be mentoring, advising on or developing their careers. I replaced that key element missing in my 'new' life with hobbies like cycling, swimming, sailing; activities that offered a wide variety of social contact to compensate. I pursued projects I wanted to do for pleasure and learning, obtaining a pilot's licence, woodworking and car mechanic work. I also took up activities for enjoyment and creativity where there was a potential of earning revenue for my endeavours – screenplay writing and movie production. I was finally doing things I wanted to do, in my own time.

From the age of forty, I decided I would work with charity organisations in an attempt to give back to the community. I volunteered any expertise I could and worked with over fifteen charities over five years. Probably naively on my part, I had assumed that those who work in the management of charities are people who genuinely want to help others. Unfortunately, in my experience, this was rarely the case, and working with a multitude of charities has done little to change my opinion. Sometimes these organisations appeared more political than those in a capitalistic, commercial environment. Of course, there are many well-managed charity organisations, but my experiences suggest they are in the minority. This was one change of life experience that was deeply disappointing.

There was a period of time during the change where I struggled with adjusting from the intense task-based time-focused life of a busy career, to just experiencing and living. Simple things like taking time to do nothing except go for a walk in a forest, reading a book (which wasn't on self-improvement) or a swim, which was not intensely exercised focused. I have seen other friends who've retired trying to fill their time with achievement-based intensive tasks, for example, master a musical instrument, complete an ironman, read a certain number of books. I didn't want to fall down that well-worn path of replacing the stress and adrenaline of the job environment with the stress of an ill-advised hobby. In my first couple of years of trying to relax, I realised I had morphed over my career into a time-hungry, self-absorbed individual and this had to be unlearned over time.

With respect to my hobby of screenplay writing ... never have I been as useless with a role that I enjoyed so much. I marvel at the skill and expertise of a talented TV series writer, being able to interweave a dazzling plot and characters. They deserve all the success in an incredibly difficult role. I struggle to write engaging dialogue or develop characters in a movie plot, but I do love researching the history behind different eras and doing detective work on shady real-life characters. I enjoy movies and TV shows more nowadays as I can relate and better understand how they were developed.

I now have time to assist others, whether it be the mundane, moving furniture or more complex financial planning for their future. This has been rewarding. I am able to impart my experience to help others with financial freedom sooner. A worthy goal in my view.

Some friends and family were concerned about my move away from a good pensionable job. I've received many suggestions of jobs over the years. Indeed, many people thought I had *failed* to be able to continue a good career into my fifties. Frequently, people ask me how I could possibly be happy without a focused career – 'You have to do something!'

So, where do I stand now on a happiness scale? I would say I am content, not stressed, fit, healthy and sleep very well. I have the flexibility to do activities with my family whenever I wish. My family receive much of my attention and, thankfully so far, seem happy and balanced. My pastimes (including some traditional work activities, lol) brighten my day. I am still financially independent and have assets that will create an income for the rest of my life. I imagine my mental health situation is better than it would be if I was still in a busy career. One can never be sure of this, but I do know I would be less fit, less rested and more stressed if I was still working and depending on that work for my income and my future. I have too many friends who have passed or now have significant avoidable health problems due to that sort of stress.

This is my story. I have little advice to impart. I don't have information on pitfalls to avoid or any religious underpinnings to my journey. I saved money and invested continuously. I would describe my life as one where opportunities were seized. My focus mid-career was to work hard to make money in the years I could, in order to avoid working later in life. My intention was to allow myself and my family to enjoy our experience on this earth. I wanted freedom, flexibility and financial independence and I wanted it at a time of my life when I was healthy and wise enough to enjoy it with my friends and family. I am grateful to have been able to achieve that with no regrets.

THE POWER OF READING

BY MARY MAHON

I didn't have a blinding flash of how my life would go, perhaps this is the same for children today. What influences us as we grow can be like a throw of the dice; how lucky can you get? For opportunities to grow and develop, we are influenced by our family's circumstances and the society we live in. With the added advantage of education today, and the amount of information available to us through various media, can anyone have an inkling of what they would like to be or do?

My main influence was my parents. My father was always working but in his free time would be interested in what we were doing. He instilled in me kindness and an interest in nature. One day while I was attempting to trap a bird in the garden, he told me the bird's heart might stop with fright, so I never did that again. To this day, nature and the environment are very close to my heart. My mother was a great reader and encouraged my brother and me to read by buying us weekly comics. Reading was a great pastime. I remember many happy hours in the library browsing through books. She always encouraged us to read, and

I remember often asking her, 'What's this word?'

'When first I fell in love, I was very, very young,
with scarce a dozen words upon this tiny tongue,
first feelings came while standing at my mother's knee,
hey mam what's this BIFF! BAM! POW! AND WHEEEEE!'
Words, Mary Scally Mahon, 1988

My mother taught me the value of the written word. She had a great regard for books and would never allow us to deface a book by scribbling or tearing pages from it. For that, she bought us colouring books, pencils and crayons. Reading became a pastime because we did not have twenty-four-hour television or many outside influences, apart from our friends who were in the same boat. Life moved at a much slower pace than today.

My other great influence, my dad, provided for us in every way. His love of nature and the environment he learned from his own parents, who kept a flowering garden in Glasnevin, where I spent many happy days under the fruit trees. The vista I loved best was our next-door neighbour's garden, full of flowers and amazing rose trees. Such was my affinity for nature, that at age nine, I dug up the neighbours prized rose tree and transplanted it to our garden. My mother kindly apologised on my behalf when our neighbour came calling for his property back!

I was born in a time when children could legally work from the age of fourteen. We came from a working-class family and my father had two jobs; his full-time five-and-a-half-day week job, and his part-time evening and weekend job, which eventually led him to a better-paid full-time job. It was just accepted as a matter of course that my brother and I would work when we left primary school. Secondary school was not free at that time, and even if one could win a scholarship, the ensuing cost of books, uniforms and sports activities would be prohibitive. Hence, off to work we went. I finished primary school in June, aged thirteen, which was under the legal age to work, but my father was able to get me a job in the company where he was working. This was very common in those days.

When I started working as a teenager in the 1950s, all my friends were working too. Workdays were Monday to Friday and half day Saturday, which was common at the time. There was no late-night shopping, and most shops were closed on Sundays. My friends and I would meet regularly for chats or go 'into town' on a Saturday afternoon, to have an ice cream in Fortes or the Rainbow Café. Overall, I don't remember anyone complaining, we just got on with it. Leaving school in our early teens, most of us spent the best part of the next ten years working and dating until we hit the next big milestone, which was more than likely – marriage. By then, it was the Swinging Sixties; famous for Mary Quant, miniskirts and platform shoes!

My work was in manufacturing. The work itself was very skilled and detailed. It required great dexterity; a skill that would come in handy later in life. However, once you'd learned the ropes, there were no prospects of advancement. I had been working for about three years when I decided to gain some other skills. I enrolled in our local technical school to learn shorthand, typing and bookkeeping. My current job didn't require any of the new skills I was learning, but that didn't deter me. To this day I still use most of those skills regularly, though shorthand less so. I also returned to the local tech to learn cooking and baking, which came in handy a few years later as a mother. My years of learning passed by, until I got married in 1967.

That was the next big phase of my life, and the time flew by. Marriage and the arrival of children change everything. Before I knew it, a few decades of my life had passed by.

'I have been blessed with five beautiful girls,
small wonder my world is always in whirls!
No boys, I almost hear you say,
yes, there was John, but only for ten days.'
My Family, Mary Scally Mahon, 1988

The next unexpected change came about when my youngest daughter entered primary school. As you would expect, this freed up part of my day. One day a friend told me about a local adult education college. I was curious but didn't realise at the time, this would be one of the most exciting opportunities to ever open up to me.

I ventured to the college and got lucky as it just so happened to be the 'open day'. I was amazed to find such a place; the hall was a hive of activity, filled with tables, a teacher at each, discussing their subject with interested potential students of all ages. I didn't know where to start or what I wanted to learn, until a kind-faced grey-haired woman approached me to help. As it turned out, she was the principal and my lifesaver! She suggested I try a PLC course, though I hadn't a clue what that was.

That September I registered as a student at Pearse College, in the Pre-Leaving Cert Course. To qualify for the leaving certificate, students had to undertake a minimum of five subjects. There were people of all ages, some taking one or two subjects and some going straight for the leaving certificate. I chose the easy route, I opted for English, history and maths with an extra leisure subject – creative writing.

Pearse College was a like a home from home. There was a great air of camaraderie where you could meet like-minded people and make friends, plus, the staff were brilliant. It was always a hive of activity. The common room was a meeting place between classes, with tea and coffee available, and there was always chat about subjects and upcoming events. For me this was *manna from heaven*.

My leaving certificate course included the three subjects I had previously chosen, which I added to by choosing economics and philosophy, of course keeping my leisure subject, creative writing. After two years, I would sit the required Department of Education exam. I could not have done this without the support of my family. I must thank my husband and five daughters for their help and cooperation in getting me through. It was hard at times fitting in all family commitments and finding time to study.

At the end of the two years, I sat the exams in all five subjects and passed. My tutor then suggested I apply for a place in Trinity College; this was something I had never dreamed of. He told me there were some places available for mature students. I applied, went for an interview and was successful in gaining entrance to a four-year degree in BESS (business economics and social studies).

The next few years were filled with new experiences. Even though the student body at Trinity was enormous, it was possible to make friends. I loved passing through College Green entrance into the cobblestone courtyard and I felt at home – this was my city, my college. The lecturers were amazing, always helpful and encouraging. I never thought about what I would do with my degree if I made it to the final year and passed. My children were growing up, the eldest working abroad and the youngest in primary school. The middle ones were at various stages of education and my husband was also undertaking a course associated with his work, so it was a very busy household. The years passed and finally I graduated in economics and politics. On graduation day, my family attended, and my mother came too. A very happy moment for me, as my father had died when I was nineteen. Mam said he would have been so proud of me that day.

So, what to do with a degree from a prestigious institution such as Trinity College Dublin? That was the next question I asked myself.

During my years in Trinity, my husband was working and taking further education courses related to his work. In his full-time job, there was no further advancement available to him, so the decision to leave his job and work for himself came easily. We were sure we could make a living. I was familiar with some aspects of his craft and had experience working in a highly skilled and detailed manufacturing facility. This experience combined with my business education from Trinity meant I could help run the business. We started off small. As it became busy, we had to look for larger premises.

Over the years we gained a reputation for producing a high standard of work. So much so, we had to expand the work force and hire additional staff, and during the school holidays our daughters would work in the business to earn money. I like to think this is how they learned the value of hard work, and perhaps it explains how successful they are in their own chosen fields today.

Our middle daughter came back into the business some years later. Originally it was to help us move into the twenty-first century. At that time, everything was paper based, and we needed to become computer literate. Initially, she was only going to help for a few months, but ended up staying much longer and took a great interest in running the business.

The business expanded yet again. This meant another increase in our workforce, employing highly skilled and technical people. Over time, having our daughter run the business meant my husband and I could take some time off to do things we never had time for before.

So, this is where we are today. The story I have laid out goes some way to explaining my early life and how my career developed. A significant factor in my development was the influence of my parents. Each in their own way showed me the value of learning. We learned through reading, a pastime my mother encouraged. What does reading do for you? Well, it can broaden the mind and, I believe, is one of the most valuable skills you can have because it is used for anything you might want to do in your life. Whatever subjects you choose in school or the work path you take, you need to ensure that you always 'read the manual'. It enables you to fully understand the options laid out before you and the choices you are making. *Reading the manual* means you are always informed about what you are doing.

In the same way my own parents inspired my love of learning, I am proud to say that my learning path has instilled in my children an understanding of the power of knowledge, and that it's never ever too late to start learning.

I am very grateful for the depth and variety of influences I've had in my life. None of it was planned, but I am happy to report, it seems to have turned out alright. Can you ever plan your life? I believe that how your career or your life unfolds depends upon many things; where you live, your access to education, your family circumstances, your ability to access advice and information.

In Ireland, we are fortunate and can avail of many opportunities through governmental grants and subsidies. Not every education will look the same. Not everyone will complete a traditional education as we know it and that's okay. My own story highlights the comparable benefit that comes from work and life experience.

Well, this is getting to the hard part. It's easy to tell you what I have been through during my life, but how do I explain how one might plan for retirement? The question arises of what to do with your time. It can be a real life-changing moment when you finally get to retire. All those years spent working, fitting life in around a career, are suddenly stretching out before you with the promise of endless freedom. It's exhilarating but it can also be frightening. So, planning for retirement is a great way to dispel some of those worrisome feelings. Perhaps you have a hobby you want to take up full-time? Perhaps you start a new one? Perhaps you work part-time or as a specialist consultant, because all those years of experience are invaluable.

I didn't think much about retirement during my life, but old age brings a slowness to life, so it's important to take each day as it comes, and fill our time with joy, doing all the things that please us. After all, we've earned it. It wasn't until it was upon me that I really began to think about it. All through my life, I was busy with raising my family, and despite retiring, that hasn't changed. In retirement, there are a lot of the usual family commitments to be met, helping when needed with grandchildren. While I no longer work traditionally, my new job is being an advocate for my physical health. There are doctor visits for ailments, aches and monitoring. Vaccines and vitamins and minor knee surgeries. A welcome perk to retirement is free GP visits, not to mention free travel across Ireland. My husband and I revisit some of our old holiday destinations in Cork, where we used to take the family.

My husband's expertise in business was still much sought-after when we reached the traditional retirement age and so we continued to work beyond sixty-five to train and develop future specialists. We had a busy life, and now a busy retirement.

My favourite pastime when I was younger was to browse through second-hand bookshops. I have collected books on many subjects, including 'some good murders', as my mother would say. Over the years, I didn't have much time for hobbies as such, reading and gardening were part of my regular routine, but now in retirement I find more time to enjoy them. We are very interested in environmental issues and are active members of a natural history club. This gets us out of the house for outings and talks about the environment, no more trapping of birds or robbing rose trees for me!

I also took up painting and went to art lessons, something I had always wanted to do and now I have the time. The National Gallery of Ireland is a great place we often go for a few hours to enjoy the wonderful exhibitions on display. There is a lovely coffee shop there as well. I could spend my life people-watching in a cafe with a good book and a large window. Retirement has many perks.

So, my advice simply is this – learn to read and write and do maths. Not necessarily at university level, but even at a basic level. This will stand with you all through your life. Reading: because you don't need anyone to tell you the meaning of the written word; you can read for yourself, make up your own mind and not be misled by others. Writing: because you can sign your own name and not use an 'X' as was common many years ago. Maths: because it plays a vital role in your financial security and can directly impact your financial independence.

A final word of encouragement: taking the first step is the hardest, but the end result will bring much confidence and independence, as well as great experiences, skills and lots of friendships.

'When I die and go to heaven,
I'll know I'm in the promised land,
if I find myself surrounded, by books,
all second-hand.'
Words, Mary Scally Mahon, 1988

I STILL DON'T KNOW WHAT I WANT TO BE WHEN I GROW UP

BY ALO BRERETON

Sitting here on this wonderfully warm summer morning, with the forecast set to reach the early thirties today and tomorrow, I'm trying to decide my best options to make the most of this exceptional weather. Will we go to the beach, take a drive into the country or just lie down and relax?

Three weeks ago, I turned sixty-two years old, and the reality is, I simply don't accept being this age. It seems that somehow thirty years have been stolen and unaccounted for. I feel like I'm in my late twenties and there's still so much to do and to be achieved.

If I'm truthful, I just don't know what I want to do when I grow up. I seem to have forgotten what I originally set out to achieve, some forty years ago.

Looking at my life, many would say I am successful. I have raised a lovely family, have a nice home and all the material possessions anyone could ask for. I am debt free, with money in the bank and a pension with enough to live on.

I seem to have spent a lifetime hoping that material success would buy me the happiness and contentment I have craved.

Carl Jung and Viktor Frankl wrote about our craving a sense of meaning; a higher purpose that would clarify what life's purpose is all about. I'm still looking for that meaning, along with most of the population.

Somewhere deep down in my psyche, I have always wanted others to like me and to admire what I have achieved. Looking back, I now realise I have spent lots of money, at times money I didn't have, buying things I didn't really need, in order to impress people I did not care about.

Because of this, it seems, I have spent a large part of my career in well-paying jobs that served a purpose but really didn't satisfy me. I wore those 'golden handcuffs' willingly, 'getting lost' in life's journey.

Now I wonder what my legacy is, and more importantly, what it could it still be. All I know is, I have plenty of energy and do not want to 'retire' or float off into the final stages of my life, with the feeling of not being in control of my destiny.

The dreaded fear of becoming 'irrelevant' has a massive impact on an increasingly fragile ego. The good news is, I am now in a position where I can choose to influence the next chapter of my life. I no longer have the responsibility of raising a family or paying a mortgage. I have the energy and the health to start again, throw the dice and gamble on something I've always wanted to do.

I drifted into my original career as it seemed the best option at the time. It was the mid-eighties, and the economic situation back then puts the current challenges into perspective. Getting a job in Ireland at the time was exceedingly difficult. Getting a well-paid job was near impossible but getting one with a career, potentially offering travel, pension and other benefits, was almost unheard of.

I remember when a major brand decided to set up in Ireland and ads started to appear for 'business developers' – nobody had heard of the term at the time. After applying twice and getting the same letter back, thanking me for my application, I decided my strategy needed to change.

Unlike today, where you might use social media to connect and subtly associate and engage with the company and key personnel, I promptly door-stepped the recruitment firm, barged into the office of the unfortunate hiring contactor and got through my three-minute sales pitch as to why he *must* get me an interview.

Three interviews later, I'm driving a brand-new Ford Sierra with a full-time job on a six-month probationary period, with expenses, bonuses, health, phone allowances (for that thing inside the hall door, and kiosks) oh … and a pension!

I started the first phase of my career in an industry that was challenging to begin with, and was not for everyone, but gave me and my family a very comfortable lifestyle. It wasn't long before I applied the 'golden handcuffs', tying myself to a job and an industry where I became too comfortable to leave, though I had quickly outgrown my position.

Somewhere along the learning curve, I made a conscious decision I would not risk moving to another company or a different industry; I chose the easier financial option and to see it out.

So, at the age of sixty, after a couple of minor moves within the industry, I found myself taking a package and enjoying that pension, sitting back and trying to get my golf handicap down to a respectable level.

And then what?

Only now do I realise how big an ego I have, and one that needs to be continuously fed. I no longer have a *big job* and the feeling of importance that goes with it. Surely, I never craved that did I? I was bigger than that, wasn't I?

The reality is, I'm a person who needs to keep busy. I have lots to offer and want to do something that will help others. I do regular volunteer work and give back in that way, but I also want to give back to the business community. I have lots of life and business experience to share that can add real value to others' business and personal growth.

The marketplace is incredibly competitive, and with my industry of origin having changed completely from a logistics, marketing and consumer perspective, I must accept, that unless I recognise this, I will become the dinosaur that years ago I swore I would never entertain, and certainly not become.

My friends ask me, 'Why are you bothering to challenge yourself at this stage in your life? Why can't you accept you're in a lucky position, knowing you have enough to live on? Go and enjoy life.'

The short answer is that deep down there is a feeling there's more to do, that there's some unfinished business I need to persue.

The actions I'm taking now are not the responses to a light-bulb moment that suddenly required a 180-degree shift in my career. At sixty-two, I still have a lot to offer a potential employer, but I know now *I need to change* to become re-employable.

THERE, I HAVE SAID IT ... I FEEL BETTER ALREADY.

What does that change need to look like? I feel my changes need to be around mindset, where I admit I do not have all the answers. I must embrace new ways of working to harness and bring to the surface my core beliefs, and make them fit for purpose in this ever-changing, sometimes frustrating, twenty-first-century environment. I'd like to encourage my belief that the ability to work on our own (remotely, anybody!) is truly valued, without a constant need for guidance, connection and validation on social media.

There was a time pre-internet, and pre-mobile phone, when someone could get into a car, be uncontactable for two days and still deliver consistently twenty-four seven, fifty-two weeks of the year.

Yes, the consumer is potentially more challenging, and business models have become more complex, but the older generation can still add valuable insights into the business world.

An old boss of mine once said, 'If you hang around long enough, the old ideas come back into vogue.'

What I want to focus on over the next stage of my career is that tweaking of the old with the new ways of working, and to support this generation to deliver consistent results.

On reflection, over the past number of years, I have dramatically changed the way I live my life physically, mentally and, indeed, spiritually. Apart from being older, I am now a different person, though sometimes I am the last one to see it.

I had prostate cancer at forty-six years old, and along with being a major wake-up call, it also made me look at the way I was living my life. When I first entered corporate life, there was a culture of heavy drinking which I dived into – headfirst. At the age of fifty-five, I quit drinking, and in hindsight, it was the best decision I've ever made.

I have always been into training and fitness, as I played competitive sport, but it was only when I stopped drinking (and smoking), that I could see what was possible. I totally changed my body shape and weight. My diet and sleeping patterns also improved dramatically.

Being the competitor that I am, my problem now is that I'm trying to achieve times and complete training programs a sixty-two-year-old should not be entertaining.

That competitive person was also very evident in my commercial life, where my drive for results and my inability to accept second best and win at all costs, very often brought out the worst in me.

However, I also need to accept that the person I presented throughout my working career may not have been the real me but more a persona I developed, suited to what I thought was the best options for my life. It was my choice to keep that chameleon alive for as long as it was working, and I fully accept the downsides that came with that decision.

I have spent my life planning for future scenarios, hitting the year-end numbers, the five-year plan, without any reference to what is happening today – in the present moment. I have always had a problem in seeing the value of living life *today*. But more importantly, I have struggled to appreciate what I experience on an hourly and momentary basis, not identifying with the good, the bad or the growth experiences each one brings.

'Wherever you are, be there totally. If you find your here and now intolerable and it makes you unhappy, you have three options: remove yourself from the situation, change it or accept it totally. If you want to take responsibility for your life, you must choose one of those three options, and you must choose now. Then accept the consequences.' – Eckhart Tolle.

For the next chapter of my life, I am working on ways to help companies and individuals discover who they really are, and to accept and believe, that this best version of themselves, can not only deliver real commercial results, but potentially achieve those results in an environment and career they are happiest in.

Recent Sources:

- *Dare to Lead* by Brené Brown.
- *Big Magic: Creative Thinking* by Elizabeth Gilbert.
- *Designing Your Life* by Bill Burnett and Dave Evans.
- *The Greatest Thing in the World* by Henry Drummond.
- *Not God* by Ernest Kurst.
- *The Sermon on the Mount* by Emmet Fox.
- *The 80/20 Principal* byRichard Koch.
- *What It takes to Be Number 1* by Vincent Lombardi JR.
- Complete Works of Henry James.
- *The Power of Now* by Eckhart Tolle.
- *The Road Less Travelled* by M Scott Peck.
- *The Upsides of Irrationality* by Dan Ariely.
- *The Monk Who Sold His Ferrari* by Robin Sharma.
- *Modern Man in Search of a Soul* by Carl Jung.
- *Man's Search for Meaning* by Viktor E Frankel.
- *SAPIENS: A Brief History of Mankind* by Yuval Noah Harari.
- *Lost Connections* by Johann Hari.

To learn more about this author: linkedin.com/in/ alobrereton

BEST LAID PLANS
BY KRIS TAYLOR

Who am I? Well, I'm a native Californian. A single middle-aged woman with no children. The eldest of two children of divorced parents. The first in my family to graduate from college. A good student. Driven. Organised. A goal-oriented planner. Traveller. Dog lover. Former corporate executive. An early 'retiree' who now works part-time job in a winery. Loyal. And, like many, a work in progress.

I was a natural student growing up and studied diligently to get good grades in high school, so I could get into college. I wanted to do well in college in order to line up a good job when I graduated. I was one of the few people in my circle of friends in college who actually knew what I wanted to do after graduation. I was laser focused on becoming an actuary in the insurance business (okay, you can stop snoring now!).

After graduation with a degree in mathematics, I started working in the insurance business in a technical arena (underwriting) while also trying to advance with my actuarial exams. But, after some years, I became less motivated to complete the exams. Instead, I became an underwriting manager at age twenty-five and was then recruited to a consulting firm in my field. Only nine months into that gig, I was recruited back to the insurance company to take on a hybrid technical/sales managerial role. Long story short, I ultimately worked in a variety of sales/account management roles and started moving up the corporate ladder. And, then I noticed something looming ...

When I was about thirty-five years old, I noticed that many of my peers were being laid off around age fifty. They were no longer valued – not flexible enough, not technical enough, not forward-thinking, not creative, etc. I concluded that there was no reason to assume this wouldn't eventually happen to me! This realisation prompted me to consult with a financial advisor for the first time. I wanted to develop an 'exit strategy' or a 'downsizing strategy' so by the time I was fifty, I could pivot when I was 'let go'. Or I could at least be proactive and move into a different career path that wouldn't require me to be beholden to my comfortable pay cheque.

THE FINANCIAL PLAN: A TO Z

The key tenets I learned early on while working with my advisor were:

- Know where all your assets are and how much each one is worth.
- Get a grip on your expenses.
- Understand your net worth and how that will develop and be used over time.

LET'S TAKE THE FIRST POINT: KNOW YOUR ASSETS.

Back then, I had a variety of retirement accounts from multiple employers, a variety of credit cards, a variety of bank accounts. After spending time tracking down all the information from so many sources, I made the decision to simplify my finances. This meant I consolidated to using just one credit card, one checking/savings bank, one brokerage account (where all retirement funds from former employers were funnelled) and one current employer retirement plan. After all the simplification, it was easier for me to regularly track my total assets and net worth. I've continued to simplify as much as possible in all aspects of my life as I've aged, as I don't want to spend my time on mundane paperwork or minutia.

Knowing that my goal was to develop the 'exit strategy' by age fifty, my financial advisor developed my financial plan. I was given a specific annual savings target I had to meet every year (starting at age thirty-five) to meet my goal. I'm going to be honest – it was a BIG number. A bit daunting at first. But, when I really looked at it, it was achievable.

It helped that I was motivated. I wasn't in my 'dream' job. One of my biggest challenges was that I couldn't even define my 'dream' job! You see, I'm the kind of person who is very goal-oriented once I set my mind to something. But, in this case, I didn't have a specific goal in mind (aka an alternative career). I was in a job where I was successful and paid well. I had developed a career that had moments that were rewarding, but by and large, it was mundane, stressful and high-pressured. I did not feel fulfilled in a meaningful way, but I enjoyed the people I worked with and made many friends along the way. I was comfortable with my income and afraid to make any major changes for fear of losing it! Let's face it, we all have bills to pay. And … I was living in San Francisco, a very expensive city.

Knowing my annual savings target helped me to create and maintain a lifestyle that had me live well within my means. Many of us (certainly in our youth) just go about making money and spending money (hopefully without spending more than we make). Now, I was making money and prioritising savings first before I set about spending money on extras. I still enjoyed vacations, hanging out with friends, treating myself to occasional pampering – all within reason! I realise this is easier said than done. Unfortunately, we are constantly bombarded by the temptations of 'instant gratification' – a shiny new toy, technology, clothing, food, drink, etc. We must make millions of little decisions every day to resist all these temptations if we are ever going to meet our goals (financial, diet, exercise, relationships, etc.). We are definitely swimming upstream!

POINT #2: GET A GRIP ON YOUR EXPENSES.

Almost everyone is very aware of how much money they earn in a year, but very few of us understand what we spend in a year.

Because I retired from corporate life at age forty-eight, I am often asked, 'How did you do it?' And the next question is, 'How do you know you can afford it?' I generally give the same answer, 'You can't know whether or not you can afford it unless you *really* understand how much you spend annually.' Next, I explain the detailed process I use to determine my *actual* expenses. Of people I've talked with on this subject, 99% have never followed my advice.

Here's what I do …

On a regular basis (annually when I was working in corporate with my sizeable income; monthly or quarterly now that my income has been slashed), I download *every single transaction* from my checking account, Visa card, Venmo, etc. I put all those transactions into a spreadsheet. I then categorise every single item into various buckets. I total everything up, then subtotal the categories to see where I have flexibility. Obviously, there are some expenses you can't do much about (rent, mortgage, property tax), but there are many categories which can be reduced (e.g. eating out) or negotiated (cable TV). I work to renegotiate anything I can each year, by setting reminders in my phone to do so when the deal is nearing an end.

Is this a fun task? No. But it is extremely eye-opening the first time you do it. And, after decades of doing this, I have an excellent understanding of where every penny of my money goes. I make sure my annual expenses are within the projections that my financial plan assumes each year.

POINT #3: KNOWING YOUR NET WORTH TODAY AND OVER TIME.

I'm sure there are probably lots of applications or programs to facilitate calculating your net worth. Personally, I've been a fan of Mint (an Intuit app)[1] for many years. You can link most of your assets (financial accounts, home value, car value) as well as your liabilities (mortgages, loans, credit cards) to the app and it will provide an updated snapshot of your total net worth. I like the

---

1   This product has been discontinued from 01/01/24. I now use Empower app.

simplicity of a single source to track my overall financial picture.

Working with a financial advisor, you can develop a plan that will outline how this net worth will be used over time, assuming inflation, expected income, expected expenses and anticipated life events. But, even without a financial advisor, you can do some quick math to determine whether your net worth can support your annual income. If your net worth is $1,000,000 and your annual expenses are $100,000, you're going to have issues funding decades of retirement if you don't have income streams to cover you.

BEST LAID PLANS

One envisions a career path, love/family life, health and the dream retirement. While it's important to have goals and dreams for our life, it's not guaranteed.

For instance, I had visions for a personal life that included a long-term relationship where I would grow old with a loved one. But fate threw me into a tailspin when my marriage ended. And I still haven't found the right partner. Now I'm older, I've reframed my expectations in this area. Always adjust.

Similarly, as I had been thinking and planning for retirement since my mid-thirties, I had a vision of how I would enter retirement. It would be an active choice I plotted out and would be happy to make the transition from work to leisure. Guess what … it didn't happen that way! I'm sure you've heard that the most severe causes of stress in life include death of a loved one, job change, moving, divorce/break-up and illness/injury. Well, as luck would have it, I dealt with all of these and more as I entered 'retirement'. In fact, I wasn't even aware I was transitioning to retirement at the time because my life was a full-on mess! There I was in my mid-forties dealing with the death of my father and a couple of close friends, overcoming a major heartbreak, had left my career for personal reasons and had no place to live, since my house was rented while I was overseas, sorting through family drama after my dad's death. I had a broken foot and then my beloved dog was diagnosed with cancer. Times were beyond tough, and I was at a breaking point. Needless to say, my situation was far from what I had envisioned at this stage of life.

Honestly, it took me years to regroup, putting one foot in front of the other to regain my footing. When you're adrift you just have to start tackling one thing at a time, at least the things within your control, until you can see straight again. So, I focused on settling my dad's estate. Then, sold my house and began living like a nomad in search of a new place to live. I floated around for about a year from Airbnb to Airbnb in different towns until I finally settled in California wine country and bought a new home. After two years of not living in my own home, it felt great to be settled!

For the first year in my new home and new town, I didn't work at all. I focused on setting up my new house and dealing with grief (in all its forms). Then, I decided I needed to work a bit to give me some daily purpose and, equally importantly, to meet people in this new town of mine. So, I started interviewing with some local wineries – a business I knew nothing about. A new startup tasting room hired me. A year later, I moved to a larger family-owned winery just ten minutes from home. That turned out to be a great move as I finally started to make some great new friends. I love to entertain, so I initiated some blind tasting parties at my house for the staff. Bonds were formed and I started to feel like I belonged. I also took a variety of classes at the local college just for fun: painting, genealogy, wine, etc.

During these initial transition years (after the logistics were sorted out), I primarily focused on my mental health. I did a lot of evaluating of what I wanted in my life – and what I didn't want. During this time, I became very prescriptive about eliminating anything, anyone, any situation that did not bring me peace and joy. This meant saying goodbye to objects or people or a job that wasn't fulfilling me in a positive way. After coming through so much trauma, what I craved most was peace, simplicity and joy in the little things. I am happy to report that five or six years later, I'm still holding strong to this mantra, and continue to simplify my life as much as possible.

Of course, something had to give …

While I sorted out a home, job, friends and finances, I let my physical health slip. I was now a middle-aged woman in her fifties who had packed on the pounds – particularly during the COVID lockdown. Something had to be done. I was tired all the time and completely out of shape! To be clear, I've never been a fit person, as exercise is not my passion; my weight has historically bounced up and down like a ping-pong ball. Sometimes I have a better handle on it, sometimes I don't. I had dieted successfully over the years but hadn't really given it any real effort in quite some time.

In April 2021, I decided to try and do something. Anything. I started dieting (using a program called Noom) in earnest. I didn't initially have any specific goal in mind, but, after a few weeks, I established a goal of losing thirty pounds in three months (which coincidentally aligned with my birthday in July). Guess what?!

After diligent dieting, walking and my weekly Pilates, I missed the target ... but, only by about two weeks. A lesson in patience, for sure. Weight loss as a menopausal woman is no picnic. After hitting that initial goal, the first person noticed I'd lost some weight. (I hadn't told anyone that I was trying to lose weight.)

Given the pace of weight loss was definitely slowing down after the first three months, I decided to try adding intense strength training into the mix, in the hopes of accelerating the weight loss again. I signed up with a local trainer. When I talked through my goals with the owner of the gym, he told me that I shouldn't expect to lose weight at my age since I was entering menopause! Well, if you want to piss a woman off, tell her she can't do something! I ignored his statement because I had already *proven* I could lose weight. So, I persevered with my approach and got stronger all the while. And while the pace of weight loss didn't accelerate, it did continue. By the end of the year, I had lost about forty-five pounds. I buckled down again in the new year and by the end of March I was down about sixty pounds. Success beyond what I could have ever dreamed a year prior. Suddenly, life seemed to be humming on all cylinders ...

Around this same time, I had one of those aha moments ...

I was feeling good. I was single and free. I wasn't working in a high-pressure job. And sadly, my beloved dog has passed away the prior year. Basically, I was in a position I had never been in at any other time in my life. I was completely unencumbered. It occurred to me that this was the optimal time to pursue a lifelong dream of travelling the world. Could I afford to do it? Where would I go? How long could I travel?

I can only think of a few times in my life when something

was so utterly clear and my mind was made up, even before I sorted out the details of 'if', 'how' and 'where'. In my experience, these rare moments in life must be seized! So, I put the plan in motion. And, as I write this chapter, I've been travelling 4.5 months thus far and still have two months to go. Travel has always been therapeutic for me. Solo travel in particular is the best time for reflection and a real opportunity to clear my mind. The biggest gift is how unbelievable the freedom feels. I can do what I want or not do anything at all. It's completely liberating! And bonus – all this freedom comes while seeing so many amazing places. Gratitude overload. Best advice … if something really sparks passion in you, don't hesitate. Just make it happen.

Eight years into this 'retirement' journey, and I sometimes marvel at the path that brought me here. The key to a successful retirement comes down to knowing what I want and need. My retirement phase of life is mine alone and it should not be compared to other's ideas of an ideal retirement. I have finally shaken off the need to feel 'productive' all the time. In the beginning years I would often feel guilty for 'wasting' my time, as I had been programmed for decades to be as productive as possible. I no longer had a life dictated by my calendar appointments, deadlines, sales targets and other obligations. Believe it or not, it's an odd feeling at first.

I love the fact that I can engage or not engage with hobbies and activities I enjoy, as my mood suits. Having the space to think about what I want is so valuable. I'm already thinking about goals and interests for upcoming years that I hope will further enrich my life. And while I feel extremely grateful that I was able to retire very early compared to most, I also recognise and appreciate that I worked very hard to earn this opportunity. May we all continue to strive to live our best lives.

PREPARATION FOR RETIREMENT

BY DUDLEY LLOYD THOMAS

Mine was a different, but probably not uncommon, end to my professional life.

In 1970, I qualified as a solicitor. A wonderful year because, that year, I also married my wife Sue and found myself in a profession which demanded great energy and staying power. I remained working as a solicitor until 1988 when I made the brave decision to transfer to the bar. For several years, I practiced as a barrister at law on the English Western Circuit. In 1990, I had the good fortune to be appointed as a Metropolitan Stipendiary Magistrate by the late Queen. For the next nine years, I sat in the Inner London Magistrates' Courts. In 1999, another change, this time of venue, when I left London to be the first Stipendiary Magistrate in the West of England.

Every part of my professional life was demanding and carried enormous responsibility, however, I enjoyed great job satisfaction and would have happily continued to work until I was seventy years old. Sadly, this was not to be the case.

In 2006, having just turned sixty, we took a well-earned holiday, flying to Thailand and onwards to Australia and Tasmania. Unfortunately, I became pretty ill on this trip and ended up in hospital in Perth, Western Australia. The care was good, but the person I saw every day, without fail, was the hospital's financial director, who wished to ensure I was in a position to pay the rather exorbitant fees for my stay.

On leaving hospital, I was looked after by some medical friends with whom we were able to stay. Then back to the UK as an assisted passenger, and quickly into the Bristol Royal Infirmary for surgery. That, happily, went well. However, as I waited to be discharged, I had an unexpected visit from a consultant cardiologist, who told me I had atrial fibrillation that required urgent treatment and that I was not to return to work until this had been treated. So, no return to work.

Time went on and the thought of returning to work became a little daunting. Although still on sick leave, I attended a two-day training course. It was noticed that I often nodded off during the lectures, and I was sent home. It soon followed that I was to provide medical reports, and my future was referred to the Lord Chancellor.

As often happens in English politics, Lord Chancellors change quite frequently. Because of this, my case did not receive attention for many months. I was interviewed by a government medical officer in Glasgow who decided I was unfit to return to work and recommended I should be offered early retirement on the grounds of ill health. The thinking was that having a judge who falls asleep on the bench is something of a nuisance! So, in January 2008, I retired.

It had been a prolonged journey and I had not given any thought to planning for retirement. In fairness to the Lord Chancellor's Department, they did send me on a course, 'Preparing for Retirement' … two years later. I attended and took my last first-class seat on British Rail to London. So, I had no preparation for retirement by the time I actually retired.

Hence, in January 2008, there I was with loads of time on my hands and no plans nor preparation for my new life. I decided to take things quietly for at least six months. I spent a lot of time touring the five or six very good charity shops nearby, occasionally finding something interesting. I had the idea that, as a judge, I had been the 'chief', and enough of that. Whatever was to come, I was going to be happy being one of the 'Indians' i.e. a volunteer, rather than an officer. I took full advantage of my free bus pass (which is less attractive than a similar pass in Ireland where trains as well as buses are free). Even so, I got great value from my pass, using it daily and journeying to different places.

However, the plan to work in the ranks did not pan out. After the relaxed winding down period, I started to receive requests to join charitable committees. One of these was a small Bristol-based charity For Ethiopia, in which my wife, Sue, was involved. Working for a worthy cause was interesting and stimulating, and took my wife and me to beautiful Ethiopia, where we made many good friends.

Then, out of the blue, I was approached by a newly established charity called Making the Change. This already had a very good group of trustees, including a Justice of the Peace, a fellow lawyer, a retired prison governor and an accountant. This charity recognised the lack of help to young men leaving prison, with no job, no home and little family support. These were youths aged between seventeen and twenty-one years. This charity was granted Charity Commission approval on the first attempt, and we worked very closely with the Youth Justice Board (YJB). We were on a three-year project with YJB. The government of the day was advocating care for released prisoners, in the way in which we were operating. However, the YJB, which had provided 40% of the funding, withdrew this after two years. We had been very stretched raising the additional 60% of funding. Despite many attempts to cover the cost of funding, we very sadly had to close the house.

Over time, I also became involved in other charities as set out below:

- **Solon**: A housing association providing accommodation in the Bristol area.
- **KWADS:** Knowle West Against Drugs – a very worthwhile charity supporting the families of addicted children or their spouses.
- **Court Friendship Scheme:** This was a multi-faith organisation to help unrepresented litigants in the Bristol Civil Centre courts.
- **Syrian Refugees:** I was involved in setting up a community scheme to provide housing and assistance to a Syrian family. My wife Sue, a retired GP, was involved with making medical arrangements with the local GP surgery, dentist and optician.

Apart from my involvement in charities, my retirement time has enabled me to swim five days a week, read for pleasure and listen to all types of music. I think my culinary skills have improved too!

So, with no preparation for retirement, I have enjoyed a very rewarding time, getting involved in worthwhile charities. Perhaps I have never learned to say 'no', but I have no regrets. I would encourage everyone to be willing to lend a hand when the right opportunities arise.

I ALWAYS KNEW I WOULD BE A DOCTOR

BY SUE THOMAS

My mother was a doctor; my father was a doctor; my uncles were doctors; my grandfather was a doctor – and I was a girl of little imagination. There was no escape!

It is a long course. I started when I was seventeen and qualified at twenty-two.

I HAD planned to be a GP but there was no Royal College of General Practitioners in those days, so I set out to train myself. Medicine and surgery were essential to be registered, then I chose obstetrics, psychiatry, paediatrics and A&E to complete my training before entering practice.

Obstetrics – tick.

Psychiatry – tick.

Psychiatry proved fascinating, and I stuck with it. General psychiatry, acute, rehabilitation, psychgeriatrics, forensic, learning disability – the jobs and promotion came thick and fast. By then, I was married and expecting my first child. A plum job came up in child guidance, right on my doorstep, so I took it.

After a year juggling an adorable baby, a nanny, my job and house, I reviewed my position – and I was pregnant again.

Enough ... Stop!

I quit the job, quit psychiatry and became a full-time mother, which was brilliant and absolutely exhausting. Community life, baby playgroups and another baby on the way ... and a voice of caution from my mother, 'Don't give up your medicine.'

There was a scheme in position, the retainer scheme, which allowed young doctors, especially women, to step back and do a few sessions of work, together with training, to keep their knowledge up-to-date and relevant. I applied and got a job for two afternoons a week in paediatrics. It was just down the road. Perfect. My mother helped with the babies and on I went. But I continued to think I really did want to be a GP.

The preschool years flashed by. As the boys became more independent, I did a little more work. I was a school doctor; six months 'inside' as a part-time prison doctor and, then, when all three were in school, I organised a two-year, half-time GP training course, a couple of miles from home. This meant long-ish hours and being on call at night sometimes, but it was all manageable.

The training completed, I didn't imagine I would get a job at the time, as locums seemed the order of the day, but within months, I was asked to join a local practice ... and the rest is history. I was, to some extent, in control of my days and hours. None of the other partners had children, so school holidays were not a problem. I had good back-up at home: a supportive husband, a housekeeper and family to fall back on. Good years. Life didn't become hum-drum, because as well as general practice, I was also doing emergency psychiatric assessments in the community, and we had a full social life.

The boys moved through their schooling; the first two went to London to university; the elder doing languages and east Asian studies, the second, medicine at Guys. When our second child was killed in a cycling accident, my world froze. I couldn't work for a year. But eventually, with great support from my practice, I eased myself back. I found I no longer wanted the responsibilities of partner, but became salaried and continued until my husband retired early on health grounds. When that happened, I retired too.

That was many years ago.

Alongside my work, I pursued many other interests – literature, travel and volunteering. When the children were in preschool, I was treasurer of their playgroup. I also worked with Bristol Victims Support Scheme, a pilot study caring for victims of crime, which has since developed into NAVSS (National Victim Support Scheme). I did courses in literature and poetry and, probably the most important, my work with For Ethiopia.

Whilst still practicing, I visited Ethiopia where a young friend had started a development project, improving water and education in an area of rural Ethiopia. I joined to help with primary health care. My practice supported me in this, and since then, in my retirement, I have continued, visiting many times. I hope to continue to do so.

I often feel I have been nowhere and done nothing. My life has been entirely local – Bristol-based, but it has never been dull. I have been lucky in so many ways – I enjoy life, but I also want to continue to put something back and plan to do so for many years to come.

CONCLUSION

REIMAGINING, REWIRING, RETIRING? ... MILES TO GO BEFORE I SLEEP

BY SANJAY GUHA

'Sixty is the new forty' is not a cliché. It is our new mindset as our generation will probably live twenty years more than our parents. We are the first YOLD (young old) tribe to break the traditional life cycle of work to sixty and die by seventy-five. This journey requires individual experimentation with no textbook model to rely on.

Reimagining and rewiring are the new reality. And then retiring. The rich and varied stories in this book are an authentic narrative of how individuals are adapting to their longer, more active lifestyles, and vividly captures the highs, lows, challenges and frustrations, as the YOLDs navigate this uncharted territory. It highlights the tensions of our evolving identity from a high-flying banker to the treasurer for a local charity. It forces us to reflect on our true purpose and quality of life. I am certain the reader will relate to many experiences in this book. It will

CREATE YOUR BEST LIFE

reassure them they are not alone on this journey and hopefully provide inspiration to lead a happier, more fulfilled life.

The stories are very different but there are several common themes that bear greater reflection:

FINANCIAL INDEPENDENCE

Not surprisingly, this dominates many stories; from just worrying about financial insecurity to detailed spreadsheets. Importantly, for many YOLDs, financial independence enables them to dream of doing something different, to follow their passion and make a difference in the community. It gives a new purpose in life. It enables them to lead happier lives and leave a legacy behind. Financial independence gives us the freedom to start an exciting new chapter in life. Innumerable studies have shown that people make the most important decisions in their lives in the fifties, sixties and seventies driven by a new purpose. Clearly, for most of us, the best is yet to come!

KNOWN UNKNOWN

We all know that often the best-laid plans in life will get disrupted. Death, illness, separation, planned or unplanned parenthood, a stressful work environment – are all issues we have seen disrupt lives. And then there are the black swan events like COVID. These events often force people to step off the speeding train and reflect on the purpose of life. The new understanding normally leads to a new phase in life, often transitioning from reimagining to rewiring. Reading these stories will make you wonder if you really need a crisis to reevaluate your life. Indeed, should you seize the initiative and reflect on what's important to you? It is often a vague notion of what you enjoyed most in your professional life or your dream from childhood. Take the risk and change course. Don't be forced by events to do so.

COMMUNITY SUPPORT

We all need to be loved. In difficult times, even more so. The authors in this book highlight the importance of close family and friends. They provide us with a hug and a shoulder to cry on when we most need one. And more importantly, they actively support us as we look to start a new journey. They help us believe in ourselves and give us the confidence to take the risks we struggle to take. Nurture your family and community in good times. They are your pillar on a difficult day.

GLASS OF WATER

Depending on your personality, the glass is either half-full or half-empty. This is an important lens that guides us through life. It is the colours we see, or miss, in our daily lives. It enables us to live in a fool's paradise or live in misery. Your reality *is* the glasses you wear. Each story in the book reflects the lens of the author. In all cases, they have built on their strengths and not allowed their derailers to cast a shadow.

LEARNING AGILITY

The importance of retraining is a common theme as people transition from one career to another or even change lanes completely. Going back to 'school' to refresh/learn a new skill or get a professional degree is often a prerequisite to progressing on our life cycle model. It reminds us that leading a long and happy life requires not just a healthy body, but an agile mind.

RETIREMENT

It is not a time of life but a state of mind. It is when you are happy without an energised purpose in life. You don't feel guilty that you are 'wasting time'. Doing nothing seems a good idea. You are enjoying the moment. And in control of your time with a rhythm to life of your own choosing. No regrets and no expectations. You have discovered true freedom – you are in nirvana. Few people in the book have got there. But it certainly is a dream to pursue.

FINALLY, MY PERSONAL STORY

Straight out of business school, I joined the Global FMCG business in India. Fifteen years later, I resigned from this excellent organisation and joined a global beverage business initially based in London. My wife had convinced me I was getting too comfortable in my previous job. It seemed a big risk, since we had just become parents. In retrospect, I have no regrets. Nothing ventured, nothing gained has been a life lesson for me. What followed was a memorable eighteen-year international career. I worked hard, experienced many highs and lows and, on most days, enjoyed going to work. I am a born optimist which has often got me into trouble, but it also gave me the belief that tomorrow will be better than yesterday.

For personal reasons, I took 'early retirement' and relocated to India. But I was in no mood to formally retire and thus started my rewiring journey. I discovered trekking, climbed Kilimanjaro and several Himalayan peaks, marginally improved my golf game and travelled extensively. I actively support two social entrepreneurs and several consumer and tech startups. More recently, I started consulting for an international beverage JV with the demands of a full-blown job! The only difference is I have better control of my time. I try and live in the moment. Retirement to me is a distant idea. I am enjoying this phase of my journey and have many miles to go ... Along the way I remind myself of Obama's advice to his kids: 'Be kind and useful.'

I hope the many stories in this book continue to inspire you to live happier lives.

To learn more about this author: linkedin.com/in/ sanjay-guha-a3203919

Val and her mum, Paula Quinn

ABOUT VAL QUINN

Val Quinn, a Dublin, Ireland, native, earned an Honours Bachelor of Commerce (BComm) degree from University College Dublin (UCD) in 1989. Following this, she obtained a Masters in Business Studies (Marketing) the subsequent year. In the early 1990s, amidst Ireland's recession, Val, like many others, moved to London, accumulating four years of experience in sales and marketing, before returning home to work for Baileys Irish Cream, Mars Masterfoods and a seventeen-year career with The Coca-Cola Company.

Since departing The Coca-Cola Company in 2021, Val has launched her own business, Tilly (www.tilly.ie), serving as a business trainer, executive and life coach. Through her work, Val is passionate about inspiring people to lead purpose-driven lives. She encourages self-reflection and proactive steps, advocating for intentional choices that can lead to a more fulfilling and purposeful life aligned with one's aspirations.

Val's debut book is a testament to her vision, where she shares her personal story and convinced others to do the same, in the quest to help inspire individuals with their journey toward fulfilment.

Picture of Val and her mum by www.maeveharringtonphoto grapher.com

ACKNOWLEDGEMENTS

A heartfelt thank you to Julie Kinch for her invaluable advice. I would also like to express my gratitude to these other dear friends, Bevin, Ciara and Mairead, who have supported this initiative and generously contributed to the funding of this book's publication.

'Inspiration surrounds us every day of our lives, yet amidst the noise and distractions, we may need to observe more closely and listen more attentively. That's why I was moved by Val's vision to curate a compilation of life stories in this book. Each narrative, each personal tale contained within resonates with readers. Through their individual chapters, we are granted the privilege of a sneak peek into their lives and can all be instantly inspired by what they share. I am grateful for the chance to support and contribute to this project.' – Bevin Mahon, Owner & CEO of Dentaltech

'Our career journeys extend beyond conventional measures of success. Personal fulfilment, growth and positive impact are equally as important and significant. To me, success is found in meaningful goals, relationships, resilience and, most importantly, in discovering purpose throughout our lives. Exploring these chapters enables us to reflect on and appreciate the richness of our own unique journeys, encouraging and inspiring us to break free from preconceived notions.

I take great pride in contributing to the realisation of this book, as Val has been a mentor to me and so many others. She has helped influence me to embrace diverse definitions of success.' – Ciara Crossan, Founder & CEO of WedPro and WeddingDates

'Val's commitment to sharing knowledge and experiences through the compilation of deeply personal and leadership stories has successfully brought this remarkable book to life. Each chapter guarantees a profound journey into the human experience, skilfully interweaving personal narratives to craft diverse and inspiring insights for all readers. Success means different things to each one of us and within each story you will find valuable perspectives on personal growth, navigating new directions and facing challenges. Participating in this transformative project is a great honour and I'm thankful for the opportunity to contribute to these impactful stories that have the power to inspire and guide us all.' – Mairead Mackle, Founder and CEO of Tarasis Enterprises.

If you enjoy and find value in this book, kindly consider sharing your positive feedback on Amazon.

Thank you for helping us to make a positive impact.